The Five Futures Glasses

The Five Futures Glasses
How to See and Understand More of the Future with the Eltville Model

Pero Mićić
CEO, FutureManagementGroup AG, Germany

© Pero Mićić 2010

All rights reserved. No reproduction, copy or transmission of this publication may be made without written permission.

No portion of this publication may be reproduced, copied or transmitted save with written permission or in accordance with the provisions of the Copyright, Designs and Patents Act 1988, or under the terms of any licence permitting limited copying issued by the Copyright Licensing Agency, Saffron House, 6–10 Kirby Street, London EC1N 8TS.

Any person who does any unauthorized act in relation to this publication may be liable to criminal prosecution and civil claims for damages.

The author has asserted his rights to be identified as the author of this work in accordance with the Copyright, Designs and Patents Act 1988.

First published in 2007 by GABAL Verlag GmbH, Offenbach as *Die fünf Zukunftsbrillen*

This edition published 2010 by
PALGRAVE MACMILLAN

Palgrave Macmillan in the UK is an imprint of Macmillan Publishers Limited, registered in England, company number 785998, of Houndmills, Basingstoke, Hampshire RG21 6XS.

Palgrave Macmillan in the US is a division of St Martin's Press LLC, 175 Fifth Avenue, New York, NY 10010.

Palgrave Macmillan is the global academic imprint of the above companies and has companies and representatives throughout the world.

Palgrave® and Macmillan® are registered trademarks in the United States, the United Kingdom, Europe and other countries.

ISBN: 978–0–230–24705–5

This book is printed on paper suitable for recycling and made from fully managed and sustained forest sources. Logging, pulping and manufacturing processes are expected to conform to the environmental regulations of the country of origin.

A catalogue record for this book is available from the British Library.

A catalog record for this book is available from the Library of Congress.

10 9 8 7 6 5 4 3 2 1
19 18 17 16 15 14 13 12 11 10

Printed and bound in China

Contents

List of figures	xi
List of tables	xii
About the author	xiii

1 About this book — 1
  The five futures glasses as a mental map for futures — 1
  Readers, goals and benefits of this book — 4
    The goals of this book — 4
    What is new? — 6
    What can this book do and what can't it do? — 6
    Remarks — 7

2 Why we need futures glasses — 8
  Man's motives for foresight — 8
  Future management: Entrepreneurial futures research — 10
    From futures research to future management — 10
    Future management as a bridge — 11
    The importance of future management — 11
    Goals and fruits of future management — 14
  Futures confusions — 15
    Goals confusion — 17
    Role confusion — 22
    Method confusion — 25
  What is required in practice — 27

3 Many futures and five futures glasses — 29
  Historical perspectives on the future — 29
  A map of futures — 29
    Futures, not future — 30
    Types of futures — 31
    How imaginable are futures? — 32
    How probable are futures? — 33
    How creatable are futures? — 36
    How desirable are futures? — 39
  The concept of the five futures glasses — 41
    From futures to futures glasses — 41

How you can easily remember the five futures glasses	44
An overview of the five futures glasses	46

4 Your blue futures glasses: What lies ahead?   49

Your blue futures glasses: Overview	50
Case studies on the blue futures glasses	52
Purpose of the blue futures glasses	58
You firm up the basis of your decisions and strategies	58
You improve your orientation and security	59
You reduce the complexity of the future	60
You better understand what is happening today	60
You make it easier to communicate about the future	61
You integrate the various perceptions of the future more easily	61
You form attractors for knowledge about the future	61
Core concepts of the blue futures glasses	62
Assumption questions	63
Future factors	64
Signals	66
Future projections	67
Future scenarios	69
Assumptions about the future	69
Attitude and principles of the blue futures glasses	71
Assume the future to be largely unpredictable	71
Direct the blue futures glasses towards your environment	73
Regard the future in a passive and detached way from the macro perspective	74
Adopt a realistic and conservative attitude	74
Consider experience as a success factor	75
You cannot carry out a complete assumption analysis	75
Use assumptions about the future as a replacement for impossible future "knowledge"	76
Remember that everyone has assumptions about the future all the time	77
You cannot delegate your assumptions about the future	77
Improve your assumptions about the future through provocative projections	78
Improve your assumptions about the future by being affected personally	78
Improve your assumptions about the future through a wide base of support	79
Methodology checklists	81
Procedure for companies	81
Procedure for life entrepreneurs	84
Checklist of methods and techniques	85

5 Your red futures glasses: How could the future surprise you?   87

Your red futures glasses: Overview	88
Case studies on the red futures glasses	90
Purpose of the red futures glasses	95
You allow for unpredictability	95
You make the future easier to think about, handle and communicate about uncertainty	95
You can see more of the possible future and are therefore less surprised by the future	96
You perceive surprising developments earlier	97

You protect yourself and your futures strategy	97
You initiate necessary changes at an early stage	100
You perceive more future opportunities	100
You improve your risk management	101

Core concepts of the red futures glasses — 101
- Surprise questions — 102
- Surprises — 103

Attitude and principles of the red futures glasses — 107
- Direct the red futures glasses to your environment — 107
- Think in a discontinuous way — 108
- Look for improbabilities — 108
- Keep surprises on the agenda — 109
- Spread possible stress more evenly in future — 109
- Don't regard surprises as being only negative — 110
- Don't expect orientation from surprises — 110
- Look for plausible surprises — 111
- The number of possible surprises is increasing — 112
- The relevance comes from the potential effects — 113
- Take the necessary time — 114
- See your vulnerabilities in flexibility sacrifices — 114
- Stake out the area of possibilities with extremes — 116
- Reduce the effect of filters and barriers — 117
- Arrange for insider and outsider knowledge — 118
- Take a pragmatic approach in the scenarios — 119

Methodology checklists — 120
- Procedure for companies — 121
- Procedure for life entrepreneurs — 125
- Checklist of methods and techniques — 125

6 Your green futures glasses: Which future opportunities do you have? — 127

Your green futures glasses: Overview — 128

Case studies on the green futures glasses — 129

Purpose of the green futures glasses — 133
- You can see more of the possible future — 133
- You increase your probability of success — 134
- You can act earlier and achieve more — 135
- You have a better view of what the competition could do — 135
- You transform threats into opportunities — 136
- You can better handle future developments — 136
- You form components for your futures strategy — 137
- You improve motivation and confidence — 137

Core concepts of the green futures glasses — 137
- Opportunity questions — 138
- Future opportunities — 139

Attitude and principles of the green futures glasses — 141
- Use future opportunities to form the basis for your competitiveness — 141
- Believe in improvement — 142

Stimulate your subconscious	142
Look through the green futures glasses with the eyes of a beginner	142
Prohibit any form of criticism with the green futures glasses	143
Prefer advantage-opportunities over catching-up-opportunities	144
Look for opportunities at an early stage	144
Big opportunities hold big risks and vice-versa	145
Don't look for opportunities that are completely new to the world	146
Recognize the danger of not seizing opportunities	147
Be more honorable than the "fast followers"	148
Make your future opportunity as simple as possible	149
Balance feasibility and competitive advantage	149
You can only determine the value of an opportunity imprecisely	149
Carefully select which future opportunities you want to leave to the competition	150
Determine an opportunity's chances of success based on the balance of pro and contra arguments	151
Think about your later cautiousness at an early stage	151
Foster modest and sensible expectations	151
Methodology checklists	**152**
Procedure for companies	152
Procedure for life entrepreneurs	157
Checklist of methods and techniques	158

7 Your yellow futures glasses: Which future do you want to form? 160

Your yellow futures glasses: Overview	162
Case studies on the yellow futures glasses	164
Purpose of the yellow futures glasses	**170**
You can manage your company as a complex adaptive system more easily	170
You provide orientation for yourself and your team	171
You determine and form the future you want to have	172
You increase your efficiency and reduce your costs	173
You activate your performance potential	173
You can set better goals	174
You decide more easily what is important and right	174
You recognize threats and opportunities earlier	175
You impart confidence in difficult times	175
You differentiate yourself from the competition	176
You become more successful overall	176
Core concepts of the yellow futures glasses	**177**
Vision questions	177
Strategic vision (vision elements)	178
Mission (mission elements)	179
Strategic guidelines	180
Attitude and principles of the yellow futures glasses	**180**
Use the yellow futures glasses for decisions	181
Benefit from self-fulfillment	181
Align your vision to your assumptions about the future	182
Develop the strategic vision from future opportunities	182

Describe the desired future situation	183
You can live without a vision, your company cannot	183
Design your vision as a picture	184
Developing your vision is your task, not someone else's	185
Believe in self-responsibility	187
Believe that the future can be deliberately created	189
Ignite and promote passion for the vision	190
Strengthen the joint vision through coherence of the individual visions	191
Acquire as many supporters as possible for your vision	193
Form harmony with the whole	193
See a homeopathic amount of challenge as ideal	194
Have the courage to set a conservative vision	197
Orient your vision on achievable competences and resources	197
Make your vision compatible with your history	198
Don't overload your customers with innovations	198
Make your vision as precise as necessary, as complex as required and as flexible as possible	199
Form the necessary differentiation with vision candidates	200
The higher the organizational level, the more general your results for the yellow futures glasses will be	202
Your strategic vision is a periodic prototype	203
What is decisive is not the achievement of your vision, but its effect on the present	203
Methodology checklists	204
Procedure for companies	204
Procedure for life entrepreneurs	207
Checklist of methods and techniques	210

8 Your violet futures glasses: What are you planning to do?   212

Your violet futures glasses: Overview	213
Case studies on the violet futures glasses	214
Purpose of the violet futures glasses	217
You form an interface to strategic planning	218
By planning your activities and resources, you bring the vision into your daily business	218
You embed responsibility in your daily routine	218
You increase the probability and degree of your success	218
You increase your efficiency by concentrating your efforts	219
You enable success monitoring and navigation towards your goals	219
You safeguard your futures strategy and your existence	219
Core concepts of the violet futures glasses	219
Strategy and futures strategy	220
Strategy questions	222
Strategic goals	222
Additional core concepts	223
Attitude and principles of the violet futures glasses	224
Notice the relationship to the yellow futures glasses	224
The quality of your strategy determines the quality of your future	224
Backcast based on your vision	224

Do *not* put the financials right at the top	225
Concentrate on gaps and surpluses	225
Be clear about the goals	225
Setting a goal means not setting ten other goals	226
Differentiate between strategic goals and routine business goals	226
Get the support of key actors	226
First think of the strategy and then the structure	226
First form the structures and the resources before you implement the strategy	227
Summarize all activities in *one* strategy	227
Choose the optimum degree of challenge	227
Balance efficiency and flexibility	227
Be open to strategy elements that arise	228
Learn from mistakes	228
Maximize the congruence of individual and common goals	228
Goals and strategies need to be important to your subconscious mind, less so to your conscious mind	229
Make your futures strategy robust	230
Choose one of seven types of eventual strategy	231
Methodology checklists	**234**
Procedure for companies	234
Procedure for life entrepreneurs	237
Checklist of methods and techniques	237

9 See more of the future — 239

The five futures glasses and the *Eltville Model*	**239**
Process model and object model	239
The core concepts of the *Eltville Model*	240
Processes and core concepts of future management	241
How to use the futures glasses in practice	**241**
Organize your thoughts	241
Communicate with a better overview and more precision	243
Help others to communicate better	243
Gain more insight from newspapers, books, lectures and films	243
Use the futures glasses as a template for designing futures projects	244
Structure your futures strategy	244
Organize your toolbox	244
See more of the future than the competition	245
Make more of your future	245

Appendix — 246

Core concepts of the *Eltville Model*	246
Notes	250

Bibliography	255
Index	261

List of figures

1.1	The five futures glasses	4
2.1	Future management as a bridge	11
2.2	The importance of future management	13
2.3	The closest thought horizon	21
3.1	Types of futures	31
4.1	Projection with pro and contra arguments	56
4.2	The blue futures glasses and their core concepts	62
4.3	Projection matrix with future factors	67
4.4	Verifying assumptions about the future on a wide basis	80
4.5	Assumption panorama	84
5.1	The core concepts of the red futures glasses	102
5.2	Scenario cube: Eight scenarios for the banking market	106
5.3	Focal points of the surprise analysis	115
5.4	Psychological causes of blind spots	117
5.5	Impact matrix on futures strategy	123
5.6	Impact matrix on fields of action	124
6.1	The green futures glasses and their core concepts	138
6.2	S-Curve as a thought model for futures devolopments	145
6.3	Developing opportunities from assumptions	154
6.4	Developing opportunities from future factors	155
7.1	The effects of a strategic vision	172
7.2	The yellow futures glasses and their core concepts	177
7.3	*Videre:* Visualization of a strategic vision	186
7.4	Within sight but out of reach	196
7.5	Personal life vision (examples)	208
8.1	The violet futures glasses and their core concepts	220
8.2	Understandings of "strategy"	221
8.3	Planned and realized strategy	228
9.1	The core concepts as a semantic network	240
9.2	The *Eltville Model* with steps and core concepts	241
9.3	The *Eltville Model* step by step	242

List of tables

2.1	The importance of future management	13
2.2	Futures glasses and key future management questions	14
2.3	The benefits of future management	14
2.4	Futures confusions	16
2.5	Requirements for practice	28
3.1	Historical relevance of the perspectives	30
3.2	Passive and active perspectives on the future	37
3.3	Types of futures and futures glasses	42
3.4	Overview of the five futures glasses	47
4.1	Overview of the blue futures glasses	50
4.2	Examples of assumption questions	63
4.3	Categories of future factors	64
4.4	Future factors checklist	65
4.5	An energy producer's projections	68
4.6	Types of assumptions about the future	70
5.1	Overview of the red futures glasses	88
5.2	Stages of prevention	98
5.3	Two types of surprises	104
5.4	Competences for the red futures glasses	118
6.1	Overview of the green futures glasses	128
6.2	A few vision candidates for banks in 2020	133
6.3	Fields of action and opportunity questions	139
6.4	Structure of future opportunities	140
7.1	Overview of the yellow futures glasses	162
7.2	Strategic vision "Trier 2020"	169
7.3	Vision questions in the narrowest sense	178
8.1	The violet futures glasses: Overview	213
8.2	Eventual strategies for the city of Trier	217
8.3	The seven eventual strategies	231
9.1	The two partial models of the *Eltville Model*	239

About the author

- Dr Pero Mićić (pronounced Mitchitch) is internationally known as a leading expert for future management, future markets and strategic foresight.
- Chairman of FutureManagementGroup AG whose mission it is to help top leaders in business, politics and administration to see more of the future and the future markets than their competitors.
- Consultant to the management teams and experts of many of the world's leading companies. He helps them to systematically elaborate and analyze future scenarios, to perceive and to seize future opportunities at a very early point and to turn this knowledge into strategic and financial success.
- Keynote speaker on professional conferences and festivities in America, Europe and Asia.
- Holds a PhD in Strategy from Leeds Business School.
- Author of six books on future management and foresight.
- Developer of the *Eltville Model* of future management.
- Lecturer at renowned universities and management academies.
- Founding member of the Association of Professional Futurists in the USA.
- President of the advisory board to the European Futurists Conference in Lucerne, Switzerland.
- President of the conference on International Trend and Future Management.
- Visit www.FutureManagementGroup.com for more information.

1 About this book

Good future management is one of the most important success factors in private and in corporate life. Regardless of whether you are the chairman of a corporation or your own life enterprise, the better you are able to perceive and use future changes, and the opportunities they conceal, at an early stage, the easier it is to build and maintain your success.

As Seneca said two thousand years ago:

> *There will come a time when we will be surprised that we didn't know such obvious things.* (Lucius Seneca)

Most of the trends, technologies and issues that will determine our future in the next ten to twenty years are already visible now. The future is already here; it just hasn't arrived everywhere to the same extent. How can we use futures research as a source of orientation, inspiration and innovation? How can we see more of the future in a meaningful and rational way?

The five futures glasses as a mental map for futures

Even among experts, there is a Babylonian confusion of language concerning the most important concepts and terms on the future. There is no conclusive language for the phenomenon of the future: much of the benefit of futures research and future management therefore remains hidden. We need a model that enables us to express exactly, or at least more exactly than usual, what we see and feel and what we think of with regard to the future. We need a map for futures terminology. A layman can only describe the taste of wine with a few words such as dry, mellow, sweet. The expert has a vocabulary of a thousand words. He has models and terms for the various occasions on which wine can be enjoyed and experienced and differentiates very clearly between the different impressions of the same wine in different situations. How much clearer and richer his perception of the world of wine must be!

Let's look at five statements about the year 2020 that could appear in your newspaper today:

1. In a research report to the government by the Federal Statistics Office, a demographer writes that thirty percent of the population will be older than sixty in 2020.

2. A WTO virologist writes that there could be a pandemic by 2020, as a result of which several million people could die within a short period.

3. A young engineer writes that virtual meetings will replace half of all business trips in 2020.

4. The Works Council writes that it will have enforced the thirty-hour week for all employees in its company in 2020.

5. A multibillionaire says in an interview that he will have donated most of his wealth by 2020.

What is the difference between all these future statements about the year 2020? Is it their intentions? Is it the methods the statements are based on? Is it the verifiability of the statements? Is it the level of predictability of the subject area? Is it a little bit of everything?

The difference quickly becomes clear if we offer each of these future thinkers a bet: if we propose that they bet 10,000 Euros of their own personal taxed money that their statement will come true. If they are right, they stand to make a substantial profit, as the rate is 1:10. How will they react?

Will the demographer accept the bet? She is possibly more likely to agree than the others. Demography is, after all, one of the few areas in which the future can be estimated with at least  some degree of certainty. The rate of 1:10 would probably convince her. The demographer has formulated a clear assumption on the future. She is looking into the probable future through the blue futures glasses.

What will we hear from the WTO expert if we offer her the bet? It is possible that she will feel insulted, show us the door. All she wanted to do was to warn people and to achieve a change  in their attitudes towards hygiene, prevention and emergency planning. She will reject our offer for moral reasons alone and perhaps even add that she wouldn't bet on the very thing she is trying to prevent. She is looking through the red futures glasses for the surprising future. This doesn't have to be negative, as in our example, it can also be positive.

How will the engineer react if we ask him to bet 10,000 Euros that fifty percent of all business travel really will be virtual in 2020? We can assume that he would qualify his statement. He didn't really mean it as a concrete forecast; he spoke about the possibility. It is simply an option, an opportunity we could already use today, if only we could get used to it. He looks through the green futures glasses and sees opportunities in the sense of possible courses of action and options.

What will the Works Council members do? They will probably say that is their vision. Money and material things are not everything. In the 1970s, one union used the advertising slogan *"Dad belongs to me on Saturdays"*. Now it's time for the next step, despite globalization. There is value in spending more time with the kids and the family. It is, of course, not certain that this vision can be realized. Therefore, they won't bet on it. The Works Council is looking through the yellow futures glasses, for the desired future, for the vision.

The multibillionaire certainly won't be impressed by the 10,000 Euros, but a game is a game after all. Will he accept the bet? Almost certainly: because he has planned it and resolved to do it. He has already announced it and no one can prevent him from doing exactly that. He is looking at the future through the violet futures glasses of planning and action.

Many problems in future management result from the different views of the future. People tend to the subconscious assumption that everyone understands how they think and talk about the future in the same way they do. They assume that everyone is wearing the same futures glasses, thus creating the premise for frustration, misunderstanding and failure.

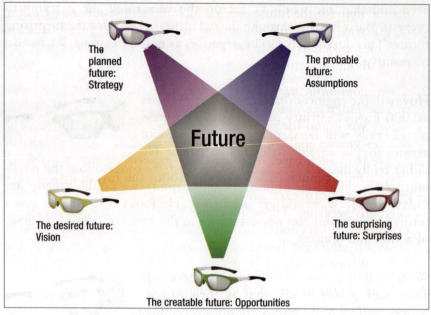

Figure 1.1 The five futures glasses

Readers, goals and benefits of this book

This book is designed for all decision-makers, be they life entrepreneurs, heads of families, chairmen of clubs, businessmen, board members, mayors or heads of government. When it comes down to it, we are all chairmen of the board of our own life enterprise, regardless of which role we have and whether we lead only ourselves or millions of people. We all need to think about our future and put on all five pairs of futures glasses.

The goals of this book

Anyone who consciously recognizes the five futures glasses, knows the characteristics of each of them in detail and is experienced in using them, will benefit in a number of ways:

1. *A holistic mental map:* This book aims to form maximum clarity on the views, the terminology and the core concepts of future management. The five futures glasses and the *Eltville Model* of future management based on them (see Appendix, Table 1) provide you with a mental model and cognitive map for your personal and business future management. You are provided with a kind of

mental map for the futures with which to form order and precision in the way you think about and work with the future. It then becomes easier to understand how people think about and can think about the future.

2. *Clear communication:* This book aims to provide you with precise language and a coherent model for your practice-based future work and for your communication about the future. The futures glasses make clear what the goal of thinking about the future is in each case. It is our daily experience that a group of people find it much easier to think about the future if they have learned to inform each other about which futures glasses they are currently wearing. There are considerably fewer misunderstandings and conflicts and the communication is more effective in the sense of achieving better results and/or more efficiency in the sense of time saved.

3. *A bridge to the future:* This book aims to help you to better understand trend researchers and futurists. It will help you to build a bridge from the present to the future and back again in order that you can more easily use their often theoretical and abstract results as a source of orientation and inspiration in your private and your working life.

4. *More realistic expectations:* This book aims to suggest clarification on what you can expect from methodologically substantiated future management – and what you cannot. It aims to make your expectations more realistic.

5. *A toolbox:* The five futures glasses and the *Eltville Model* are not dependent on any specific method. In principal, you can use any future management method or tool. The sound knowledge of the five futures glasses and the *Eltville Model* provided in this book aims to make it easier for you to assess the suitability of the different methods, techniques and tools for the various phases and goals of future management, and to put them into the correct compartment of your toolbox.

6. *See more of the future:* Using the five futures glasses and the *Eltville Model*, this book aims to strengthen your futures competence and give you a competitive advantage in the face of increasing competition for foresight. Anyone with a good map has a significant advantage over those with just a vague idea and can see more of the future than the competition.

7. *A design template for future projects:* This book aims to serve as a template for future projects. The five futures glasses are descriptive as they characterize the commonalities between people in thinking about the future. By precisely systematizing what people already carry in them anyway, the five futures glasses are also prescriptive. They show the steps and phases in which you can think in a sound and pragmatic way about the future and answer the key questions of future management (see Table 2.2).

The five futures glasses are simple, yet sufficiently complex to be an unbelievably valuable thinking tool.

> *The real journey of discovery does not consist of looking for new landscapes, but in looking at the world through new eyes.*
> (Marcel Proust)

What is new?

The futures glasses are not a development that needs to be painstakingly learned. They are more of a discovery of what can be found in the thinking of people. The perspectives that are illustrated by the five futures glasses are familiar and peculiar to each person in a very natural way, except that the terms are defined a little differently in each mind. The core concepts are sorted in a different way and both perspectives and concepts are connected in an individual way.

> *Every intelligent thing has already been thought, you just have to try to think it again at the right time.* (Johann Wolfgang von Goethe)

Until now, there has been no consistent model in practice or in theory which completely integrates the more or less natural thought processes and core concepts for the future in a simple way, describes them with clear definitions and relations and makes them applicable in practice. The *Eltville Model* is the result of an attempt to form such a model. This attempt is based on the systematic evaluation of more than 250 interviews with managers and around 1,000 workshops and seminars with management teams from various industries and of different sizes.

What can this book do and what can't it do?

A book can neither work miracles nor replace the effort of practical implementation. Although this may seem obvious, it apparently does not appear so to some critics. We are not promising that it will be easy to solve all future management tasks with this book. If it were easy, then anyone could do it and there would be nothing special about it anymore.

We do however promise that the five futures glasses and the resulting *Eltville Model* will significantly improve your future management in the ways we have outlined above and that you will therefore be able to see more of the future.

Remarks

1. The five futures glasses are not based on other concepts that also use colors and objects in an allegorical way as has already been done numerous times in theory and practice. The five futures glasses differ significantly from de Bono's thinking hats[1] in particular, as they:
   - are solely intended for futures analysis (the thinking hats can be used for anything)
   - look at different objects (the thinking hats look at the same thing from different perspectives)
   - are not only perspectives, but also contain a results model (see *Eltville Model*, in Table 1 in the Appendix)
   - were developed through research in futures workshops with management teams
   - are not even comparable in the number and colors of the perspectives.

   The futures glasses are also not comparable with the six thinking modes developed by Hall before de Bono, or with spiral dynamics.

2. The occasional references to our other books are not surreptitious advertising, which wouldn't work anyway, but are well-meant links within a complete work.

3. The use of the male pronoun is used only for ease of reading: both genders are obviously addressed, so please take no offence.

4. There is a companion website to this book: www.Futuresglasses.com

2 Why we need futures glasses

Man's motives for foresight

Why do human beings actually want to look into the future? Even the earliest civilizations tried to see more of the future. They were and are driven by four basic motives:

1. *Curiosity*
   We humans are curious about the present if something is unusual, different to or contradicts what we know.[1] Then we want to know about it. We are curious about the future because we know or suspect that it will or can be different from the present. That's why things we hear about the future fascinate us. It appears to be of little significance whether the future shown is really meant as a prediction or is just supposed to be entertaining.

2. *Fear*
   We talk of fear when we expect significant disadvantages from a certain event, person or phenomenon. Kierkegaard[2] clearly distinguished fear from anxiety, which is not connected to a concrete threat. We adopt this differentiation from the practical observation that it makes a significant difference to motivation whether a concrete threat is the reason for studies of the future, in which case they are clearly focused, or whether non-specific anxiety leads to a broad scan of the future for potential threats.

   According to Heidegger,[3] we try to escape our fear by gathering knowledge about the threat, integrating it into our knowledge system and thus developing or improving our strategy for dealing with the threat. In the 1980s for example, there was a lot of research on forest dieback and appropriate measures were taken. We have occupied ourselves for an amazingly short number of years with the subject of aging, which is a threat in many people's eyes, and looked for ways of maybe slowing down aging itself or at least alleviating its consequences. The fear of the effects of climate change also drives many experts, entrepreneurs and politicians to research the threats and

opportunities it offers. In 1972, Shell discussed the possibility of a rapid and high price increase in crude oil. Once the gravity of the potential effects had been recognized, systematic preparation began, essentially through flexibilization (see also page 93).

3. *Anxiety*
Humans want to be informed about changes and the dangers they present, even if they can't name them. There is no clear, concrete reason for anxiety as defined by Kierkegaard. It is a feeling of vulnerability based on the assumption that uncontrollable threats could surface. As opposed to fear, anxiety does not lead to a focused investigation of specific issues, but to wide-ranging scanning for potential threats. According to our observation, anxiety is the most important motive for leaders of large organizations to concern themselves with the future. The search for opportunities often plays a surprisingly small role.

The goal is to reduce the anxiety to an acceptably low level by gathering knowledge on the type, probability and potential effects of threatening events and developments. After all, the goal cannot be to eliminate anxiety totally: anxiety makes and keeps us alert.

4. *The pursuit of happiness*
Human beings intuitively know that they will gain an advantage by knowing the future better than others. The motive for the pursuit of happiness[4] as we call it, drives us towards achieving absolute advantages over the present situation or relative advantages over our competitors by seeing more of the future. Companies can achieve absolute progress in their pursuit of happiness if they improve the situation of their company compared to a previous point in time by perceiving future opportunity at an early stage, with the help of new technology for example. A life entrepreneur who recognizes that a certain qualification will be highly rewarded in future can establish himself as one of the first experts in this field. Relative progress is achieved when the situation (only) improves compared to the competition. In addition to the less significant absolute advantage, the first energy and electronics company able to use superconductors at room temperature will above all have achieved a relative advantage, which is particularly important if the lead can be expanded through rights and patents. The advantage can be exclusively relative if a company discards an old technology before the competition. Even without investing in new markets, the company will be in a better position than its competitors.

Happiness is often defined through comparison with others, meaning it is more often relative than absolute. Various indices that indicate that the people in materially rich countries are often unhappier in total than people in the materially poor so-called developing and emerging markets show that such comparisons can often lead to false conclusions.[5] However, this does not change the fact that people's pursuit of happiness is a motive for wanting to know the future better.

Future management: Entrepreneurial futures research

Before we were able to talk specifically of future management in the narrowest sense of the word, futures research had first to become established as a discipline. We started using the term future management in the mid-1990s when professionally managed companies increasingly systematically concerned themselves with analyses of the future beyond strategic planning.

From futures research to future management

Futures research is the interdisciplinary discovery and analysis of possible, plausible, probable and creatable long-term futures.[6] It aims to help us to:

- understand the (present) world
- improve the well-being of the human race
- increase awareness for the long-term future
- make better decisions
- understand thinking about the future.[7]

The word "research" is much discussed: many people dispute the fact that futures research is a science as the word implies. Futures research is not scientific if you support the positivistic science paradigm that only things that can be measured, counted, weighed and generally confirmed or refuted can be researched. But the future does not exist in a strict ontological sense. If the quality of being scientific means that the methods used meet the demands of validity, reliability, replicability and generalization, then futures research *can* indeed be scientific. After all, no one can exactly measure history either.

Future management as a bridge

Managers and entrepreneurs often consider futures research and the related trend research as imprecise, noncommittal and unreliable. There is often a huge gap between their need for knowledge and the knowledge offered by futures and trend researchers. Future management, which we define as follows, closes this gap:

> Future management is the bridge between futures research on the one side and strategic management on the other. It describes the totality of all systems, processes and methods for early perception and analysis of future developments and their inclusion in strategy.

Future management is entrepreneurial and corporate futures research. Compared to futures research, future management is a more practical concept and fundamental to human nature as it turns futures research, which is primarily focused on anticipation, into a holistic concept with interfaces to strategic and operative management. It closes the gap between futures research, which is often abstract and theoretical, and the practical requirements of companies, by systematically recognizing the future of markets and developing practical and implementable strategies out of these findings. Future management builds on the findings of general futures research and creates the connection to (business) decisions and actions in everyday life.

Figure 2.1 Future management as a bridge

The importance of future management

Interestingly, if you ask any audience with some degree of understanding of business, how much of their business success depends on long-term decision-making, you always get more or less the same answer: seventy percent. No one can measure, let alone prove this figure, but you get a feeling for the importance of future management. Even if in reality it is only fifty or sixty percent, that still makes up a significant part of our success. Long-term decisions on direction, taken consciously or unconsciously, determine how we invest, compete, work and decide. Corporate culture particularly cannot be changed quickly. Whether you want to build up a global high-tech company, or operate in your domestic market and offer customer benefits with no unnecessary technical items, is to a large extent a decision on the corporate culture needed for your strategic vision, which is often then binding for the next ten years. The example of Mao Zedong and his "great leap forward", given on page 164, shows how one man's decisions on strategic direction can cost the lives of thirty million people.

> A human being or a management team use long-term decision-making to decide which mountain they want to climb long-term, whereas operative management only serves the purpose of climbing the chosen mountain well.[8]

It is interesting to find out how much time top decision-makers usually spend on thinking consciously and systematically about these major decisions. According to research by the American professors Hamel and Prahalad, senior managers spend no more than 2.4 percent of their time working on the vision.[9] Two to three percent of work time in most countries is still five to six working days, quite a lot we would say. Who spends six full days per year systematically and consciously working on the future? That figure is probably also seldom achieved in private life. At this point, many people say that can't be true; after all, dozens or even thousands of people are employed in R&D and in the strategic planning department, which is the ultimate in futures work. What we are talking about here, however, is not the research and analysis delegated to specialists on how to climb the mountain in a better way, that is, to achieve greater success in the existing business with existing goals. We are talking about entrepreneurial future management in the sense of directional decision-making on the mountains to be climbed.

> You cannot delegate your future management. We're talking about the rare entrepreneurial directional decisions, which are most certainly not made by researchers or analysts.

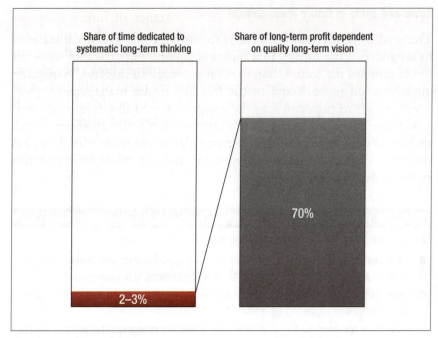

Figure 2.2 The importance of future management

Table 2.1 summarizes the above discourse.

Table 2.1 The importance of future management	
Good future management is the best investment	■ Your future management provides you with a strong lever for success. ■ A large part of your success depends on a small part of your time budget. ■ Time and finance-based investments in sound future management will probably guarantee the highest possible returns.
Future management can also ruin a company	■ The lever for success also works in the opposite direction. ■ Bad future management leads to the death of the business. ■ Future management is not a simple technique for success, but a responsibility you bear for your family, colleagues, employees or fellow citizens.
Two or three percent of your time is sufficient	■ There is a reason for the two to three percent in practice. This figure has proved its value. ■ There are more than enough hurdles facing systematic future management without building a further one by demanding a higher investment in time.
Future management requires professionalism	■ The two to three percent must be invested with the same professionalism as used in daily business. ■ Future management needs to be done equally as professionally as projects and processes are organized and carried out nowadays.

Goals and fruits of future management

The goal of future management is to assist people and organizations to see more of the future. In a business context in particular, we want to see more of the future than the competition. To this end, systematic answers need to be found to the five key future management questions, which in turn can later be assigned to the five futures glasses, which are described in detail at a later stage. Of the questions listed, questions one, two and three in particular relate more to the futures research aspect of future management and questions four and five more to the strategic aspect.

Table 2.2 Futures glasses and key future management questions	
Future glasses and work stage	**Key future management question**
Blue futures glasses (Assumption analysis)	How will our market, work and life environment change in the next five to ten years?
Red futures glasses (Surprise analysis)	How should we prepare ourselves for possible surprising events and developments in the future?
Green futures glasses (Opportunity development)	Which opportunities and threats to our markets, products, strategies, processes and structures will arise out of these changes?
Yellow futures glasses (Vision development)	What do we want our company to look like in five to ten years in terms of a strategic vision?
Violet futures glasses (Strategy development)	How do we need to design our strategy to realize our strategic vision?

Seeing more of the future means first and foremost having more time to gain, develop or keep a leading edge. The resulting benefit of future management can be summarized in the following six points (Table 2.3):

Table 2.3 The benefits of future management
Better competitive position   Future management provides knowledge of future developments resulting in a lead over the competition concerning the development and implementation of strategies, products, processes and systems.
Ensuring the company's continuation   Changes to the market that are noticed late or misjudged can quickly threaten a company's existence. Those who identify possible dangerous developments at an early stage can prepare more easily for them with eventual strategies.

Table 2.3 (cont'd)

Increased earnings
Future management identifies a large number of high-quality future opportunities and thus extends your scope for action, enabling you to develop and utilize earnings potentials.

Cost savings
If you and your employees have a clear strategic vision of the desired future, then the amount of agreement and directional differences needed will be dramatically reduced. The resulting higher efficiency can be measured in relative cost reductions.

Improvements in strategic decisions
The more sound and robust your assumptions about future developments in your business environment, the higher the quality of your strategic decisions will be.

Improvements in motivation and confidence
The certainty of having answered these key questions soundly and in detail improves the motivation of your employees and confidence in the future of your company.

Futures confusions

Futures experts and their clients often speak different languages, even after decades. Even futures researchers, trend researchers and future managers often do not understand each other. The following lamentations from entrepreneurs and managers illustrate this point:

- *We have looked at earlier forecasts and are very disappointed by the quality.*

- *We can't cope with all of these forecasts, scenarios and visions – we have no clear picture.*

- *We know the results of futures research, but haven't been able to translate this knowledge into our language, our concepts and practicable strategies.*

- *We have worked with scenarios, but it didn't meet our needs.*

- *We have listened to the futures researchers, but what they had to say didn't have enough new, helpful and reliable information for us specialists.*

Numerous projects and plans in future management practice fail thanks to such confusion, which is summarized in Table 2.4.

Table 2.4 Futures confusions

Goals confusion	**Forecast versus creation** ■ The more strongly humans are able to form their own future, the less predictable the future becomes. ■ Forecasting and creating the future are opposing, mutually exclusive goals. ■ Since people can create their future to a large extent, the future cannot be predictable. **Forecast versus warning** ■ Scenarios of extreme and surprising futures are misunderstood as forecasts. ■ They should however, serve exactly the opposite purpose, namely to prevent these futures. **Vision versus plan** ■ The description of a long-term future to be aimed for is understood as planning and rejected. ■ Planning in the narrowest sense can nowadays only be done for a very short period. Vision is not planning. **Pragmatism versus science fiction** ■ Many people understand the future as being only what is new, utopian and never imagined before. ■ However, the future is usually already here. Most of its ingredients can already be seen today.
Role confusion	**Prophet or future manager?** ■ The client usually sees the futures expert as a prophet or forecaster. ■ The futures expert sees himself more as a future manager in most cases. **Prophet or inspirer?** ■ Trend researchers' trend creations are understood as forecasts. ■ In reality however, they provide inspiring ideas and thoughts rather than predicting the future. **Universal expert or innovator?** ■ Futures experts are often assumed or expected to know the future better than the specialists. ■ Their competence is much more their interdisciplinarity and their methodological knowledge.
Method confusion	**Tool catalog without a construction drawing** ■ The suitability of the methods and tools for various approaches to the future is hardly mentioned in the catalogs of methods. ■ Hence, some methods are overused and misused for purposes that they were not aimed for. **Limitations of classic scenarios** ■ The classic scenario method does not cover many of the requirements for practice. ■ As scenarios are considered to be state of the art, the result is often disappointed expectations.

Goals confusion

At the core of futures confusion lie the dilemmas and irrationalities that people display when looking into the future.

Forecast versus creation

Many people express two wishes in the same breath. They want to have the future predicted, yet at the same time want to shape their future. Only a few notice that these two wishes are mutually exclusive. If anyone or something could exactly predict the future, then we would be condemned to live exactly that predicted life. Have another baby, learn something new, change your mind, emigrate, start all over again, behave like a teenager again? None of that would be possible if it hadn't been predicted. The future isn't like that, nor do we want it to be.

We should be pleased that the future isn't predictable. We can shape it because it is open.

As all 7 billion people on this earth can shape their lives within certain limitations and change their views and their behavior, the future cannot be predictable. When it comes to it, we don't even know exactly what we will be doing in two weeks' time. We must learn to differentiate between passive and active perspectives on the future.

Forecast versus warning

In 2003, the US Department of Defense commissioned a study on the future of climate change.[10] The experts from Global Business Network, led by Peter Schwartz and Doug Randall, are great scenario fans. They use a very simple scenario method, essentially based on a four-window matrix in which two uncertainty factors are combined to give four scenarios. Schwartz and Randall didn't want to settle for the common assumption that climate change will gradually develop and that humanity will adjust to it. They wanted to show it more dramatically, to make people aware of how serious the situation is. They therefore developed a scenario called "rapid climate change", which described severe cooling in the North and significant warming in the South. It consisted among other things of the following forecasts for 2010 to 2020:

- The Gulf Stream in the Atlantic, Europe's heating system, changes its direction in a complex reaction.

- Dryness and aridity characterize the whole period in important agricultural regions and in the areas around the major conurbations in Europe and North America.
- The average annual temperature falls by up to five degrees Fahrenheit (2.8 degrees Celsius) in Asia and North America and by up to six degrees Fahrenheit (3.3 degrees Celsius) in Europe. That represents a dramatic cooling.
- The average annual temperature increases by up to four degrees Fahrenheit (2.2 degrees Celsius) in Australia, South Africa and South America. That represents an equally dramatic warming.
- Desert storms and winds dramatically increase and amplify the effect of the cooling.
- At the end of the year 2020, the climate in Central Europe is the same as the climate in Siberia in 2000.

Dramatic consequences were described for the period between 2010 and 2020: military skirmishes for water and food in Europe, a massive exodus of people from Holland and Germany to Italy and Spain, an influx of immigrants enter the USA from Japan and the Caribbean, Chinese military intervention in Kazakhstan to secure the pipelines against rebels. Humanity returns to the old pattern of permanent battles for resources. Life is once again determined by war, this time with the strongest weapons ever available to man.

It was a scenario of a possible, yet improbable future, which was supposed to serve as a warning. And what did practically all the papers and magazines say after publication? Correct, "futures researchers predict radical climate change".

> Futures researchers paint scenarios of extreme futures in order to prevent them. The public however thinks only of forecasts.

Schwarz and Randall specifically stated that their goal was to think the unimaginable, to dramatize the situation in order to show the horrendous consequences that could occur if we do not prepare for such a possible future. It was a calculatedly pessimistic approach. After all, the researchers claim, history has shown that sometimes the extreme happens and if this possibility exists, then the Department of Defense should prepare for it. Schwartz uses the term "inevitable surprises" here.

In the weeks following publication, the media and a number of our business partners regarded the study as nonsense. The climate would surely not change that quickly. The Pentagon spent 100,000 dollars on such a nonsensical prediction? Schwartz and Randall developed their study using the red futures glasses for the unexpected future, whereas the mass of the recipients did what they always do. Every statement on the future is understood to be a prediction (using the blue futures glasses), which automatically leads to a discussion on probability.

Another well-known case is the study *Limits to Growth* published in 1972 by Dennis and Donella Meadows. On behalf of the Club of Rome, a group of seventeen researchers used a computer model to unmistakably describe that our environment would be in a catastrophic state around the millennium. Virtually no one heard that the theories were always marked with the remark "ceteris paribus". Meaning, if we carry on as we are, then that will be the result. They were warnings, seen, spoken and written with the red futures glasses. In this case again, the public saw the scenarios through the blue futures glasses, as predictions. Just as if the authors had written "100% probability, whatever else may happen" behind each sentence, The inside cover of the edition published in 1973 by Rowohlt-Verlag states: "The MIT study uses the new techniques of scientific system analysis and computer simulation[11] for the first time , in order to be able to provide precise predictions on the long-term development of global problems through the combination of large quantities of information."

> It is often forgotten that our actions can precipitate or exclude the occurrence of the prediction.

You could think at this point that it was their own fault for using the word prediction, because most people understand that to mean a statement that will definitely come true, whatever happens. And a simple means of communication, such as the five futures glasses, with which you can quickly clarify what is meant wasn't available.

Vision versus plan

2020? We are often told that it is courageous to plan that far into the future. You can't even plan the day in such a way that everything goes according to design. What we are doing is amazing, they say. Again, we are faced here with another example of language confusion. It becomes particularly interesting when a host has to introduce a speaker on a futures issue.

> With charming naivety, possibility is confused with prediction and vision with plan.

The urgent need for a clarifying model for thinking and communicating about the future becomes clear once again.

Pragmatism versus science fiction

So what then? Everyone knows that people are becoming older and that society is therefore aging, that a sixth of all physical products contain nanotechnology components, that memory capacity will have exploded exponentially, that fuel cell technology is slowly but surely progressing, that global energy requirements are increasing and functional food is a future market. So where is the new mega trend?

Many people only understand "future" to mean things that are new and not yet imagined. To many, speculation on the personal fabricator, the 3-D printer for home use with which you can print any product, or the space station hung on geostationary satellites or the transatlantic bridge are the future. The more science fiction, the better. In practice however, we are concerned more with serious analysis of things that are already visible on the horizon.

The fuel cell has been around since 1837, Svante Arrhenius wrote about global warming through carbon dioxide in 1896, hybrid drive has existed since 1902, the German railway company used the first mobile phones in 1932, there were vegetarian restaurants in the 1920s, Reinhold Lotze wrote about the upcoming aging society in Germany in 1932, the first online diaries (blogs) were published in the 1970s and as early as 1995 at the Vienna Marathon, the times of the runners were recorded using RFID chips in their shoes.

> *The future is already here – it's just not evenly distributed.*
> (William Gibson)

In the pragmatic sense, the starting point for futures work should be primarily what we can already observe today. We are talking about the phenomenon of the diffusion of innovation, the s-curve of innovation diffusion from the innovator to the general public. What represents an innovation, and to whom, is conceivably relative. For an energy corporation, the introduction of a knowledge management system is part of its history. For a medium sized construction company on the other hand, the same opportunity represents a huge challenge. The future is rarely something absolutely new to the world. The future is much more often something relatively new to the beholder, but which has already existed for a long time elsewhere. Don't impede yourself by searching for something revolutionarily new. Sufficiently new is whatever you have not yet implemented in your company.

A mega trend is strong, global and long-term. It describes comprehensive change processes. Examples are aging in developed countries, the increase in global energy requirements and the increased performance levels of computers. Mega trends can be helpful if you want to think of probable futures through their continuation. However, when someone talks "new mega trends" they claim to be able to predict the future, for a mega trend can only be seen in a speculative thought mode. Either we are talking about the mega trends that are really effective or we are talking about new trends. But *new mega trends* is not a coherent concept.

> To achieve a better understanding and for successful future projects, we need to differentiate whether we are talking about probabilities or possibilities.

It makes a significant difference whether you want an orientation basis for real life (blue futures glasses) or whether you are just looking for inspiration (green futures glasses). With the blue futures glasses we are looking for probabilities, with the green ones for possibilities. Someone who is wearing the blue futures glasses doesn't want to inspire, he wants to be right. He wants to know and/or show how the future will be based on his assumption. He would even bet a significant amount that it will happen that way. Someone who is wearing the green futures glasses doesn't want to be right with his assumptions about the future, he wants to communicate something interesting and expand the imagination of his clientele. He is unlikely to bet that it will happen the way he presents it. The futures glasses

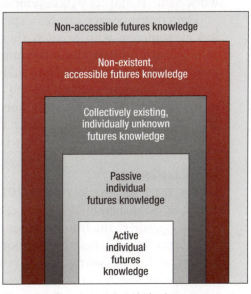

Figure 2.3 The closest thought horizon

can help to understand these relations better and communicate them more easily.

Role confusion

The roles of the futures experts, be they trend researchers, futures researchers or future managers, are often misunderstood.

Prophet or future manager?

As soon as someone occupies himself professionally with the future, most people imagine his core task to be one thing above all: predictions! The quality of these people's work must, so goes the general assumption, first and foremost be measured according to how accurately they are able to predict events and developments in the future. The accuracy of the prediction should be checked critically in ten years' time and if things haven't turned out the way they said they would, then they should be denounced or, at best, laughed at. Futures experts are still considered to be prediction machines, whose right to exist, and primary quality criterion, is the accuracy of their predictions. Even if it is common knowledge that the future cannot be precisely predicted, even if the chaos researchers confirm this assumption, the work of futures experts is burdened with false expectations. The clients expect clear statements from them as to how their field of work or their market will develop in future.

The contemporary futures expert on the other hand, sees himself less as someone who *predicts* things about the future and more as someone who *thinks* about the future. As a result, futures researchers like to think in scenarios. They enable them to work on the future and inspire innovations without having to make unrealistic predictive statements. Their clients, however, stubbornly understand their scenarios to be predictions. Disappointment on the client's side and ridicule or even contempt are the regular consequences of unclear role perception.

Prophet or inspirer?

If you read the book *Trends 2015* by Gerd Gerken and Michael Konitzer, published in 1995, you can check how well the authors were able to "predict" the future (although they certainly didn't claim to do so). Experts agree that the working week will continue to become shorter without a corresponding reduction in wages (p. 124), down to twenty-nine hours in 2030. Other futures experts are cited, for example the BAT-Leisure Research Institute or the Institute for Work and Job Research. Almost all of them believed over a period of several decades in the coming of the leisure society, so that we shouldn't be too strict or gleeful here. There is nothing wrong after all in extrapolating a trend that is several decades old.

The end of the printed word has also not yet happened (p. 88) and definitely won't have happened by 2015. Let's take a look at a few more unusual subjects we have selected:

- "Art in future will be a kind of companion to ecstasy ... Art will no longer be used as a guarantee of meaning, but will impart a feeling of existence. Ecstatic means that there is no longer meaning, no complaints, no complaining thinking. Introducing ecstasy leads to the departure of evaluation." (p. 101)
- Today's (1995) borderline patients are the multi-minds of the future. They are actually the ones who are more fit. They are an elite progressing onwards, which is able to deal with several realities. "Such people never end in the blind-alley of having to really believe in something at some point." (p. 39)
- "Fashion will become an individual loudspeaker of one's own feelings and mental state, a means of transport for mental intimacy and personal imagination." (p. 167)

In *Clicking*, a Popcorn Report published in 1997, Faith Popcorn writes:

- Clanning is a trend. People organize themselves in clans and groups (p. 84 ff).
- Fantasy adventures are booming. To escape stress and boredom, consumers feel the need to experience adventure and stimulation in a risk-free environment. (p. 103)

When a mechanical engineer, with his positivistic mind looks at the work of trend researchers, he can only shake his head. Charlatanism, you hear him shout. More or less nothing in the above statements can be measured or proved. Even some of the words themselves cannot be clearly understood. The predictive value, if the statements have one at all, can't even be proven afterwards, let alone a priori. In any case, simple present phenomena are often described as trends, as is the case with Faith Popcorn and most of the other trend researchers.

■ Use trend researchers as providers of ideas, not as predictors and prophets.

A person reading the same statements with the mind of a constructivist, looking for open ideas, will be pleased to find several helpful suggestions. The difference is simple and mundane; unfortunately it is drawn too seldom. Trend researchers' statements should never be taken as predictions (blue futures glasses) but as inspiring ideas and inventions. The trend researchers cannot provide you with orientation in the narrowest sense. Faith Popcorn states openly that most of what she does is to form "entertaining predictions" (p. 66).

These are two different futures glasses. One wants to see a probable future, the other wants to point to ideas for the future. Without being aware of it generally, the trend researcher wears the green futures glasses, whereas the engineer, for example, and many others along with him, believes that the trend researcher at least claims to wear the blue futures glasses.

Universal expert or innovator?
Many futures experts work as generalists in very many areas. Because of their interdisciplinarity and method competence, they are able to be highly inspiring and to expand and enrich the thought horizons of their clients.

Unfortunately, many futures researchers and future managers don't draw a clear line and act as experts for cosmetics one day, give lectures as experts on climatology the next and put on a brilliant show as pedagogic and psychology experts the following day. The futures specialist is therefore regularly in competition with experts in these fields whose specialist knowledge will always be better. This universality of futures researchers leads to two serious problems:

1. Many experts are rightly disappointed when the futures researcher presents ideas that have already been talked about for years at specialist conferences.

2. The futures researchers feed the prejudice that the future of a specialist area can be analyzed without any real expertise in that area. Many clients assume that they can ask a futures researcher about the future of virtually anything.

No model can solve this potential conflict. It would need to make clear that appropriate expertise in an area or market is necessary in order to be able to analyze its probable future, yet at the same time interdisciplinarity and experience in completely different areas are beneficial to the analysis of the possible or potential surprising future.

> The trend researcher shines through interdisciplinarity and creativity, but rarely through depth of knowledge and expertise in a specialist area. There he is less capable than the experts.

Method confusion

The third section of futures confusion describes the methodological problems and challenges.

A tool catalog without a construction drawing

There are a number of lists and catalogs with methods, techniques and tools for futures research and future management. What is remarkable, other than the variety, is the fact that almost no differentiation is made between the methods with regard to how they can be actually used in practical projects. With amazing inconsistency, methods such as simple brainstorming are mentioned in the same breath as scenarios and comprehensive situation mapping. As a result, a method you have got along well with quickly becomes a universal tool for future management tasks, which inevitably leads to disappointment and irritation. Only when a differentiation of perspective (futures glasses) is made do such lists and catalogs make sense.

Limitations of classic scenarios

The world experienced an enormous economic boom after the two World Wars. Anticipation was relatively easy in a growing economy, and if you made a mistake then no one really got upset about it, as growth had generally occurred anyway. When the growth engine started to sputter at the end of the 1960s and beginning of the 1970s, an increasing number of futures researchers crashed into the wall of reality with their predictions.

The dawn of the scenario methods

In the search for alternatives, Herman Kahn of the RAND-Corporation and his scenarios came at exactly the right time. The book he published together with Anthony Weiner in 1967, *The Year 2000 – A Framework for Speculation on the Next Thirty-Three Years*, introduced the principle of the scenario method. It described alternative scenarios of the world in the year 2000. The futurists quickly realized that scenarios provided the intellectual tools enabling them to take the increasing complexity and turbulence of the future into consideration and still analyze the future. They freed themselves from the dilemma that although the future is not predictable, there is a great demand for orientation knowledge on what we can expect in the future. They found a path between the clients' desperate desire for predictions on the one hand and a reality that doesn't permit this on the other. Scenario methods enabled them to keep doing their jobs again without having to be measured on specific predictions.

From then on, more or less all futurists worked with scenarios as pictures of possible futures. All they needed to do was to convince their readers and clients of the meaning and value of scenarios. That was relatively easy: after all, Edward Lorenz (1963) and others had already made some progress in the understanding of complex adaptive systems, to which, among other things, practically every system in which people play a role belongs. Such systems cannot be predicted (see *The FutureRadar*[12]). Since the end of the 1960s, classic scenario methods have continuously gained in importance as futures research and planning tools.

Classic scenario methods are only a partial solution

Scenarios enable the futures researcher to remain noncommittal. You, however, as a decision-maker in life or in a corporation do need to commit yourself. Long-term decisions on business areas, locations or managers can hardly be made in such a way that they fit all possible scenarios. This point can be illustrated by the weather forecast. We listen to the weather forecast because we want to be prepared for the coming weather. Three scenarios, according to which the weather will be hot, stormy or cool and windy, are not much help to us. Anyone who wants to be prepared for all possible weather conditions, as the futures researchers demand, needs to carry a lot of excess baggage with him. In practice that would mean that only those strategies that meet all scenarios would be considered robust. This is too costly and also leads directly to increased comparability with the competition, since strategies that are suitable for all scenarios tend to be very similar to each other. This in turn would minimize differentiation between competitors and thus minimize operating margins.

Decision-makers need assumptions about the future, with given expectation probabilities, as well as inspiration and decision-making tools to be able to perceive future opportunities and develop visions. After all, you need to find good ways of actually implementing the goals and strategies based on them. Scenarios include probable, improbable, desired, feared, doable and invented futures. This is a mix of various future characters, which does not permit clarity or orientation. It has proved to be useful to differentiate future scenarios more clearly than is usually the case.

Managers' complaints

We repeatedly come up against the same complaints from practitioners:

- We have used the scenario method, but with three or five equally probable futures we had no real orientation. In real life it is impossible to be prepared for everything at the same time.

- We have discussed future scenarios, but it didn't lead us to a really innovative perspective on our opportunities in the futures in the way we had expected.

- We have determined and analyzed the implications of the scenarios, but what we really wanted was a clear vision specific to our company that we could work towards.

- Our scenario project ended with recommendations for key strategies, but that's exactly where the real work begins in practice. We would have liked a better connection to our scorecards.

- What we needed in addition to the scenarios was an approach with which we could have tested the solidity of our strategies on a wide basis. Two or three scenarios are OK, but we fear completely different surprises from the real world.

- We used computer-aided scenario methods, but that turned out to be a very complex, time-intensive and expensive exercise.

The five futures glasses help to clarify and extend the perspectives of the classic scenario methods.

> The *Eltville Model* (see Chapter 9) based on the five futures glasses is a new, holistic scenario method for business practice.

What is required in practice

Dilemmas, irrationalities and future confusions can be positively reformulated into requirements for practice. The five futures glasses and the *Eltville Model* are intended to meet these requirements as far as possible.

Table 2.5 Requirements for practice

A holistic approach: Above all, the method needs to be holistic in the sense that it integrates all necessary process steps and all results types in one model and links them with each other.

Futures differentiation: The method must clearly differentiate between the various perspectives of the future (possible, probable, feared, surprising, planned and so on).

Active–passive clarity: It must be clear in the process whether one is regarding oneself or one's environment: mixing the active and passive views is systemically not practicable.

Orientation: The method must provide an orientational picture of a probable future, even if the future cannot be (exactly) predicted.

Variety of surprises: The method needs to consider a large number of potential surprises.

Opportunity focus: The method needs to guarantee a strong element of creative identification and development of future opportunities and options and thus support competitive differentiation.

Vision: The method needs to provide a comprehensive picture of the future desired by the actor or the team.

Strategy and planning: The method needs to have clear connections to the operative business.

Permanence: The method needs to be suitable for supporting a permanent radar process in daily business.

Efficiency: The method needs to be efficient in the sense that the above-mentioned requirements can be met with an appropriate amount of time and money.

Independent application: The method needs to be suitable for independent use by an averagely qualified team, at least in its basic functions.

3 Many futures and five futures glasses

This chapter describes the development and concept of the five futures glasses. We start with a short historical review of the relevant perspectives of the different futures in order to identify the five futures glasses in them.

Historical perspectives on the future

There is evidence of various perspectives on the future in the history of mankind. People have consciously tried to see the future since antiquity, and then more extensively since the Renaissance. People have always adopted all five perspectives on the future and therefore worn all five futures glasses, but those concerned with the long-term future of markets and the world on a professional basis have had a focus.

Table 3.1 gives an overview of the typical perspectives on the future in various eras.

A map of futures

The future. If all we mean by that is the time in front of us, then the definition of the future seems simple and any further inquiry superfluous. However, if we look at it more closely, then it quickly becomes clear that this initial unambiguous and exhaustive understanding of the future is often unsatisfactory and hardly does justice to the complexity of the future. Futurists try to categorize the future, using terms such as possible, probable and preferred. Yet this structure also remains unsatisfactory. As the future is a very complex concept, it is dangerous to look at it with too radical a simplification. Complexity can only be understood and handled with complexity.

If we look through the relevant literature, we notice with surprise and disappointment, that hardly any futures thinker has ever attempted a comprehensive categorization of the future that goes beyond probable, possible and preferred futures. The map presented here can be seen as such an attempt.

Table 3.1 Historical relevance of the perspectives

Period and role of the future	Perspectives / Futures glasses				
	Know the probable future	Know possible surprises	Creatively recognize future options	Determine a better future	Plan the doable future
Stone Age: the eternal present					
Bronze and Stone Age: Interpreters, seers and diviners	○				
Antiquity: Modern futures wisdom	●		○	●	
Middle Ages: Enforced standstill	○				
Renaissance: Utopias in distant places in the present	○		●	●	
Reformation: Creating the future through criticism of the present	○		○	●	
Enlightenment: Utopias at the same place in the future	●		●	●	
Industrialization: Technical visions and social change	●		●	●	
World Wars and Depression: Military and government planning and intervention	●	○	○	●	○
Post-War Years and 1950s: Vision and planning of reconstruction	●	○	●	●	●
1960s: Dawn of futures research	●	○	●	●	●
1970s: Popularization and disenchantment	●	●	●	●	●
1980s: Crisis and trend period	○	●	●	●	●
1990s: Catharsis and revival	○	●	●	●	○
2000s: Establishment and recognition	○	●	●	●	○

Futures, not future

The implication of a singular future suggested by the word future is quite obviously a fallacy. The future is plural. We generally don't think beyond a single imagined future. In the 16th century, the Spanish theologian Molina used the made-up word "futuribles" (later picked up again by Bertrand de Jouvenel in France), a combination of the words "futures" and "possibles", to mean possible futures. He was already aware, as opposed to popular understanding today, of the purpose of the conscious and preferred use of the plural of future: futures.

The futures experts started to speak about the future in the plural a few decades ago.[1] It is a linguistic pointer to the openness and, in principle, lack of predictability of the future. The plural term much better accommodates the fact that the future can have numerous possible outcomes. The plurality of the future makes it clear to us that in addition to the "standard future" there are, in principle, an endless number of alternative futures.

Types of futures

Figure 3.1 shows the types of futures from our viewpoint. The initial complex categorization enables appropriate simplification by bringing structure and a system into the term and the nature of the future. Let's therefore accept the temporary confusion in order to then develop a simple and practicable model. It is only possible to comprehend and understand why it is important and necessary to get to know and use the five futures glasses when you see how many different terms and definitions there are for the future.

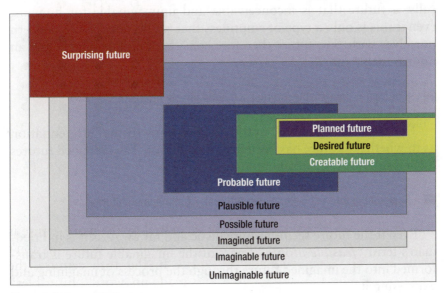

Figure 3.1 Types of futures

The types of futures suggested here need to be regarded under the following assumptions:

- The futures are defined from the perspective of an individual actor, meaning a person, a team or an organization. The content of every type of future is therefore contingent on the subjectivity and incomplete knowledge of each individual.
- The definitions of the types of futures are dependent on the time at which they are considered. The contents of the categories change over time. One future, such as contact with extraterrestrial life, can develop from the imaginable future to the possible future and plausible future to the probable future, before it falls out of the futures and into the present or the certain due to factual evidence.
- The types of futures depend on the sequence in which they are looked at. If you begin with the planned future, you can make a well-argued case for a different categorization.

How imaginable are futures?

It would seem obvious that every future that a person deals with, and could deal with, must be imaginable.[2] Imaginable is used synonymously with conceivable, knowable[3] and potential[4] here. If there is a conceivable or imaginable future, then there could be, at least theoretically, a future that is inconceivable and unimaginable for humans, even if this is only a type of emptiness that we do not need to concern ourselves with. The future therefore consists of an imaginable and an unimaginable future.

■ [Futures] = [imaginable futures] + [unimaginable futures]

The term "imaginable" automatically leads to the differentiation as to whether a future has been imagined or not. The imagined futures form a subset of the imaginable futures.

■ [Imaginable futures] = [imagined futures] + [unimagined futures]

Even if the future seems as unrealistic and far away as it is in Friedman's term *"feasible utopia"*,[5] part of the imaginable future is transformed into the imagined future through the process of imagining and expressing it.

A statement by Donald Rumsfeld, the former US Secretary of Defense, shows that even politicians concern themselves with the problem of imagined and only imaginable futures:

> As we know, there is the known known, i.e. things which we know that we know. We also know that there is the known unknown, which means that we know that there are some things that we do not know. But there is also the unknown unknown – the things which we don't know that we don't know.[6]

How probable are futures?

When most people think about the future, they do so in the category of probability.[7] This is because we know intuitively how valuable it would be to know the future.

Imaginable futures and possible futures

In order to be probable, a given future must first be physically possible.[8] A world economy based on hydrogen, the elimination of hunger, and long-term balanced government budgets are without a doubt physically possible. The question of their probability, however, is open to debate. The frequently discussed installation of space elevators "hung" on geostatic satellites is theoretically possible, but their possibility has been neither proven nor disproved in practice. Until 1995, this was also true for the existence of planets outside the sun system. Anyone who disputed the possibility was considered to be ignorant or blind, even though there had been no evidence of it before 1995. Nowadays, around two new planets are discovered every month. Until 2005/2006 the manufacture of cloaks of invisibility was considered impossible. Now, in physics at least, there are significant indices and even experiments that indicate that invisibility is actually possible through the deflection of light rays using appropriate equipment.[9]

■ [Future] = [possible futures] + [impossible futures]

If something is possible, it *must* be imaginable. If something is imaginable, it *may* be possible. For the time being, actual beaming seems to be imaginable but physically impossible, even if there have been a number of successful experiments on the teleportation of characteristics, which is not beaming in its real sense of teleporting a unique body.

■ [Possible futures] is a subset of [imaginable futures]

We can assume that not everything that is possible has already been imagined. We obviously have no proof of this: first, no one can know everything that has already been imagined and second, the evidence would turn the unimagined possible into the imagined possible, thus destroying what was to be proved.

Something that has been imagined may be possible but doesn't have to be. Something that is possible, may, but doesn't have to, have been already imagined. The possible and the imaginable futures therefore intersect.

■ [Possible futures] has an intersection with [imagined futures]

In this way, we can also define utopia as a future, which is imaginable, yet impossible to realize.

■ [Utopias] = [imaginable futures] − [possible futures]

If something is possible, it is also imaginable. Something that is imaginable *may* be possible. Something that is not imaginable cannot be possible.

Plausible futures

In addition to pure physical possibility, it seems meaningful to introduce the category of plausible futures.[10] A future is plausible when it can be described with arguments that make it seem evident that this future *could* actually happen. It is in principle possible that your new product may achieve one hundred percent market share within the first year: as a rule however, this is not plausible, at least not within one year. Futures can therefore be possible in principle without being plausible.

■ [Possible futures] = [plausible futures] + [implausible futures]

Something that is possible *may* be plausible. Something that is plausible *must* be possible, at least when using a strict measurement of plausibility.

■ [Plausible futures] is a subset of [possible futures]

Probable futures
Plausible futures are possible and, at the same time, imagined futures, that is, a subset of this category. If a future is possible and plausible, it can still be rather improbable. You could plausibly demonstrate how you want to achieve ninety percent market share within one year with your new product, or how, within the same time frame, you want to save eighty percent of the world's starving people. However plausible your arguments may appear and however brilliant your strategy may be, the probability would be considered as low by any reasonable standards.[11] Probable futures would therefore be a subset of plausible futures.

■ [Probable futures] is a subset of [plausible futures]

The further the time horizon reaches into the future, the more the probability of futures is a person's subjective evaluation and less something that can be mathematically substantiated. This is particularly true for the futures determined by humans in society, politics and business. Probability calculations for earthquakes on the other hand, can be done quite accurately, even if they leave open whether "one in 10,000 years" means tomorrow or in 20,000 years. To reduce it to a short formula: *The probability of futures is the result of human estimates that can only be partially substantiated mathematically.* The probabilities meant here are therefore more "expectation probabilities" than mathematical probabilities.

If we observe people thinking and communicating about probabilities, three categories emerge. We consider something to be either probable or improbable, or neither probable nor improbable, meaning "semi-probable".

■ [Plausible futures] = [probable futures] + [semi-probable futures] + [improbable futures]

Futures experts' definitions of probable futures have in common that they are generally interpreted as passive futures that happen to us and that we can change to a relatively low degree.[12]

Surprising futures
When considering futures, we have until now always assumed that we can deliberately look at possible and plausible futures and then

estimate their probability. But what about the futures we haven't imagined but which nevertheless happen? Almost no bank foresaw the fact that there would one day be peer-to-peer money markets for private individuals, such as Zopa (www.zopa.com) and Prosper (www.prosper.com). Let's call such cases surprising[13] futures. However, the occurrence of a future that we looked at, but then consciously or subconsciously classified as improbable can also be surprising. The thought of an airplane crash imagined at the check-in desk, of a tsunami in Indonesia as in 2004, of an HIV infection with a risky lifestyle or of the bankruptcy of a decisive client that was rejected as improbable, belong to the category of surprises if the unexpected does then occur. There are therefore unimagined surprises and imagined surprises.

■ [Surprising futures] = [imagined surprising futures]
+ [unimagined surprising futures]

As we can never exactly know what is possible and what isn't, there can also be surprising futures that we considered not to be physically possible before they occurred. The same then also applies to plausible futures.

■ [Surprising futures] has an intersection with [possible futures]
(according to current knowledge)

■ [Surprising futures] has an intersection with [plausible futures]

How creatable are futures?

If we think about futures in the category of probability, then it would seem reasonable to look at the future of the non-influenceable areas in our environment. If however, we think about our own future, whether as a person, a team or an organization, then we are primarily concerned with the dimension of being able to "form" it (which is synonymous with feasibility[14] and practicability[15]) and later also with "desirability".

The *passive perspective* on the probable future assumes that our environment will largely develop without our intervention and that this development will have a noticeable effect on us. The basic assumption of the passive perspective on the future is that we need to foresee what is coming in order to be able to prepare in good time for what the future will do with us. We think the future from the outside to the inside: we are passive and react.

The *active perspective* on the creatable future assumes that our environment will largely develop as we want it to. The basic assumption of the active perspective on the future is that we need to form or even make the future we want to have. We think the future from the inside to the outside: we are proactive and act.

Everyone can form his or her future within certain limitations. The wider these limitations are, the better a person and every group of people, be it the family, the company, the organization or the state, will feel. Yet not everyone can design their own happiness and reality. Not only the helpless child who is hungry and thirsty, but also every person without the necessary physical, mental, financial or other prerequisites, has limited possibilities to improve his own future.

The legal system of the European Union or the USA, the global military security situation and climate change are beyond the possibility of direct influence for any one individual and for most companies and organizations. Water can of course break stones, as one of the rallying cries of the alternative scene in the 1970s and 1980s claimed. If we join up with others, then imagination, resources and time are the only limiting factors to what we can change. However, looked at realistically, it is more sensible to accept that a significant part of our environment is beyond our targeted and direct influence. If we believe recent brain research, then even a significant part of our self is beyond our influence.

Table 3.2 Passive and active perspectives on the future

Criterion	Passive perspective	Active perspective
Focus	■ Actor's outside world	■ Actor's inside world
Direction of thought	■ From the outside inwards	■ From the inside outwards
Main idea	■ Anticipate the future and adjust oneself and the inside world	■ Invent the future, form it and adjust the outside world
Degree of creatability	■ Minimal ■ The future can hardly be influenced by the actor	■ Relatively high ■ The future can be influenced to a great degree by the actor
Methodic approach	■ Analytical	■ Creative

Table 3.2 (cont'd)

Mindset	■ Observing ■ Analytical / logical ■ Critical ■ Conservative ■ Fatalistic ■ Pessimistic / realistic ■ Evaluating	■ Imaginative ■ Intuitive ■ Creative ■ Progressive / transformative ■ Acting ■ Optimistic / realistic ■ Deciding
Assignable categories of the future (see next section)	■ Imaginable futures ■ Imagined futures ■ Possible futures ■ Plausible futures ■ Probable futures ■ Surprising futures	■ Creatable futures ■ Desired futures ■ Planned futures

The future as a whole always consists of both the active and the passive future. We need to assess the future of our environment in order to be able to design our own actions, which in turn have a certain, if mostly relatively low influence on the environment. Friedrich Rückert best expressed that and how human beings need both the foreseeable and the uncertain future.

> *Man's happiness consists of two things, that the future is equally certain and uncertain.* (Friedrich Rückert)

Two thousand five hundred years ago, Pericles suggested a clear prioritization. He claimed that it was not our job to predict the future, but to prepare for the future. If we look a little deeper at the logic of this statement, then we can see that we can only prepare for the future if we have assessed it to a certain extent; therefore it is initially part of the task to anticipate the future after all, if not to predict it. The same basic difference is also made by Cunha,[16] who differentiates between "foresight as prediction", meaning the passive-anticipatory future and "foresight as invention", meaning the also active-creating future.

In order that futures can be created, they must be imaginable and possible.

■ [Creatable futures] is a subset of [possible futures]

As human beings can also think and act in an irrational way, the creatable future does not necessarily have to be plausible, even if the argument of irrationality might make it appear plausible.

■ [Creatable futures] has an intersection with [plausible futures]

■ [Creatable futures] has an intersection with [probable futures]

Plausible futures and probable futures can be created to a certain extent. It is highly probable that the birthrate in many developed countries will remain at less than two, but it can only be influenced to a tiny degree by the individual even with a great deal of will and effort. If we work in a sector that is obviously and probably heading towards a crisis, we can hardly divert the crisis from the sector, we can however, change our probable future by looking for a task in another sector.

How desirable are futures?

Most people have a more or less exact idea of what the future, above all their own, should be like.[17] Many know exactly what they want with regard to health, a partner, wealth and so on. Anyone who cannot determine his desired future himself can generally say which of a number of options he would prefer for his own future.[18] Possible directions of professional development or even just the options for the next vacation are prioritized in this way. And those who have difficulty in prioritizing their desired futures, at least know what they don't want.

Perhaps the easiest way of classifying the future is into optimistic, pessimistic and realistic.[19] However, we see a significant semantic and ontological difference between the desired future and the optimistic attitude towards the future. The optimistic attitude sees "the future" more as a whole, whereas the "desired future" relates more to the future concerned with the person who desires it. The same difference applies to the pessimistic and the feared future.

Desired futures

Creatable futures may, but do not have to, also be preferable or even desired futures. Whereas this is easy to understand, we have to think a little more closely about whether the desired futures should also be creatable. Success coaches recommend setting only achievable goals, and claim that anything else leads to frustration. To generalize this principle, a small but important difference between preferable and desired needs to be made. Desired, in the sense of really being followed as a goal, is generally a subset of preferable. Humankinds' dreams and desires may be limitless, yet what we really want is less than that which we could want. Living to be 150 may be desirable, yet hardly anyone really wants it. The amazing wealth of a Bill Gates (the majority of which he will soon have donated) is perhaps desirable, but rarely actually wanted by those not in close sight of Bill in the wealth rankings.

■ [Desired futures] is a subset of [preferred futures]

If a person or a team desires a certain future, then this future will not correspond exactly to the probable future, or it wouldn't need to be desired. If the top management of a company determines and announces its vision for a desired future, this has something of a normative[20] function – a binding basis for orientation is created – and something of a prescriptive[21] function – how and in which direction the employees should act is demonstrated in order to realize the future that management desires.

If we understand desired futures to be a binding goal, not just as desirable, then, as the philosophers and success guides all suggest, we will select the desired futures from the mass of creatable futures.

■ [Desired futures] is a subset of [creatable futures]

Planned futures

If we recognize something as creatable and classify it as desired, then we can also plan it. Through planning, we break the desired future down into a series of planned actions.[22]

■ [Planned futures] is a subset of [desired futures]

Feared and frightening futures

The opposite of desired futures are feared futures.[23] Why does our model only contain the category of desired futures but not the feared futures? Which futures do we fear? We fear those futures that would question our current corporate strategy or our life concept. This is the case when assumptions about the future on which we base our important decisions for the future are shown to be incorrect. If you assume that a computer cannot do your work, you fear a future in which this assumption is shown to be wrong. If you assume that your key technology, rubber membranes in automobile motors for example, cannot convincingly be replaced by electronics, then you fear a future in which exactly that happens. And we of course fear futures that we know would physically or psychologically harm us.

But we also fear the type of future we haven't concretely imagined. We know that the future can also surprise us in a way we haven't yet imagined but we can at least imagine that our previous strategy could prove to be wrong or unfavorable in this surprising future. We experience fear of concrete threats, and anguish when we do not know the concrete threat.[24]

It appears that we fear everything that is surprising in some way, whether we expected it to be different or we didn't expect it at all. But we also fear the non-surprising if it can harm us. The thing that we fear can be probable, semi-probable, hardly probable, only plausible, only possible or even just imaginable. One is almost tempted to characterize as feared or anguishing everything that is not desired. If we want to display reality well, we also need to identify the indifferent futures, meaning futures that we neither particularly desire nor particularly fear, which we are basically indifferent to. Then we can formulate that the feared futures can only be defined through the other futures, so that they do not need to expressly appear in the model. Feared futures are equal to the total future minus the desired futures and the indifferent futures.

■ [Feared futures] = [futures] − [desired futures] − [indifferent futures]

The concept of the five futures glasses

The map of the futures creates a good understanding of the complexity of the seemingly simple and unambiguous term "future". It also gives us a reason to apply a portion of modesty and humility when wanting to manage the future. However, in order to be able to master the complexity shown in the map of the futures, we need a simplified model that helps us to understand the future without being oversimplified.

From futures to futures glasses

Table 3.3 summarizes the types of futures into the considerably simpler model of the five futures glasses.

Table 3.3 Types of futures and futures glasses

Types of future	Active/Passive	Five futures glasses
■ Probable and improbable futures ■ (Plausible futures)	Passive	**Blue futures glasses** Assumption analysis: Knowing about the probable development of the environment
■ Surprising futures	Passive	**Red futures glasses** Surprise analysis: Knowing the possible surprises
■ Creatable futures	Active	**Green futures glasses** Opportunity development: Knowing the possible courses of action for the future
■ Desired futures	Active	**Yellow futures glasses** Vision development: Determining the long-term orientation
■ Planned futures	Active	**Violet futures glasses** Strategy development: Determining the action necessary for the future
■ Imaginable futures ■ Imagined futures ■ Possible futures	Active and passive	Futures unable to be clearly assigned to one pair of futures glasses

The colors are assigned to the futures glasses intuitively. Blue reminds us of clinical, reserved and logical analysis. Red is for surprise and (usually) for threats. We think of green as the color of creativity, opportunities and options. We understand yellow as the color for a decision in a certain direction, in the sense of a vision. And finally, violet is considered as the color of planning and action.

The categories "imaginable futures", "imagined futures", and "possible futures" are so basic and relevant for every perspective that they cannot be clearly assigned to any pair of futures glasses. They can be included in all five perspectives and provide the mental raw material for different ways of looking at the future.

The best sequence

Theoretically, the five futures glasses could be shown in a total of 120 sequences (permutations) $(5! = 5*4*3*2*1)$[25] to describe a process or method. The sequence shown in Table 3.3 is generally the most useful. How do we know which sequence is most suitable for most applications? We derive it from five principles.

1. *Think from the outside towards the inside first:* We need to know our environment in order to orient ourselves.

2. *We have to see the probable in order to define the surprising:* The blue futures glasses must come at the beginning. The assumptions fulfill the orientation function, which in conventional scenario approaches is met by scenarios, and which is insufficient since scenarios, by definition, describe rather improbable futures.

3. *Strategy follows vision:* Strategy is understood here as the path to achieve goals. Therefore, the yellow futures glasses come before the violet ones, which have to be at the end in order that practical action can be based on all futures glasses.

4. *Vision follows opportunities:* We need options in order to be able to make decisions. The green futures glasses therefore need to come before the yellow futures glasses.

5. *Potential surprises imply opportunities and help to solidify the vision:* The red futures glasses therefore need to come before the green ones. The red futures glasses need to be used again and improved after developing a preliminary vision with the yellow futures glasses, since it is necessary to develop scenarios of surprising futures that directly challenge the vision. We need a line of sight in the sense of an interim strategic vision in order to be able to develop relevant scenarios.

The seven benefits

You have already read about the benefits of the five futures glasses in detail on page 4:

1. They are a mental map for futures, bringing order and precision to future management.

2. They guarantee clear communication through precise language and a coherent model.

3. They build a bridge to the future, enabling you to use the results of futures research as a resource.

4. They enable more realistic expectations of future management.

5. They are a toolbox you can use to apply methods, techniques and tools more precisely.

6. You can see more of the future with them.

7. They are a template for practical futures projects.

How you can easily remember the five futures glasses

The following story aims to provide you with a mental picture of the five futures glasses, so that you can easily remember them. The story is not supposed to be taken literally and the maritime details are not always correct. It serves as a memory technique.

> #### The windjammer captain's five futures glasses
>
> Imagine the captain of a tall ship, who sets out with his crew to distant, unknown destinations. In order to steer his ship towards a good future, he needs to regularly get a picture of how the sea and the weather will develop over the coming hours and days. The captain and his crew are dependent on natural forces. They cannot influence them, let alone steer them in a certain direction. Thinking creatively about the future weather is of no help to them either; fantasy is out of place here. The captain needs to get hold of available weather data and process it into his own personal assumptions about the future weather in the coming hours and days using his experience, powers of observation and logic.
>
> A clever captain will not rely solely on his own estimates. He will ask his officers and weather specialists for their personal assumptions about the future. He will not fully understand it and his crew, in turn, will not necessarily understand every aspect of his assumptions. A common picture of the future weather situation will only be arrived at gradually after discussions. A sail strategy can be developed based on these common assumptions about the future although there may be a certain variation, on assumptions about the wind direction for example. Ideally, it should also be possible to implement the sail strategy even if the deviating assumptions about the future later prove to have been more correct.
>
> **What color does the captain see when he looks at the sea and the sky? Blue! He is wearing the blue futures glasses for the probable future.**
>
> The captain knows that only one thing is more or less certain on his journey into the future: that the future will surprise him. A lot of things could surprise him: monsters (freak waves more than thirty meters high, which really do occur twice a day),[26] heavy storms or pirates, who still make life difficult for seafarers today, in the Strait of Malacca for example, where hundreds of pirate attacks take place every year. All this is unlikely, yet possible.
>
> The sailors can avoid such threats if they know about them. They can choose a less risky route or, if the risk of pirates is too great for example, even decide on the second-best but less risky strategic vision for the ship. The captain and his officers will in any case take protective equipment and weapons with them and train their crew to prepare for encounters with pirates or freak waves. The captain can only protect the ship against surprises if he prepares for them using eventual strategies.

If pirates attack without warning, what is shed? Correct – blood. And blood is ... red! The captain is wearing the red futures glasses for the surprising future.

In the next step, the captain needs to consider possible destinations that he could head for with his crew, based on his assumptions and the possible surprises. Which fertile countries and islands can be reached and conquered? This is not a scheduled trip, but an expedition into unknown territory. No one has ever been there before; none of the crew, but also no one else from their country. They only know the possible destinations from hearsay and in the case of some destinations it is doubtful if they actually exist and are not just a product of the imagination of visionaries and gurus. Furthermore, the captain and many of his crew develop their own fantasies and paint such colorful pictures of worthwhile destinations that they are convinced that these fertile countries and islands really exist. What is needed when thinking and talking about possible destinations is the crew's imagination and creativity rather than its experience. Experience-based logic often even prevents excellent opportunities from being developed.

What color does the captain see when he thinks about fertile countries and islands? Green! He is wearing the green futures glasses for the creatable future.

If the captain and his officers do not decide on one of the destinations they have imagined, they can only drop anchor or waste time, energy and money by sailing aimlessly. They have to decide which of the possible and worthwhile destinations they want to head for. They cannot steer their ship towards several destinations or several visions. A vision is always singular. The destinations they imagined are quasi vision candidates. Which vision candidates fit the assumptions on the weather and the sea? Which vision candidates fit the potential and capabilities of the crew? Which vision candidates can be reached with this ship in an appropriate amount of time and with an appropriate amount of effort? After all, there are several competitive ships and every destination can only provide a living for a small number of ships. Which vision candidates do the crew eagerly accept? The captain will finally decide on one of the vision candidates with his crew and thus arrive at a strategic vision, albeit a temporary one at first. Having a concrete, fascinating, jointly strived for and yet achievable vision is like sailing towards the sun.

What color does the captain see when he sails towards the sun? Yellow! He is wearing the yellow futures glasses for the desired future.

Once the captain, with his team, has made assumptions about the probable development and future of the sea and the weather, conceived of and evaluated the possible destinations as opportunities, determined the vision, thought through surprises and developed eventual strategies, he can start planning – creating the most obvious future. The seafarers now determine strategic subobjectives on the way to the strategic vision and support all of this, in modern terms, through the introduction and adjustment of processes, projects and systems. Pragmatism and realism are what are called for here. At this point, the seafarers think about opportunities again. How can the strategic vision be achieved in an efficient and intelligent way? This creative phase is similar to the one in which they looked for destinations. But the opportunities being looked for here are of a more operative nature: they are concerned with the "how". Finally, they need to plan and implement.

When you plan and then act on a sailing ship, you are going to get bruised. And the worst of those bruises are which color? Violet! The captain wears the violet futures glasses for the planned future.

The tasks of the captain and his officers are very similar to those of an entrepreneur and his management team. And, as in principle everyone is the Chairman of the Board of his own life enterprise, the sailing ship example can be applied to almost everyone's future management. Someone who is on a journey by plane, train or automobile has a known and exactly described route in front of him. When we move towards the future, these trodden paths or even paved roads do not exist. That is why the example of a windjammer on a journey of discovery is so suitable, even if it seems a little contrived in detail.

An overview of the five futures glasses

Table 3.4 provides a comprehensive overview of the characters of the five futures glasses. They are the fundamental tools for your future management.

> *Give someone a fish and he will feed himself once, teach him fishing and he will feed himself all his life.* (Laotse)

Each pair of futures glasses will be described in the following chapters using the same structure:

1. *Overview:* Tabular overview of the most important issues.
2. *Cases:* Insights into the character of the pair of futures glasses.
3. *Purpose:* What this pair of futures glasses is for.
4. *Core concepts:* What you see through this pair of futures glasses.
5. *Principles:* What you need to know about this pair of futures glasses.
6. *Attitude:* How you approach this pair of futures glasses.
7. *Methodology:* Which work steps and methods are available.

Table 3.4 Overview of the five futures glasses

Futures glasses	The blue futures glasses	The red futures glasses	The green futures glasses	The yellow futures glasses	The violet futures glasses
Primary goal	■ To know the probable future developments in the environment	■ To know the possible surprises the future holds	■ To know the possible options for action	■ To determine the desired future	■ To determine the necessary action to achieve the desired future
Secondary goal	■ To improve assumptions ■ To make better decisions ■ To reduce risks	■ To prepare for surprises ■ To be less surprised; to reduce peak level of stress ■ To secure existence	■ To expand the potential for success ■ To increase the number and quality of ideas for the vision and the strategy	■ To follow a clear direction ■ To seize potential for success ■ To initiate and coordinate action	■ To link the futures strategy to operational strategy ■ To coordinate action
Example	■ In 2020, one third of the population will be 60 or older.	■ A pandemic with an unknown virus could kill millions of people. ■ September 11, 2001, November 9, 1989 (fall of the Berlin Wall)	■ We can increase our efficiency by using videoconferencing.	■ We will be the first provider of a conversational user interface for simple communication between man and computer.	■ We will establish a cooperation with a software research institute to develop the conversational user interface.
Objects of thought (concepts) concerned	■ Assumption questions ■ Future factors (trends technologies, issues) ■ Signals ■ Future projections ■ Future scenarios ■ Assumptions about the future	■ Surprise questions ■ Surprises (event-based) ■ Surprises (process-based)	■ Opportunity questions ■ Future opportunities ■ Vision candidates	■ Visions questions ■ Mission (mission elements) ■ Vision (vision elements) ■ Strategic guidelines	■ Strategy questions ■ Goals ■ Projects ■ Processes ■ Systems ■ Development opportunities ■ Eventual strategies

Table 3.4 (cont'd)

Futures glasses	The blue futures glasses	The red futures glasses	The green futures glasses	The yellow futures glasses	The violet futures glasses
Perspectives	■ Macro perspective ■ Outward orientation	■ Macro perspective ■ Outward orientation	■ Micro perspective ■ Inward orientation	■ Micro perspective ■ Inward orientation	■ Micro perspective ■ Inward orientation
Attitude	■ Detached ■ Passive ■ Observing	■ Detached ■ Passive ■ Observing	■ Involved ■ Active ■ Intervening	■ Involved ■ Active ■ Intervening	■ Involved ■ Active ■ Intervening
Mindset	■ Realistic ■ Critical ■ Analytical ■ Experience-based ■ Conservative	■ Calculatedly pessimistic ■ Analytic ■ Creative ■ Imaginative ■ Progressive	■ Optimistic ■ Creative ■ Intuitive ■ Imaginative ■ Progressive ■ Transformative	■ Optimistic and realistic at the same time ■ Intuitive and analytic at the same time ■ Progressive	■ Realistic ■ Pragmatic ■ Analytic ■ Experience-based ■ Progressive
Destructive factors	■ Wanting to creatively develop the future ■ Wishful thinking ■ Being too optimistic ■ Being too pessimistic ■ Including one's own action	■ Probability thinking ■ Underestimating the benefits ■ Suppression and avoidance	■ Critical thinking ■ Experience-based thinking	■ Being too ambitious ■ Not being ambitious enough	■ Being too ambitious ■ Not being ambitious enough ■ Under or overestimating the importance of finance and resources
Typical methods	■ Projections and scenarios ■ Delphi ■ Roadmapping	■ Assumptions reversal ■ Scenario methods ■ Wild Card analysis ■ Wargaming	■ Impact analysis ■ Creativity techniques	■ Decision techniques ■ Conception techniques (e.g. morphologies)	■ Planning ■ Project management ■ Roadmapping

4 Your blue futures glasses: What lies ahead?

No one can predict the future, but it is dangerous not to try to do so, for we base every decision in our lives and in our companies on our image of the future. These are either assumptions about the present, meaning abstractions of reality we consider to be the truth, or assumptions about the future, in which case we are more aware of their uncertain nature. Philosophy, and epistemology in particular, has been concerned with assumptions about the present for millennia. Aristotle, Heraclitus, Descartes, Kant, Popper and Habermas are the great names associated with considerations on the importance of assumptions about the present. Assumptions about the future on the other hand are a relatively new area of research. Every human decision is based on assumptions.

> If our assumptions are wrong, we can lose our economic existence. If they are right, the winds of change drive us to success.

Assumptions about the future can be made on more or less any thought-object in the future, on future:

- facts
- rules
- causes
- effects
- assumptions of other people
- values of other people
- goals of other people
- expectations of other people
- existence of something
- state of something
- development of something
- quality of something and so on.

As shown in the story of the windjammer captain, the point of the blue futures glasses is to see which developments and which futures in our environment in general we can expect. People use the blue futures glasses to satisfy their age-old need for advance information without having to fall back on a crystal ball or other mystic aids. With the blue futures glasses you ask yourself two main questions:

1. How much do you know about the driving forces of change and the possible changes in your environment?
2. Which changes and developments do you consider to be probable, which to be improbable and which to be semi-probable?

As the past colonizes the future to a certain extent through a person's own projective thinking, as described by Ernst Bloch, the view through the blue futures glasses doesn't need creative drafts of the future. However, even if the view of the probable future is not innovative, we need it for orientation.

Your blue futures glasses: Overview

Table 4.1 summarizes the characteristics of the blue futures glasses.

Table 4.1 Overview of the blue futures glasses
Objective: To estimate the probable future development of the environment.
Work step and key question: ■ Assumption analysis ■ Which changes will we probably face and which not?
Purpose: ■ You firm up the basis of your decisions and strategies. ■ You improve your orientation and security. ■ You reduce the complexity of the future. ■ You better understand what is happening today. ■ You make it easier to communicate about the future. ■ You integrate the various perceptions of the future more easily. ■ You form attractors for knowledge about the future.
Attitude and principles: ■ Assume the future to be largely unpredictable. ■ Direct the blue futures glasses towards your environment (not internal aspects). ■ Look at the future in a passive and detached way from a macro perspective. ■ Adopt a realistic and conservative attitude with the blue futures glasses. ■ Understand experience as a success factor.

Table 4.1 (cont'd)

Attitude and principles (cont'd):
- You cannot carry out a complete assumption analysis.
- Use assumptions about the future as a replacement for impossible future "knowledge".
- Remember that everyone has assumptions about the future all the time.
- You cannot delegate your assumptions about the future.
- Improve your assumptions about the future through provocative projections.
- Improve your assumptions about the future by being affected personally.
- Improve your assumptions about the future through a wide base of support.

Core concepts:
- Assumption questions
- Future factors
- Signals
- Future projections and future scenarios
- Assumptions about the future (expectations, non-expectations, eventualities)

Typical methods:
- Forecasting
- Delphi survey
- Scenario techniques
- Games and simulation

Procedure:
1. Put together a futures team.
2. Get an overall idea of the character of the blue futures glasses.
3. Determine a uniform futures horizon.
4. Ask your assumption questions.
5. Determine the relevant future factors for your assumption questions.
6. Look for information and signals on the selected future factors.
7. Develop a minimum of three and a maximum of six future projections for each of your future questions.
8. Draw up a list of arguments for and against each projection.
9. Bring the assumptions about the future of each individual member of the future team to the surface.
10. Prepare an assumption panorama.
11. Discuss the assumption panorama.
12. Carry out a second evaluation round.
13. Gain more confidence in estimating the probable.

Results:
An assumption panorama will develop with the most important assumption questions and answers to them that are formulated as assumptions on future developments and are marked with expectation probabilities.

Case studies on the blue futures glasses

The following examples attest to the role that the blue futures glasses play in the economic existence and success of individuals and companies.

The Allies' assumptions about the future of Hitler's demise

An early assumption analysis that finally ended in concrete ideas for action (opportunities) can be found in a study carried out for the CIA in 1943. It contains nine possible answers to the question of how Hitler could be removed from power. Based on an analysis of Hitler's behavior and convictions, the psychologist Henry A. Murray developed nine scenarios of Hitler's demise. He presented them as possible outcomes, but designated them as predictions to which he allocated degrees of probability.[1]

1. Hitler could be seized by the military or some revolutionary fraction and imprisoned in a fortress (improbable).
2. Hitler could be shot by a German (improbable).
3. Hitler could arrange his murder by a German, possibly by a Jew, in order to become a martyr in the same way as Siegfried, Caesar and Jesus (slightly probable).
4. Hitler could arrange his death in battle as the leader of his army in order to be seen as the defender of the Aryan people against Bolshevism and the Slavs (probable).
5. Hitler could go completely insane, in view of his psychological dysfunctions (slightly probable).
6. Hitler could commit suicide, at the very last moment and in a very dramatic way, through a silver bullet or a huge explosion on the Obersalzberg for example (highly probable).
7. Hitler could die of natural causes.
8. Hitler could flee to a neutral country to write his long planned Bible for the German people (improbable).
9. Hitler could fall into the hands of the United Nations (here: the Allied Forces) (least probable).

These scenarios led Murray to both original and crude recommendations, such as the spreading of the information that all German leaders would be executed, except Hitler who would be banished to the island of St Helena as a more terrible punishment. Hitler, who greatly admired Napoleon, could then see how he could write his plan for German military action in the future and paint landscapes on St Helena, while creating his own legend. Unfortunately no one knows which strategy the Allies developed based on this assumption analysis.

The billion-dollar bet between Airbus and Boeing

In the aircraft industry, there has been a bet on the future for decades, involving billions of dollars in investments and hundreds of thousands of jobs. Airbus and Boeing are engaged in a grim battle. In the middle of the 1990s, the different assumptions made by the top executive teams were shown clearly in their product strategies.

Airbus made the future assumption that cost not time would be the determining factor in the airline industry. Based on this assumption, Airbus developed the A380, claiming "cost will count", with a special focus on increasing the productivity of airlines and airports. Airbus saw capacity problems, with the airports' large hubs in particular, that would be solved by the new super jumbo. At the same time, Boeing's management made fundamentally different assumptions, stating that smaller and faster planes would provide the airlines with a competitive advantage in future. Claiming "time will count", Boeing concentrated its efforts on the "Sonic Cruiser" concept, which would enable fast direct flights between smaller airports.

Boeing's assumptions about the future on the importance of speed proved to be wrong. As a result of the lack of interest on the part of its clients, Boeing had to discontinue the development of the Sonic Cruiser at the concept stage. The Airbus management's assumptions about the future were more correct. In view of the strong competition, costs are a decisive success factor for airlines. The A380 made its maiden flight in April 2005. After that however, various operative problems led to a number of delays with the result that the initial delivery planned for 2006 had to be postponed several times. Even the most accurate assumptions about the future require excellent operative performance.

In December 2003, Boeing opened a new round in the clash of the titans with its decision for the 787 Dreamliner (then 7E7). The management partly revised its assumptions about the future. Boeing still assumes that the number of direct flights will increase, but time as a decisive competitive factor has moved into the background. In its current new development, Boeing is assuming the decisive significance of fuel efficiency in future. The basic assumption "cost will count" has therefore been retained. The early order situation looked highly promising. However, the Boeing 787 has also been subject to repeated rumors about delays in the schedule.[2]

The airlines play a decisive role as the clients of the two rivals. Their assumptions about the future are, in turn, fundamental for Airbus's and Boeing's assumptions. In November 2006, Japan Airlines announced that purchasing the A380 made no sense and expressed the assumption about the future that the A380 was going against the market trend in which the airlines increasingly preferred to purchase more fuel-efficient, medium sized planes such as the Boeing 787. The A380 was a highly controversial concept on the current aircraft market. JAL plans to reduce the share of large planes in its fleet from sixty-two percent to thirty-eight percent within five years. The billion-dollar bet on the future between Airbus and Boeing will continue to be full of suspense.

Changing assumptions about the future at Daimler

Edzard Reuter, former Chairman of the Daimler-Benz Board, decided to attempt to transform the company from an automobile manufacturer into an "integrated technology corporation". This plan was based on the assumption that the automobile market was approaching saturation, making further growth and, as a result, an adequate level of profitability impossible if Daimler were present on this market alone. Reuter's efforts ended in a long period of substantial losses for Daimler-Benz. An incorrect assumption led the company into a crisis.

After the management changed in the corporation, Reuter's successor, Jürgen Schrempp, concentrated on building automobiles again. He assumed that only a few, very large companies would survive in future. As a result, he formed one of the world's largest automobile manufacturers, culminating in the purchase of Chrysler and the merger of the two companies. A few years later, the total market value of both companies was lower than the value of Daimler-Benz before the takeover. Either Schrempp's assumptions about the future on the market development were wrong, or his assumption that Chrysler was a good acquisition candidate.

Will book publishers suffer the same fate as the music publishers at the hands of E-Books?

In 2006, the Philips subsidiary iRex introduced the iLead onto the

European market, the first E-Book-Reader whose use is not limited by so-called DRM software (Digital Rights Management). The iRex management's assumption was that customers will acquire the necessary content themselves, as they have done in the music industry. As it has been difficult until now to acquire a sufficient amount of digital reading material by legal means, the dark corners of the internet could make the product into a success. In the same way, illegal file-sharing networks helped the digital distribution of music in MP3 format to become accepted, until the music industry and outsiders such as Apple eventually provided attractive, legal offers of music. The iRex management expected a similar development. Willem Endhoven, the company's marketing manager, was quoted as saying: "The Iliad will be to reading, what the MP3 player is to music."[3] The coming years will show if his assumption is correct.

BASF sells the pharmaceutical division

Based on the assumption that a company with a turnover of only two billion Euros has no chance of operating sufficiently profitably in the pharmaceutical market of the future, BASF sold its pharmaceutical division in 1999. The sale enabled the chemical company to concentrate on areas of business in which it saw its strength and had positive assumptions about the future. They then named themselves "The Chemical Company". Its economic success has proved these assumptions to be correct so far.

Advisory software for financial services

German tax law, by far the most complicated tax law in the world, was already available in the mid-1990s in software packages, which enable people to complete their taxes in dialog with the program. Nowadays, these software programs even provide a moderator, who guides the user through the program and patiently explains everything.

One could now confront financial advisors with the thought that advice on retirement provisions is less complex than tax advice and derive the following futures projections from that: in 2018, a significant number of clients, meaning around twenty percent, will also use mobile software for financial advice solutions and for developing a long-term financial strategy. Most financial advisors react to this with a pitying smile and, at best, incredulity. However, if we systematically analyze the arguments in Figure 4.1, the financial advisors' arguments begin to falter. Many of them suddenly realize that advice doesn't necessarily have to be a personal service. The result is regularly that the assumption basis is shaken and they start to think about completely different futures strategies.

Future question	How will the value process change in the financial services sector?
Future projection	2018: A significant number of customers use self-advisory software (with mobile availability) to solve their financial questions and to develop a long-term finance strategy.

Pro arguments	Contra arguments
■ Home banking is increasing the use of software for personal financial management in private households. ■ An increasing number of people complete their taxes on their computer and transmit them digitally to the tax authorities. ■ Analysis functions enable software to develop from being a purely administrative instrument to an interactive advice and optimization tool. ■ The borders between software installed on a local computer and internet applications are becoming increasingly blurred. ■ Internet access is becoming increasingly cheap. ■ A lot of people already rely primarily on their own judgment on financial issues. ■ Self-advisory software guarantees a high level of discretion. ■ The software also offers elements of learning and fun.	■ The time required to get used to the software could be too much for many people. ■ Computer manipulation is increasing and making people suspicious of technical procedures.

Figure 4.1 Projection with pro and contra arguments

Commercial buildings in Frankfurt

In 1990, Ulrich Cartellieri, former member of the Managing Board and Supervisory Board of the Deutsche Bank, borrowed a statement from a French entrepreneur that is now famous in the banking world: "The banks are the steel industry of the 90s." The number of employees has in fact sunk dramatically since 2001. The signals have been more than clear for a long time.

The city Frankfurt am Main is dependent on banks as leasers of its commercial buildings like no other German city. There is a saying that when the banks cough, the Frankfurt property market immediately gets pneumonia. Banks lease almost a third of the area. In a study in 2004, the Deutsche Bank[4] itself forecast a twenty percent lower demand by 2050. The increase in the number of home offices thanks to better technical infrastructure and the declining population are two of the influencing factors in the falling requirement.

What were the assumptions about the future of those who built the office blocks? Which consequences did they foresee from the clear signals? None. They kept on building until 2004! In 2006, the level of vacant buildings in Frankfurt was around 17 percent or 2.1 million square meters. Of this, 0.6 to 0.7 million square meters is so-called base vacancy. The figures in all other major German property cities were much lower: Düsseldorf 12.4, Munich 10.4, Berlin 10.3 and Hamburg 8.0 percent. In 2005, forty percent less office space was completed than in the previous year.

> If the assumptions about the future are incorrect, if therefore the steering instruments are set in the wrong direction, then even the best captain will lose his way.

The extremely high liquidity resulting from disappointed stock market expectations after 2001 cannot alone justify the level of property investment. What would have happened if someone had taken each individual decision-maker aside and asked him to bet a large sum of his personal, after-tax money that this or that building would really achieve its planned return? We can assume that many a square meter would never have been built.

Well-known wrong assumptions

Numerous books of quotes have been published which testify to the limitations of the human imagination and wrong assumptions. Charles Duell, Head of the US Patent Office in 1899, is alleged to have requested that his office be closed as everything of importance had already been invented. In 1963, *Newsweek* quoted the British astronomer Sir Harold Spencer as holding the view that it would take generations before man landed on the moon. And if it did happen, then there would be little likelihood of also returning.[5] In 1985, when Microsoft Windows 1.0 was introduced, the *New York Times* described it as "a totally useless product". In July 1989, a few months before the fall of the Berlin Wall, Gerhard Schröder, former German Chancellor, assumed self-confidently: "Forty years after the founding of the German Federal Republic, we should not lie to a new generation about the opportunity of reunification. It does not exist."[6] The renowned

German newspaper *Die Welt* wrote in 2001, that the internet would not become a mass medium, "because in its soul, it isn't one".[7]

Purpose of the blue futures glasses

You wear the blue futures glasses in order to satisfy a number of needs and to achieve certain goals.

You firm up the basis of your decisions and strategies

The quality and meaning of a strategy concept or an individual decision can only be verified if the assumptions about the future they are based on are known.[8] Strategy concepts are rarely illogical or meaningless as such. If entrepreneurs and managers fail with their strategy, it is rarely due to the strategy itself, but much more frequently due to incorrect assumptions about the future.

Every decision and act that reaches into the future is based on assumptions about the future. You base practically your whole life concept on your assumptions about the future. Your profession, the professions you didn't choose, your choice of partner, your personal investment strategy for your retirement provision, and also the place where you live are all to a large degree the result of your assumptions about the future. Where you live may well depend on where you grew up, but you basically periodically make the mostly subconscious decision that it makes sense for you to continue living there. Even the direction of your children's education depends partly on your assumptions about the future, or at least on those occasions where your opinion was important.

The existence and the strategy of your company or your organization are even more obviously essentially based on assumptions about the future. They form the basis of the mission, the vision, the strategies and the decisions. You evaluate the future more or less consciously when deciding which products your company develops, which markets it serves, which people are recruited or dismissed. A not insignificant part of a company's investments are geared towards ten or even twenty years. These include decisions on production locations, particularly in the chemical industry for example, or on the desired corporate culture. Whether you do it consciously and systematically or more in passing, decisions on such cornerstones of your existence cannot be made without assumptions about the future.

■ With the blue futures glasses, you do not forecast futures; you diagnose assumptions about the future.

Careers and companies flourish and wither with the quality of the underlying assumptions about the future. Our assumptions about the future, consciously or subconsciously, almost constantly influence what we do, what we don't do and how we do something.

The point of the blue futures glasses is to bring assumptions about the future up to the surface of our perception, to diagnose their quality and finally to improve them. By working on your assumptions about the future, you achieve quite a feat. You become surer that you assess the future correctly, although you cannot predict it. It sounds paradoxical at first. When you bring your assumptions about the future to the surface[9] and thus make them deliberate, you have created the possibility of continuously checking and controlling their correctness. You can invite colleagues, experts, employees and friends to verify your assumptions about the future using questions such as the following:

1. Which questions would you ask?
2. Which projections are missing in your view?
3. Which assumptions would you make?
4. How would you assess the probability?
5. How do you rate our arguments for and against a certain probability of a projection?
6. Which arguments have we overlooked?

You improve your orientation and security

As we can, strictly speaking, know nothing about the future, substantiated assumptions about the future help to give us a certain degree of orientation towards the future. The result of looking through the blue futures glasses is a picture, developed either individually for an individual person or collectively for a team, of an assumed probable future for the most important field of observation and objects. You can have customers, the market, competitors, technologies, the environment or laws in your sights.

Working with assumptions about the future reduces the number of probable futures. Assumptions about the future work like the constraints in a linear or non-linear optimization in mathematics, which are also used to narrow down the solution space.

> Assumptions about the future are the mental tools with which we satisfy our need for advance knowledge without being able to predict the future.

The more uncertain the future is, the more necessary and important it is to carefully develop and analyze assumptions about the future. Incorrect assumptions about the future lead to dangerous strategies and, as a result, to risky situations. Good assumptions about the future are like sextants for a good strategy.[10] They ensure that more than fifty percent of your decisions are right, which Hans-Peter Keitel, member of the Board of Hochtief, once formulated as a goal.[11]

You reduce the complexity of the future

Social, economic and political change is a highly complex phenomenon. Assumptions about future trends, developments and conditions can help to reduce the complexity that inevitably results from looking at the future and thus simplify the thinking process. In practice, there is never as much time available as would be necessary to comprehensively analyze the future. Assumptions about the future, based on solid arguments and embedded in a total model as recommended and shown here, are intended to help to cover the essential points.

One could say that a really useful assumption about the future must be incorrect to a certain extent: incorrect in the sense that it hides part of the future in order to be able to really reduce its complexity.

With the help of well-developed assumptions about the future, a whole network of details and sub-assumptions can be meaningfully pulled together. The degree of aggregation you choose for your assumptions about the future depends on your point of view.

You better understand what is happening today

The development of assumptions about the future inevitably leads to considerations as to how your market, and in a wider sense your environment, functions both in the past and in the present. It is necessary to develop and use an understanding of the mechanisms and the logic of change. This is an indispensable precondition for the development of assumptions about the future. Your assumptions about the future need to be consistent as a whole, meaning at least with few inconsistencies. Not even the present is completely free of inconsistencies.

You make it easier to communicate about the future

If the reasons for assumptions about the future are clear, then significantly fewer misunderstandings will occur when communicating about the future. Those involved in the discussion better understand on which assumptions about the future the other party is basing his opinions, judgments and decisions. In this way, you can exchange ideas on the future more easily and precisely, with your employees for example. Facilitating communication about the future will also be discussed in Chapter 5, "Purpose of the red futures glasses".

You integrate the various perceptions of the future more easily

Every opinion on the probable and possible future, however peculiar and unsubstantiated it may be, can be expressed in a future projection. Future projections are theses. Using future projections in a workshop can help a moderator to avoid offending the sensibilities of contributors with strange ideas. Every opinion on the future can be made easy to handle as a well-formulated future projection.

You form attractors for knowledge about the future

Looking through the blue futures glasses has a heuristic character. Assumptions about the future are theses about the future, whose value lies, among other things, in the fact that they can be regularly, if not continuously verified on the way to the future. As soon as an assumption about the future has been formulated and documented, it creates a perception category. It is said that we only perceive what we know. Even if this is not true in such an extreme way, there is still a lot of truth in it. It is similar to the assumption questions. As soon as they have been asked, we perceive more possible answers than before. Assumptions about the future are therefore starting points for the monitoring of possible changes in your environment. If a management team from the IT department assumes that computers will be able to be operated by voice at the linguistic level of an adult in ten years' time, then these experts will invest less in keyboard-based solutions and be much more attentive to signals that can confirm or refute their assumption. Assumptions about the future thus become attractors for signals about the future.

Core concepts of the blue futures glasses

If you want to think and communicate about the future in a structured way, then you need to be aware of the most important core concepts of future management and their definitions at a very early stage. You see the following objects through the blue futures glasses, which we want to briefly characterize and define:

- Assumption questions
- Future factors
- Signals
- Future projections
- Future scenarios
- Assumptions about the future (expectations, eventualities, non-expectations).

As the following figure shows, the core concepts above are developed as part of the process steps future radar and assumption analysis (blue futures glasses). The "future radar" step serves to detect future developments and changes in your environment systematically and at an early stage.

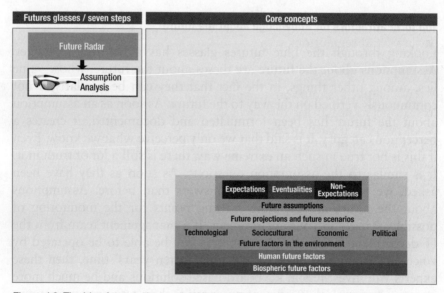

Figure 4.2 The blue futures glasses and their core concepts

Assumption questions

There is a special form of future question for each pair of futures glasses. Future questions create natural access to the contents of future management that is much appreciated by entrepreneurs and managers.

> You use assumption questions to determine the most important knowledge requirements for the probable development of your environment.

When you put on the blue futures glasses, you ask assumption questions. These are questions about the future development of your environment. In the story about the windjammer captain, these were questions on the developments of the sea and the weather, that is, the external factors with the greatest influence on the existence and well-being of the ship. They must be questions with which you can capture and appraise the future of the most important influencing factors of your economic existence. What do you need to know about the future development of your environment in order to be able to make decisions today that will be robust in the future? Generally it concerns changes in:

- your customers' behavior
- relevant technologies
- market conditions and competition
- laws and regulations
- natural living conditions.

Which five assumption questions would you ask a group of futures researchers known for the accuracy of their forecasts (if there were such people), if each question cost 100,000 Euros and you were able to invest 500,000 Euros in five questions? Even the boards of major corporations would probably have to think hard about it before being able to determine the most important assumption questions.

Table 4.2 Examples of assumption questions

Industry	Future question
Aircraft (1990s)	What will be most important to airlines in future – flight prices (and therefore large efficient aircraft) or flight times (and therefore small, fast aircraft)?

Table 4.2 (cont'd)

Industry	Future question
Electricity	How much of the required electricity will be generated by the consumers themselves in decentralized power plants in future?
Banks	How many financial services purchases will be completed through e-banking in future?
Dentistry	Will higher levels of personal responsibility lead to dramatic reductions in turnover or make dental-wellness into a mass market?
Business travel	To what extent will the increase in video calls and video conferencing technology lead to a decrease in business travel?
Logistics	To what extent will continued dematerialization and virtualization lead to a reduction in transport volume (as in the music industry)?
Construction	How important will the "intelligent house" really be in the total market?

Future factors

In the windjammer captain story, the future factors were the high and low-pressure areas, the winds, the celestial bodies and other factors that determine the environment; these are the ingredients for the future.

> Future factors are trends, technologies and issues that act as driving forces for future changes.

The three types of future factors also need clear definition, the more so as the term *trend* in particular is used in a variety of ways.

> A trend is a clearly directed change to one or more variables in the environment.
>
> A technology is a tool for expanding human capabilities.
>
> An issue refers to a phenomenon that causes future changes in one or more directions.

As shown in Table 4.3, we differentiate six categories of future factors:

Table 4.3 Categories of future factors

Category	Explanation and examples
Human future factors (need factors)	Basic motives of human beings which drive them to develop ideas, technologies and tools, to keep house and to organize themselves in communities and societies

Table 4.3 (cont'd)

Category	Explanation and examples
Biospheric future factors	Changes to biospheric relationships such as shrinking biodiversity, global warming or the destruction of rainforests
Technological future factors	Technological–methodical developments and innovations such as microchips, the internet, nuclear energy, nanotechnology or genetic engineering
Political future factors	Changes in the balance of power such as the takeover of power, the development of terrorism, increasing international cooperation or Europeanization
Economic future factors	Changes of strategies, systems and practices to satisfy human needs such as globalization and the polarization of markets
Sociocultural future factors	Changes in sociocultural circumstances, cultures and ideals, for example individualization, knowledge growth, the increased speed of change or aging

The future factors checklist in Table 4.4 provides you with a comprehensive overview of some of the most important trends, issues and technologies of the future. A future factor is objectively relevant for your company if it has a clearly recognizable influence on the response to one or more of your future questions. Formulate your future questions in such a way that they are neither too general nor too specific from the viewpoint of your market. For an energy generator, "energy innovations" is too general, for a construction company on the other hand, "tidal power stations" is too specific.

Table 4.4 Future factors checklist[12]

Biospheric future factors

- Climate change
- Diminishing biodiversity
- Soil erosion and desertification
- Forest destruction
- Shortage of drinking water
- Shortage of oil
- Environmental pollution

Technological future factors

- Increasing computer processing power
- Higher performance data transfer systems
- Display innovations
- Informatization
- Internetization
- Dematerialization and virtualization
- Human–machine interfaces
- Automatization and robotics
- E-Business
- Biometrics
- Microsystem technology
- Microprocessing technology
- Nanotechnology
- Biotechnology and genetic engineering
- Bionization
- Energy innovations
- Logistics and traffic innovations
- Medical innovations

Table 4.4 (cont'd)

Technological future factors (cont'd)

- Artificial intelligence
- Knowledge systems
- E-Learning
- Photonics
- Sensor technology
- Material innovations
- Production and process innovations
- Functional food
- Mass customization
- Mobilization

Political future factors

- European integration
- Government financial problems
- Economization of the state
- Liberalization
- Increasing international cooperation

Economic future factors

- Interdisciplinarization
- Globalization
- Global economic growth
- Asian boom
- Market saturation in developed countries
- Increasing global demand for energy
- Tertiarization and quarterization
- Network economy
- Productivity growth
- Fragmentation of markets
- Polarization of markets
- Polarization of prosperity
- Polarization of work
- Sustainable business
- Digital money
- Customer emancipation
- Marine economy
- Outer space as a business area
- Management innovations

Sociocultural future factors

- Aging
- Population decline in some countries
- Population growth and urbanization in developing countries
- Knowledge growth
- Individualization
- Entrepreneurization
- Flexibilization
- Ethicalization
- Feminization
- Convenience trend
- Thirst for experiences and excitement
- New families
- Interculturalization
- Religious and ethnic conflicts
- Crime and terrorism
- Increasing speed of change
- Increasing complexity
- Salutogenesis and life-balancing
- Spiritualization

Signals

Signals are descriptive and constitutive elements of future factors. We define them as follows:

> A signal is a piece of information about possible developments and events in the future.

An example of a signal would be: *Twenty percent of young foreigners and ten percent of young home nationals leave school with no formal qualifications.* When it comes to it, every message relevant to a futures study or futures strategy is a signal. The concept of a signal also denotes the term prognosticon, an Ancient Greek word meaning a pointer to a future development. For the sake of simplicity, we assign signals to the future factors.

Future projections

Your assumption questions are answered with future projections first. If your assumption question is more complex, then you will summarize several projections into a scenario (see below).

> A future projection is a statement about the possible state of an observation object in the environment at a certain point in the future.

The simplest method of developing projections is the direct derivation of projections from future factors. Future trends, technologies and issues provide rather obvious answers to your assumption questions based on the principle shown in Figure 4.3. If the future factors can be described using numbers, then these are used as so-called predictors, that is, as variables for projecting future developments.

Future factors	Assumption questions on developments in the environment			
	Assumption question 1	Assumption question 2	Assumption question 3	Assumption question n
Aging		●		
Individualization	●		●	●
Dematerialization		●		
Automatization		●	●	●
Mobilization		●	● ●	
Convenience orientation	●			●
Regionalization	●	●	●	
Flexibilization	●			●
Biometrics		●	●	●
Customer emancipation	●			
Knowledge economy		● ●	●	●
...				

● Future projection

Figure 4.3 Projection matrix with future factors

Using derivations from future factors, the assumption questions of an energy producer could be answered as follows (Table 4.5):

Table 4.5 An energy producer's projections

Assumption question	Future factors	Projection 1	Projection 2
How much electricity will be generated decentrally by the customers themselves?	■ Energy innovations (fuel cells, optimized photovoltaics etc.) ■ Shortage of oil ■ Climate change	2020: Virtually no customers are generating their own energy (0%).	2020: 80% of customers are generating a significant percentage (approx. one third) of their own electricity.
To what extent will the "intelligent household" become accepted?	■ Informatization ■ Individualization ■ Dematerialization ■ Human–machine interfaces ■ Terrorism and crime	2020: Household technology is virtually unchanged.	2020: Every new house and every refurbishment will result in an intelligent, highly networked household.

The projections in Table 4.5 show that a projection does not necessarily have to appear probable to everyone and, as a result, is not the same as a prediction or a forecast. Many projections are only made as a provocative thesis with the sole purpose of stimulating thinking about the future or of showing that the future can be completely different than we think.

Further examples of future projections are:

- Sixty percent of the population of city X will live in single households in 2020.
- The capacity of microchips will grow by 1,000 percent in the next seven years.
- Extreme sports will have become popular in almost all social groups by 2015.
- The number of graduates will have grown by ten percent in ten years.
- The share of internet-based administration files between citizens and public authorities will be over fifty percent in ten years' time.

Future scenarios

Projections can be regarded as mini scenarios.[13] They provide answers to a single question, whereas scenarios as such answer several questions at the same time and thus encompass an entire system of projections. Scenarios integrate several projections and make it easier to consider the influencing factors, the mechanisms or simply the logic of change.[14]

The *Battle of Dorking* describes a fictitious future battle and is a good example of a scenario (see also page 91). However, this scenario was created with the red futures glasses.

> A future scenario is a system of projections that describes a complex picture of a possible future and maybe the path to it.

Using the blue futures glasses, scenarios are not looked at in a significantly different way than projections. Scenarios play their special role when looking at the future through the red futures glasses (see Chapter 5).

Assumptions about the future

Assumptions about the future are the core concepts of the blue futures glasses. An example of an assumption about the future is the statement: *We assume with eighty percent probability, that sixty percent of the population of city X will live in single households in the year 2020.*

> An assumption about the future is a conviction about the probable future, expressed as an expectational probability attributed to a projection or a scenario.

It is remarkable that the term "assumption about the future" has been relatively seldom researched and discussed by futures experts. Even standard works[15] do without a definition of the concept of assumptions about the future, apparently on the *assumption* that everyone already knows what an assumption about the future is.

Assumptions about the future are debatable, but plausible convictions about future states, processes or facts. An assumption about the future according to the definition above presumes there is a projection or a scenario to be evaluated as a thesis. You can delegate the preparation of projections or scenarios or purchase them from a third party, but you can only make assumptions about the future yourself.

An assumption about the future expresses that someone considers a statement about the future (projection or scenario) to be:

1. somewhat probable (expectations) or
2. semi-probable (eventualities) or
3. rather improbable (non-expectations).

Figure 4.2 (above) shows the classification of assumptions about the future.

Table 4.6 Types of assumptions about the future		
Type	Definition	Meaning
Expectations	An assumption about the future which expresses a high degree of expected probability	The futures strategy is based on this future happening.
Eventualities	An assumption about the future which expresses a low degree of expected probability	The futures strategy is based on this future not happening.
Non-expectations	An assumption about the future which expresses a medium degree of expected probability	The futures strategy takes both possibilities into account: that this future will happen and also that it will not.

One either believes that the projection or the scenario describes future reality, or one doesn't believe it, or one believes that there is an equal opportunity of it happening or not. Assumptions about the future are therefore not forecasts, but heuristic statements (meaning for the purpose of gaining knowledge) about something believed.

With the non-expectations, there is basically the same level of certainty as with the expectations, which is a little confusing at first. One is certain at both ends of the probability scale that this future will either happen or it won't. It would therefore be surprising if the opposite happened in each case. Non-expectations are optional outcomes, such as the increase or decrease of certain market prices for example. As opposed to the surprises (see Chapter 5), non-expectations are analyzed very consciously and rationally as at least potentially probable futures.

Eventualities as the third type of assumption about the future express the highest degree of uncertainty. Eventualities are not there to show indecisiveness or ignorance. Declaring a futures statement such as "nanotechnology components will represent around twenty percent of the market volume in ten years" as an eventuality with an expectational probability of fifty percent is a clear decision that has consequences for the futures strategy.

When we talk about probabilities for assumptions about the future, we mean expectational probabilities. Probabilities in the statistical sense would require historical data that generally does not exist for strategically relevant assumptions about the long-term future. Expectational probabilities are substantiated, subjective expectations on whether the statement concerned will be true at a given point in time in the future. We use an ordinal scale from 1 (very improbable) to 9 (very probable) to describe expectational probabilities. We do not use a zero or a ten, because nothing is impossible in the future and nothing is certain. This subject is discussed further in "Procedure for companies", later in the chapter.

Attitude and principles of the blue futures glasses

With the blue futures glasses you are looking outwardly from a macro perspective at the future you assume to be probable for your environment. You adopt a detached, observing view. Your attitude is realistic, analytical, experience-based and rather conservative.

Assume the future to be largely unpredictable

The blue futures glasses look at the probable future, yet this cannot be forecast accurately enough. The results of chaos research (and not only chaos theory!) suggest we abandon any attempt at completely understanding current change, let alone forecasting future change. Markets and society are characterized by and organized according to quite clear principles (deterministic chaos), yet their complex structure means that they generally behave chaotically, meaning they cannot be completely understood or forecast.[16]

Even simple complex systems cannot be foreseen. Where a leaf will exactly fall from a tree, how a heartbeat will appear on an ECG in the next second, or how three bodies, planets for example, will affect each other with their power of attraction, none of this can be foreseen. Even the direction of a ball in a pinball machine cannot be predicted, although everything can be measured and recorded, be it the weight or volume of the ball, the angle of incidence and reflection, the strength of the initial thrust, the dynamics of the active triggering elements, the player's reaction speed and so on. Complex systems cannot be adequately explained with the description of their elements and functions, and certainly not predicted.[17] Each round delivers a different result. This is even more the case with complex adaptive systems, and would be the case if the ball in the pinball game was guided by emotion, made decisions and could adapt to its environment.

> Wherever humans play an active role, we are concerned with a complex adaptive system, which as such is by nature not predictable.

Before chaos research, it was assumed that we only needed to be able to record the elements and coherences of a system accurately enough to be able to predict its behavior. Nowadays, we know that due to the sensitive dependence of system behavior, of markets for example, minimal deviations at atom level (the butterfly effect)[18] are sufficient to arrive at completely unexpected results.

Some futures experts nevertheless claim that almost everything that happens now has been foreseen. Sometimes it is just a question of syntax: *Foreseen or just seen before?* Without a doubt, a line or two on current events can be found in the universe of historical writings, from the Sumerians to yesterday's newspaper. Unfortunately a lot more can also be found on things that haven't happened (yet). Once again there is a lack of precision in looking at the future. Are we concerned with someone considering it to be possible or being able to imagine it (green futures glasses)? Or do we mean that someone predicted it for this time and place and in this shape or at least assumed it from his point of view (blue futures glasses)?

When our clients (using the blue futures glasses) think about probable futures, they are not satisfied with ideas and visions that someone considers to be possible in the distant future. It only becomes interesting if they see opportunities for themselves in it (green futures glasses). Knowing the probable future (blue futures glasses) is above all of particular value if the time, place and quality of this future are known in advance. And complete accuracy is not the most important thing here. It would, for example, be immensely valuable for a chemical company to know if equipment for additive fabrication (a kind of three-dimensional printing) will have a market volume of seven to twelve billion Euros in ten years' time. That would be accurate enough. But this level of accuracy of "knowledge" about the future will never exist. We can have and need to have assumptions, but assumptions are neither knowledge nor forecasts. Claiming that such developments can be predicted, requires an extremely lax understanding of the word "prediction" which most people would not share.

Therefore, anyone who claims that everything has been foreseen could just as well claim that every drawn combination of numbers in the lottery has already been predicted. Of course it is helpful to know everything that has been predicted and said about the future. But to draw the possibility of prediction from this is epistemologically simply not possible. We would need to ignore that many people have also predicted exactly the opposite. Otherwise there would only need to be a sufficiently large number of forecasts to later be able to claim that it had already been predicted.

There are however areas whose future is not completely subject to the unpredictable behavior of chaotic (complex) systems. There, either the future is the result of current ratios and relatively reliably calculable functions (in demographics for example) or the future is the result of human expectations, as can largely be assumed for the social product, for turnover or for the diffusion of technology.

> Anyone who identifies and analyzes assumptions about the future of participating and affected people, and in doing so takes typical human behavior into account, can recognize earlier than others if his estimation of the future is correct.

Direct the blue futures glasses towards your environment

In the example of the windjammer captain in Chapter 3, the blue futures glasses were concerned with the ocean and the weather, that is, about the circumstances in his environment that the captain cannot influence. If the captain looks through the blue futures glasses, he almost needs a fatalistic attitude.

The well-being of your own family or of your own company cannot be imagined with the blue futures glasses, and therefore not thought about in the category of probability, because you yourself have a strong influence on the development.

Assumptions about the future should only be made concerning independent observation objects, typically the development of the market, generally available technologies, the biosphere, customer behavior or legislation.

> We can only meaningfully think about probabilities if we as the observer have no influence over what is being observed.

Regard the future in a passive and detached way from the macro perspective

"A desk is a dangerous place from which to watch the world", John le Carré is alleged to have said. Ideally you look at your environment from a macro perspective through the blue futures glasses. Your desk and your company are not the focus of your observation, but the circumstances in the world, on your continent, in your country and in your market. That is the only way you can understand the bigger context.

You need to "externalize", disengage yourself from the system you are looking at in order to watch and appraise it, even if in reality you are an integral part of the system. This is exactly the apparent error in reasoning that makes it easier, and often possible at all, for us to think about probable futures.

The necessity of the macro perspective demands a passive and detached attitude. You can generally not significantly and purposefully change the circumstances in your market in the direction of your choice. Even if you have a large market share, you cannot control the activities of competitors, government actors and researchers. From a systemic point of view, one could object that the observer always has an influence on the object he is watching; Heisenberg's uncertainty[19] principle has after all virtually become public property. Nevertheless, although total passivity and neutrality are impossible, you should formulate your assumptions about the future as if you *were* able to behave passively and neutrally.

Adopt a realistic and conservative attitude

The blue futures glasses appear to some people as boring or even unnecessary, because the point of them is less to identify the latest trends and hypes than to form a basis of orientation for the life of people and companies. Creativity and fantasy are of no great significance when looking through the blue futures glasses. The captain cannot change anything of significance concerning the ocean and the weather. It therefore makes little sense for him to be particularly creative when trying to find out how his environment will develop, for he cannot be creative, in the sense of creating something, in connection with the weather.

> Wishful thinking, exaggerations, creative ideas, glossing over things and pessimism have no place in your assumptions about the future.

It goes without saying that an assumption about the future will be the sounder, the more well founded it is. The more unclear, emotional, narrative and complex it is, the lower its quality will be. You should, as far as possible, back up every assumption with figures and data. There can be no facts in the narrowest sense about the future, yet the more fact-like your assumptions about the future are, the better you will be able to review them and have them reviewed. In practice, it has proved valuable to draw up a list of pro and contra arguments,[20] with and without weighting the arguments. People are, of course, incapable of purely rational, let alone "objective" judgments on the future, but the closer we come to this attitude the better, at least with the blue futures glasses. Creative ideas and longings are reserved for the other futures glasses.

We tend towards too much optimism in particular with regard to technology. In the history of futures research, the breakthrough of most major technologies was expected much too early. When you look through the blue futures glasses, it is not a sign of an estimable breadth of thought and creativity to answer the serious futures questions concerning a company with science fiction. This is much more a sign that someone has not yet understood the blue futures glasses and, above all, the difference between them and the other futures glasses.

Consider experience as a success factor

Anyone who has thirty years' experience in his business can quickly and intuitively assess which futures are more probable and which not. The beginner and layman can creatively come up with a lot of imaginative ideas and illuminate the possibilities of the future, but the person with experience regularly has a higher success rate in assessing real probabilities. This is certainly true as long as the world being looked at has not significantly changed since the experience had been gained.

You cannot carry out a complete assumption analysis

In view of the notorious lack of time in futures work, the blue futures glasses must be directed at the strongest relevant assumption. You can basically equate relevance with the strength of the anticipated effects of the futures development being investigated. The more dependent you or your company are on the object of an assumption about the future, on a certain demand or a certain habit for example, the stronger the effect of the changes will potentially be.

You already fall back on assumptions about the present when choosing the environment factors to be recorded. The way you determine important and relevant things is already inevitably based on deeper lying assumptions on the way your own business works. If a publisher is convinced that only the specialist content quality of books determines sales success, then he will probably make a selection of assumptions about the future which those who are convinced that bestsellers are "made" and not written will fail to understand.

> The ideals of completeness and perfection rarely match the thought-object "future", at least not in practice.

It goes without saying that focusing on a small number of assumptions also means that important environment aspects must be taken out of the analysis. Therefore concentrate your blue futures glasses on:

1. environment factors which have a strong influence on your future existence (relevance)

2. environment factors of a long-term nature

3. changes to the environment factors.

When looking at trends in particular, it is advisable to concentrate on those that you can assume to be durable for a number of years. For time and effort reasons, it is simply not possible to include every short-term development in a well-founded assumption analysis.

A captain is less interested in having the dark shadows on the radar screen explained than he is in the moving light points. You shouldn't spend your scarce time on extrapolating the present. Although many, if not most things will remain the same, despite all the claims of turbulent change, it is the differences, the changes to the present that are of most interest.

Use assumptions about the future as a replacement for impossible future "knowledge"

The problems that appear in connection with assumptions about the present, particularly the problem of incomplete and colored perception, are much greater still with assumptions about the future. The present can at least be partly checked for figures, data and facts. You can never check the future, for as soon as you can do so, it has become the present.

> There can never be knowledge about the future in a strictly scientific sense. As the future does not really exist at the point in time it is looked at, it cannot be measured, counted or weighed.

We can neither falsify (refute) nor verify (prove) anything about the future, which according to Karl Popper is a precondition for scientific knowledge. Declaratory knowledge about the future is impossible. We can therefore only have subjective knowledge about the future, meaning conjectures structured with the help of clear argumentation.

Remember that everyone has assumptions about the future all the time

You don't have to form your assumptions about the future. They are already there, either consciously or unconsciously. You don't have the choice of doing without assumptions about the future. As we have already described, every decision you make is based on your assumptions about the future, even the decision not to make a decision.

You cannot delegate your assumptions about the future

There is a huge amount and variety of futures information available. The internet is not the only inexhaustible source. Printed literature in particular provides extremely good futures studies at acceptable prices. As the head of a company, you possibly have access to a whole range of specialists who provide you with analyses and studies about the future. There is an abundance of projections, scenarios and ideas. You can also contract external experts and futures researchers. But one thing you cannot do: you cannot buy assumptions about the future. You cannot delegate your assessment of future developments. You can take the assessments of other people into your own assumption about the future without checking them. But then you ignore your very own values, your vision and the circumstances of your life and work.

Assumptions about the future made by third parties, employees, consultants and experts, for example, are therefore initially only projections for you or, if they are more complex, scenarios. You haven't developed or checked your assumption about the future until you have assessed the expectational probability of a projection.

Improve your assumptions about the future through provocative projections

The projection "2020: The market volume has fallen by thirty percent" can be very valuable, even if you know beforehand that everyone will assume the opposite. The discussion and reasoning lead to a considerable learning effect. It is just as valuable to assume that a projection will not occur, as it is to assume that a projection will occur. In both cases, the feeling of certainty in the perception of the future increases.

Improve your assumptions about the future by being affected personally

The blue futures glasses are used to realistically assess the probable future. Someone who makes an assumption about the future generally wants to be right. As you have no possibility a priori – meaning before the described future happens – to check, let alone prove the reliability of an assumption about the future, auxiliary criteria are needed.

It is a highly interesting and fruitful process to establish the assumptions about the future of the individual members of a management team independently of each other, then to compare and discuss them in detail. It is our daily experience that people manage a company together for several years, yet have completely different assessments of how the market will develop in the future. Imagine the officers of a windjammer each having completely different assessments of the future weather conditions.

In the prolog to the five futures glasses in Chapter 1, we used a bet to differentiate between the characters of the statements of five people. Asking them to wager a significant sum of money affected their decisions. Prediction markets that involve betting real money are generally more reliable than those in which authors and evaluators risk nothing if their predictions are wrong.

The case studies earlier in this chapter, and in particular the example of the commercial property market in Frankfurt, show that being affected personally is a significant quality criterion for an assumption about the future.

> Someone who suffers a loss if the assumption turns out to be wrong makes more realistic and therefore better assumptions.

The loss or damage must be painful, whether financial or immaterial, for example damage to reputation. Unfortunately, many people only start to think in the face of impending disadvantages. Someone who knows that he will later be critically questioned in the media on his assumptions about the future will describe the probable future very differently to someone who makes anonymous comments on the internet. Make sure therefore, that the employees, colleagues, consultants or even futures researchers you ask for their assumptions about the future know that you will check what they said at a later date.

Mind you, no one can know the future. The point is therefore not to interpret every incorrect assumption about the future as a failure. If someone says that something will happen with ninety percent certainty, then he can be questioned about it later if it doesn't happen. But even ninety percent isn't one hundred percent. The future is open, so we have to concede that someone can make a mistake – not, however, after several failed attempts. If the person asked spoke about sixty or seventy percent expectational probability, then there is nothing to reproach him for.

Who is most affected if the assumptions about the future of a company turn out to be incorrect? Who is most affected if they turn out to be correct? This would make an excellent subject for discussion. We will assume that it is those whose economic existence depends on the success of the company. As the members of the management team are those most likely to lose their jobs for incorrect assumptions about the future and most likely to benefit from correct assumptions about it, they are the people you should first ask about their assumptions about the future. If these assumptions about the future need to become sounder, then you can additionally ask the employees and the owners or stockholders.

> The most valuable assumptions about the future are the really personal ones that you tell hardly anyone about.

As the example of the commercial property market in Frankfurt shows, it is essential that those affected are able to first state their assumptions about the future without the influence of others. This is the only way to achieve and benefit from their being personally affected.

Improve your assumptions about the future through a wide base of support

The more people you can get to verify or falsify your assumptions about the future, meaning to confirm or refute them, the better. The Delphi method developed by Olaf Helmer[21] at the RAND Corporation uses panels of experts who are questioned in two to three rounds. After each round, the experts are told how their judgment compares with the others and are given the opportunity of revising their judgment. The principle is that the more people assume the same thing, the more likely they are to be correct. It has been shown that even the Delphi method is not immune to serious mistakes. A wide-ranging Delphi study in 1964 showed up as many mistakes as the German Delphi reports from 1993 and 1998. There is nevertheless hardly a more sound possibility of assessing probable futures than the iterative questioning of people who have substantial knowledge about the subject concerned. Experience is useful when looking through the blue futures glasses. It is a well-known fact that experts, in particular, can get it very wrong. A famous, probably Chinese, proverb says that there are a million possibilities in the mind of a beginner, but only very few in the mind of an expert. Experts have separated much as being ridiculous and impossible, but they are often not in a position to recognize changes in the landscape and consider their map to be the real landscape for far too long. Experts and the people affected are nevertheless extremely valuable for the blue futures glasses' concept – the best are the experts who are really affected and who are presented with provocative projections to widen their mental horizon.

> The best way to develop solid assumptions is to question affected experts on both reasonable and provocative projections.

The higher the degree of consensus in a group of experts or affected persons is, the higher the quality of an assumption about the future can be estimated to be.[22] This is valid at least when looking through the blue futures glasses at the probable future.

When considering the issue of being personally affected and the need for wide support, the most important thing is the totality of your management team's personal assumptions about the future.

The quality of the assumptions about the future will be improved further if you extend the assumption analysis to additional employees and internal experts. The assumptions of external experts rarely fulfill the criterion of being affected; on the

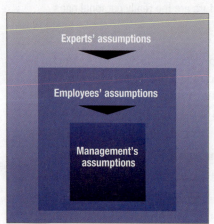

Figure 4.4 Verifying assumptions about the future on a wide basis

other hand they can improve your assumptions about the future through further projections and supporting or doubting arguments. In this way, you can use experts as sensors for a future radar to regularly check your assumptions about the future.

Methodology checklists

This section provides you with step-by-step guidelines for use in practice. The first checklist describes the steps for you as the head of a medium size or large company, or as the person with responsibility for strategy. The second checklist shows a more simplified process for you personally in your role as a life entrepreneur. The third checklist is aimed at the professionals, that is, future management experts.

Procedure for companies

1. **Put together a futures team**, where the core consists of the first management tier of the company or unit being investigated (division, section, area, department), as many strategy relevant representatives of the second management tier as possible, a few creative people, a few internal experts, and, on a temporary basis, customers, suppliers and partners.

2. **Get an overall idea** of the character of the blue futures glasses using the overview in Table 4.1.

3. **Determine a uniform futures horizon.** As a rule of thumb: the length of time needed to build up a business area from the idea to the first income, multiplied by two. In most cases, ten years is a good basis.

4. **Ask your assumption questions** as described on page 63. The first time you do it, concentrate on a maximum of five assumption questions.

5. **Ascertain the fundamentally relevant future factors for your assumption questions** (future trends, technologies and issues) using the checklist in Table 4.4.

6. **Determine the future factors** (trends, technologies and issues) that are most relevant for your assumption questions using the criteria listed for the future factors.

7. **Research information and signals** on the selected future factors. A list of useful links and tips on sources of knowledge on future

factors can be found on the website accompanying this book (www.FuturesGlasses.com).

8. **Develop at least three and at most six futures projections for each of your assumption questions** (see Core concepts section) as possible answers. Start first with two extreme projections, as shown in Table 4.5. You will need three and more futures projections for the assumption questions that are not so one-dimensional. You can develop the projections in the following way:
   (a) The projection matrix in Figure 4.3 shows you a structure for determining possible influences of the selected future factors on your assumption questions.
   (b) Develop projections with the help of thought models, mechanisms and creators of change. Information on these can be found at www.FuturesGlasses.com.
   (c) Take projections from futures studies, of which a large number and variety are available in book form. A number of sources can also be found at www.FuturesGlasses.com.
   (d) Ask experts in your company for their suggested answers (projections) to your assumption questions.
   (e) Ask external experts.

9. **Form a pro and contra list for your arguments for each projection,** as shown Figure 4.1. At the beginning, you should not include a weighting of the arguments for reasons of time and complexity. A pro and contra list can help to structure a complex thinking process in a simple way, which is why they are frequently used in practice.

10. **Bring the assumptions about the future of each individual member of your future team to the surface.** Have every decision-maker in your future team assess each projection on a scale from 1 to 9. The scale from 1 to 9 can be divided into three areas of expectational probability:

    1–3: Non-expectations
    (low expectational probability)
    4–6: Eventuality
    (medium expectational probability)
    7–9: Expectation
    (high expectational probability).

The evaluation process takes place in two stages. You and your other contributors can first decide whether you consider the projection in question to have a low, medium or high expectational probability. In the second step, you can make your decision more precise and select the interim values. By doing so, you have applied the Delphi method for your assumption analysis.

For the mathematicians: Correct, from a purely mathematical point of view, you cannot calculate averages with an ordinal scale. Nevertheless, millions of schoolchildren are also assessed with average grades from an ordinal scale, even by mathematics professors.

11. **Form an assumption panorama,** as shown in tabular form in Figure 4.5. The assumption panorama consists of:
    (a) Your assumption questions
    (b) The projections
    (c) The arguments (hidden in the figure)
    (d) Each individual's assumptions about the future
    (e) The joint assumptions about the future (mean values)
    (f) The level of contention of the assumptions about the future (statistical spread in the form of standard deviations).

    In this way, you can get a good picture of the averages and the spread of your team's assumptions about the future. In later stages, a graphic presentation of your assumption panorama is to be recommended.

12. **Discuss the assumption panorama,** make the assumptions more precise and add to them using a consistency matrix, where the assumptions about the future are possibly contradictory. Although not even the present is free of contradictions, really obvious contradictions can be smoothed out in this way.

13. **Carry out a second assessment round,** to get even more sound results. A third round generally tends not to achieve better results.

14. **Get more certainty into the assessment of the probable,** by having a further circle of your employees check and add to the assumption panorama. Ask them to provide additional projections and further arguments. Also determine the assumptions about the future of this additional circle and compare the results. You can thus expose your assumptions about the future to a systematic and extremely valuable process of verification and falsification.

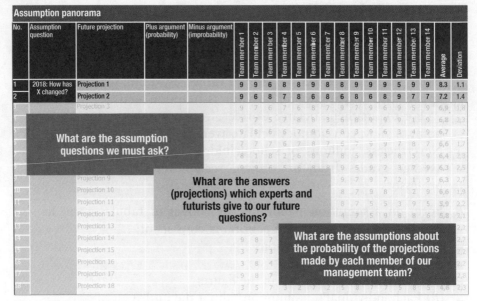

Figure 4.5 Assumption panorama

15. **Gain even more certainty**, by inviting external experts, your customers, suppliers or your partners to discuss and add to your assumption panorama.

Procedure for life entrepreneurs

In principle, you can also use the above procedure for companies as a life entrepreneur. Admittedly, a simplified approach is advisable at the beginning. The minimum procedure for individual people consists of the following steps, for which you should record the results in writing if possible:

1. Ask your assumption questions.

2. Determine which relevant future factors you know well enough.

3. Find out which future factors you need to know better or additionally.

4. Ascertain the effects the future factors will have on your (professional) life based on your assumptions about the future.

5. Ask other people who are important to you and competent which additional effects they see.

Checklist of methods and techniques

The following method checklist for professionals is a maximum list of the methods, techniques and tools that can be applied in the individual work steps of the blue futures glasses. Those readers whose interest goes deeper, can tap into the method universe of future management with little effort using the literature references and the list of references in the Appendix.

Professional checklist:
Methods for the blue futures glasses with literature suggestions
(see Bibliography)

Developing assumption questions
- Assumption questions / Delphi (Mićić, 2006)
- Structure analysis (Geschka and von Reibnitz, 1981; Godet, 1994; Gausemeier et al., 1996)
- Comprehensive situation mapping (Georgantzas and Acar, 1995)

Developing projections and scenarios of possible developments
- Trend extrapolation (time series analysis) (Armstrong, 2001)
- Multivariate regression (Armstrong, 2001)
- Scenarios (Schwartz, 1996; de Geus, 1988; Godet, 1994; Georgantzas and Acar, 1995; van der Heijden, 1996; von Reibnitz, 1991; Gausemeier et al., 1996) and others
- Decision modeling / conjoint analysis (Armstrong, 2001)
- Morphology (Glenn and Gordon, 2003; Godet, 1994)
- Field anomaly relaxation (Coyle, 2003; Rhyne, 1981)
- Futures wheel / mind mapping (Glenn and Gordon, 2003; Buzan, 2006)
- Cross impact analysis (Glenn and Gordon, 2003)
- Trend impact analysis (Gordon, 2003b)
- Historical analogies (Armstrong, 2001)
- Precursor analysis / leading indicators (May, 1996)
- Statistical modeling (Glenn and Gordon, 2003; Armstrong, 2001; Makridakis, Wheelwright, Hyndman, 1998; Martino, 1993)
- Simulations (Rausch and Catanzaro, 2003)
- Games (Rausch and Catanzaro, 2003)
- Agent modeling (Gordon, 2003a; Godet, 1994)
- Role playing (Armstrong, 2001)
- Genius forecasting / expert interviews (Glenn, 2003)
- Evaluation of speculative literature and art (May, 1996)
- Brainstorming/writing

Increasing the plausibility of projections and scenarios
- Argument pro and contra lists (Breiing and Knosala, 1997)
- Judgmental bootstrapping (Armstrong, 2001)

Professional checklist (cont'd)

Increasing the plausibility of projections and scenarios (cont'd)
- Expert systems (Armstrong, 2001)
- Strategic conversation (van der Heijden, 1996)
- Causal layered analysis (Inayatullah, 2003)

Assessing expectational probabilities
- Delphi (Helmer, 1983)
- Opinion poll (Armstrong, 2001)
- Multiple perspective concept (Linstone, 2003)
- Future panorama / assumption panorama (Mićić, 2005)

Presenting results
- Roadmapping (Möhrle and Isenmann, 2007)
- Future panorama / assumption panorama (Mićić, 2005)
- Illustrations, charts and mind-maps

5 Your red futures glasses: How could the future surprise you?

With the red futures glasses, the captain turns his attention to the future's possible surprises, to prepare his crew and his ship for them, to protect them and possibly to profit from them through early perception. He recognizes for example, that his ship could be hit by a freak wave or attacked by pirates.

Only one thing is certain in the future: that the future will surprise us. The future will be different to the way we can imagine it today with the blue futures glasses. Developing assumptions about the future using the blue futures glasses is commensurate with the naive but valid longing for a foreseeable future. Your assumptions about the future will prove to be wrong to a greater or lesser extent, which you cannot "know" today. Neither the strongest will nor the best method can change that. The future is open, untamable and incalculable. If your assumptions about the future prove to be fundamentally wrong, the mental construction of your future strategy threatens to collapse if it is not properly secured.

■ *It is probable that something improbable will happen.* (Aristotle)

You use the yellow futures glasses, and later the violet ones, to formulate a clear strategy for the future. Yet the more unambiguous the strategy is, the larger and less opaque the blinkers are that you can penetrate with the red futures glasses.

You need to use the red futures glasses to identify possible surprising events and developments and thus to improve and safeguard your futures strategy. Like the blue futures glasses, they are used for an analysis of the environment, but consciously look for improbable yet possible surprises rather than probabilities.

The surprises that are recognized are then used to:

1. recognize opportunities
2. firm up the results of the yellow futures glasses; that is, improve the mission, strategic guidelines and vision

3. firm up the results of the violet futures glasses; that is, improve the goals, projects, processes, systems, developing opportunities and eventual strategies.

The surprises as such are initially beyond the boundaries of your perception, or they would not be surprises. You need to actively look for them. Surprises are by definition very improbable and are generally not even discussed as an option with the blue futures glasses. The statement "laser technology replaces razor blades" could describe a potential surprise for Gillette. A decrease in market size of fifty percent within five weeks is generally also not included as an option for an assumption about the future. Such a future must be introduced by the red futures glasses.

> *The world we live in is dominated by trends and punctuated by surprises.* (John L. Petersen)[1]

In traditional future management methodology, scenarios and wild card analysis are generally used for the surprising future as visible through the red futures glasses. Scenario methods are useful here, whereas they neglect or even completely disregard the view through the blue, green and yellow futures glasses.

Your red futures glasses: Overview

Table 5.1 summarizes the characteristics of the red futures glasses.

Table 5.1 Overview of the red futures glasses
Objective: To get to know the future's possible surprises.
Work step and key question: ■ Surprise analysis ■ How could the future surprise us and how can we prepare for it?
Purpose: ■ You allow for unpredictability. ■ You make it easier to think about, handle and communicate about uncertainty. ■ You can see more of the possible future and are therefore less surprised by the future. ■ You perceive surprising developments earlier. ■ You protect yourself and your futures strategy. ■ You initiate necessary changes at an early stage. ■ You perceive more future opportunities. ■ You improve your risk management.

Table 5.1 (cont'd)

Attitude and principles:
- Direct the red futures glasses at your environment.
- Think in a discontinuous way.
- Look for improbabilities.
- Keep surprises on the agenda.
- Spread possible stress more evenly in future.
- Don't regard surprises as being only negative.
- Don't expect any orientation from surprises.
- Look for plausible surprises.
- The number of possible surprises is increasing.
- The relevance comes from the potential effects.
- Take the necessary time.
- See your vulnerabilities in flexibility sacrifices.
- Stake out the area of possibilities with extremes.
- Reduce the effect of filters and barriers.
- Arrange for insider and outsider knowledge.
- Take a pragmatic approach in the scenarios.

Core concepts:
- Surprise questions
- Surprises (event-like and process-like)

Typical methods:
- Scenario methods
- Wild cards
- Assumption reversal
- Games and simulations

Procedure:
1. Gather together your futures team.
2. Determine your surprise questions.
3. Develop projections and scenarios of surprising events.
4. Develop scenarios of surprising developments or alternative futures.
5. Add the standard surprise "5–50".[2]
6. Determine the potential effects on your (preliminary) futures strategy.
7. Alternatively: Determine the potential effects on your current company.
8. Prioritize the surprises by the strength of their effect.
9. Prepare a surprise panorama.
10. Improve your vision, your mission and your guidelines.

Results:
Projections and scenarios of surprising developments and events and eventual strategies to immunize yourself against the most important strategic surprises.

Case studies on the red futures glasses

The examples from the *GBN-Study*[3] on climate change and the study *Limits to Growth*[4] (both discussed in Chapter 2) are two prominent examples of the application of the red futures glasses. Numerous possible surprises (wild cards) are discussed in the literature. A selection can be found below:

Biospheric surprises
- Change in the direction of circulation of the Gulf Stream and abrupt climate change
- Super quake in Japan or the USA with worldwide consequences
- Contact with extraterrestrial intelligence
- Super tsunami in the Atlantic
- Pandemic with 100 million dead

Technological surprises
- Cyber attack paralyzes computer networks and the internet
- Invisibility becomes possible
- Cold nuclear fusion becomes possible
- The end of encoding techniques
- A solution for the CO_2 problem is discovered

Political surprises
- Abolition of intellectual property rights
- The Euro fails
- Insurrections in western countries
- The use of nuclear weapons

Economic surprises
- Global stock market crash
- World economic crisis
- The ascendancy of Africa

Sociocultural surprises
- War of the old against the young
- Baby boom in aging countries
- Massive infertility

In our personal and business lives, we are generally more interested in the less fundamental and dramatic surprises. Questions such as: what will the city do if the neighboring city ends all forms of cooperation after a change in government? What will the leisure park operator do if he loses his visitors to computer games and videos? What will the bank do if it becomes superfluous thanks to the omnipresent financial services offers from other sectors? What will the gym do if a large number of its weight reduction oriented members stop going thanks to a diet pill with no side effects? What will the church do if complex extraterrestrial life is discovered? What will the saver do if, as has happened repeatedly in the past, there is a currency devaluation and his wealth shrinks to a fraction of its worth?

The Battle of Dorking

In 1871, G.T. Chesney published the fictitious story *The Battle of Dorking. When William Came* in *Blackwood's Magazine*. It was one of the first targeted uses of a future scenario. The essence of the plot is a German invasion of Great Britain in 1872, that is, a year into the future. The foundation of the second German Reich and its victory over France created the setting for the story. William is meant to be Emperor William.

Chesney described the following: The British army is dispersed all over the world. It defeats rebellions in India, protects Canada against the United States and safeguards Ireland against attacks by Napoleon III. Meanwhile, the Germans have developed new technologies such as torpedoes with which they quickly overpower the remaining British fleet. The final resistance in the battle of Dorking also fails and the inevitable happens: the Germans conquer Great Britain. That's how the scenario ends.

The text caused a great deal of commotion in Great Britain. The Prime Minister was outraged at what he considered to be its lack of plausibility. Nevertheless, *The Battle of Dorking* started a discussion as a result of which British military strategy was rethought and considerably more attention was paid to the defense of the country.

LOEWE misses out on flat screens

LOEWE, the traditional German TV manufacturer, went into a tailspin in 2003, so the press said. LOEWE had recognized the new flat screen technologies but hugely underestimated their importance in the TV business and was therefore surprised by the rapid change in the market. Sales of tube TVs in Germany fell by 23 percent in June 2003 compared to the previous month and the sale of flat screens increased by 152 percent. Apparently, the company was only saved from insolvency by equity participation from its Japanese competitor Sharp, one of the leading manufacturers of flat screens.[5]

VoIP places a question mark over the business of classic telecommunications companies

New technologies such as VoIP (Voice over Internet Protocol) are seriously threatening traditional telecommunications companies. The number of fixed line connections fell dramatically in 2005 alone. In addition to landline calls, cell phone communication will also be done via the internet in the near future. One of the last sources of profit would thus disappear.[6] The telecom companies have recognized the threat, but not yet taken it seriously and therefore not reacted. According to an internal study by the German Telekom's own consultancy company Detecon, the basis of the company's business could collapse within two years.[7] That speed is very surprising. It remains to be seen what consequences will ensue from this development.

"Finance-Ebay" threatens the banks' credit business

The small British internet company Zopa.com operates an online marketplace for peer-to-peer-lending and borrowing. According to the company's own information, it had far more than 100,000 registered members at the beginning of 2010. Prosper.com started business with a similar concept in the USA in February 2006. Both companies enable lenders and borrowers to carry out business without using the banks as an intermediary. The majority of the banks' profit margin thus goes to the customer. The fee for borrowers is only one percent (instead of around three percent interest difference with the banks) and half a percent for investors.

Prosper takes the concept even further than Zopa. Whereas Zopa distributes its customers' investments over at least fifty borrowers and therefore carries out a certain amount of risk management for the lenders, the latter can, or rather have to operate freely at Prosper and are therefore responsible themselves for spreading the risk over several borrowers according to their own needs.

Should the internet platforms establish themselves worldwide, traditional banks would face serious competition in the deposit and credit business. The internet marketplaces are currently limited to transactions at relatively low levels. Potentially however, project and company financing is imaginable. Half a dozen companies were established with a peer-to-peer concept. They are punishing the bankers who try to hide behind the fact that all of this is not possible in their country for legal reasons.

European global player discovers surprising substitution technology

With the red futures glasses, a well-known global European company has discovered and is investigating a not yet marketed possibility of completely replacing its own products. A physical solution that solves an acoustic problem in vehicles could be completely replaced by an electronic process and an appropriate component. By recognizing this at an early stage, the company was able to develop and implement eventual strategies before the potential surprise became reality.

Shell and the oil crisis

Royal Dutch Shell is considered to be one of the pioneers in the use of scenario methods to safeguard itself against potential surprises. Relevant techniques have been used there since the beginning of the 1970s. In one of the scenarios of the "group planning" department at the time, Pierre Wack and Ted Newland analyzed the possibility of a dramatic increase in the price of oil. At the time, with a price of around 2.80 US dollars per barrel (159 liters) and the fact that sudden changes in price were more or less unknown, imagining an oil price of six dollars was considered to be a daring scenario in the early 1970s. As OPEC had been established as an oil cartel twelve years previously, this scenario was certainly not completely unfounded.

The scenario was the trigger and starting point for a number of flexibilization measures. Shell carried out an inventory of its vulnerabilities. It was discovered among other things, that tanker capacity was booked in long-term contracts without utilization components. A sudden fall in demand as a result of a price increase would lead to a high level of empty capacity having to be paid for. Shell came up with the simple measure of adding a clause to contracts with tanker operators giving Shell an extraordinary cancellation right at an oil price of six dollars.

> *But here, as always, it will not happen in the way we expect.*
> (Wilhelm Busch)

When the oil crisis happened in 1973 and the oil price rose to significantly over six dollars, Shell was much better prepared with this measure and various other eventual strategies than the other six big oil companies. Before the oil crisis, Shell had always been one of the worst placed of the so-called seven sisters with regard to income. As a result of the oil crisis, Shell shot up to the top position in income and remained there, with the exception of one year, for twelve years. The oil crisis had made Shell the most successful oil company in the world.

War games against blind spots

One of the world's largest automotive supply companies used war games to identify possible attacks by competitors and to reduce blind spots in the management's attention. Attack strategies of real and fictitious competitors were developed in several rounds together with the company's own defense strategy. Dynamic competition scenarios were used to identify vulnerability to competitor activity and opportunities to strengthen its own business developed. The broad approach of war games and the thinking in improbabilities, the methodically supported reduction of blind spots and the evaluation of the potential impact of various competitive scenarios effectively safeguarded the strategy and competitive position. Many of the potential surprises recognized hadn't previously come up on the radar screen.

Government war games in cyberspace

The American National Security Agency (NSA) is the largest and most powerful secret service in the world. It is attached to the US Defense Department. The NSA has been carrying out the so-called Annual Cyber Defense Exercise since 2000. The goal is to recognize possible surprises at an early stage by inviting other services and agencies to set up a computer network that is attacked by the NSA experts with all available means. The network's functionalities, such as ongoing e-mail traffic, instant messaging, data server, internet and other important services have to be sustained at the same time.[8]

Similar projects have been and still are implemented in the USA and other developed countries to protect the national infrastructure. The potential surprises being looked for are not to be found in the attacks themselves, but in the dynamic developments and reactions triggered by them.

In Germany, a cyber war was simulated in order to protect the infrastructure. Authorities and large companies simulated a massive terrorist attack on the power supply system and communication network, including the media. It is comparatively easy to resist the demands of terrorists who threaten to murder a number of citizens. However, when the threat consists of bringing public life, including air traffic and medical provision, to a standstill through paralyzing the power and communication networks, then governmental rigor looks a little different. If anyone were successful with such a cyber war attack, they could effectively demand whatever they want, and certainly a withdrawal of all troops from extraterritorial areas of action such as Afghanistan or the release of hundreds of terrorists.[9]

Purpose of the red futures glasses

The red futures glasses are primarily intended to sensitize us to the certain part of the future, for the surprises. We need the red futures glasses for that which is not obvious.

You allow for unpredictability

As generally known and already discussed in the principles of the blue futures glasses, the future is largely unpredictable and therefore essentially open. If only the blue futures glasses existed, you would fall prey to a false sense of security. It would just be the appearance of security, because you hadn't thought about it sufficiently.

■ Transform ignorant security into reflected insecurity.[10]

The blue futures glasses do not visualize surprises. The red futures glasses correct this error. Whereas you can only look in a projective, that is, continuing way into the future with the blue futures glasses, the red futures glasses concentrate your view on the futures that are beyond your usual thought horizon. They are futures we will come up against in the form of surprising events and developments that we have considered to be very unlikely or even totally impossible.

You make the future easier to think about, handle and communicate about uncertainty

The red futures glasses help you to recognize how uncertain the future is and in what way it is uncertain. Projections and in particular scenarios of surprising futures make it easier for you to think about the uncertainties of the future and to handle your lack of knowledge.[11] The huge variety of improbable yet possible futures can be reduced to a few, comprehensible projections and scenarios. These projections and scenarios become common mental pictures and terms for a possible surprising future.[12] Projections take on the role of mini scenarios,[13] which provide answers to a single question, whereas the real scenarios answer several questions at the same time and therefore cover whole bundles of projections.

In the same way that the blue futures glasses with their assumptions about the future reduce the complexity of the probable future and ease communication about it (see pages 60 and 61), the projections and scenarios of surprising futures seen through the red futures glasses also function as a means of communication. They summarize manifold and, at first sight, confusing data in a structured and consistent way[14] and thus enable simplification and acceleration of the thought and discussion processes.

You can see more of the possible future and are therefore less surprised by the future

The future is multiple (see Chapter 3). The red futures glasses expand your perspective and help you to recognize more possible futures in your environment beyond the blue futures glasses. Thanks to the red futures glasses, you will be less surprised by the future because you will have seen more of what can happen. Someone who has been confronted with the scenario that their own products could be made superfluous by a technology from another sector which suddenly appears from nowhere, such as razor blades replaced by laser technology, or that two competitors could merge, will be less surprised by such events. Someone who furthermore goes beyond scenarios and also thinks about eventual strategies, is not only less surprised, but also better prepared than others.

> The red futures glasses are a tool for overcoming barriers to perception and thought. They increase the imagination and stimulate the user to think more imaginatively and boldly about the possible.

By broadening horizons, the red futures glasses make lateral thinking beyond standard practice easier, which some people somewhat exaggeratedly refer to as paradigms. Barber[15] sees three intensities of the effects of scenarios of surprising futures on your thinking and your strategy:

1. *Stretching* the existing paradigm: You see more alternatives, without essentially changing your strategy.

2. *Expanding* the existing paradigm: You change your strategy and your behavior, but only on a situational basis, not permanently.

3. *Cracking* the existing paradigm: You destroy the existing paradigm and start searching for a new one.

You perceive surprising developments earlier

The first element of early perception with the red futures glasses is the fact that they are being used. The mere effort of thinking about and imagining the surprising allows you to perceive futures that remained closed to you previously.

The second element of early perception, to a certain extent second level early perception, is similar to the attractor function of the blue futures glasses. One of the goals of the blue futures glasses is to use the assumptions about future developments as attractors for futures information, so that you can perceive more signals and messages that speak for or against the correctness of the assumption (see page 61). The projections and scenarios of surprising events and developments work in the same way as attractors and attention categories[16] for references to increasing or decreasing probabilities of their possible occurrence. These references are known as weak signals[17] or as prognostications.[18] If you have considered the bankruptcy of your largest customer as a possible surprise, then you will be much more alert to signals and messages, be they in conversations, in newspapers, on the radio, on television or in the internet. This attractor function of the red futures glasses also helps you to be less surprised by the future.

You protect yourself and your futures strategy

Through the red futures glasses, you see projections and scenarios of surprising futures which serve as simulations of the possible but improbable[19] and can show how you and your organization will cope in different futures. With projections and scenarios of surprising futures you can safeguard:

- your existence as a person or a company,
- your futures strategy and
- your individual decision

against these possible and effective but improbable futures and significantly improve their chances of success in this way.

> Surprises demand too much of our normal ability to react and our reaction speed.

A primary goal of the red futures glasses is to learn a priori to cope with surprising situations that are otherwise impossible or difficult to manage. If you don't learn this early enough, you have not enough experience, nor enough time or neither of these to get control of the new situation when it actually happens. Thinking about the implications and effects of possible surprises early, and storing this for later use, improves your experience in dealing with them and reduces the amount of time you need to develop and carry out eventual strategies.

In 1964, Gerald Caplan[20] developed the trichotomy of psychological prevention shown in Table 5.2, which is used in more or less all fields of medicine and is also supported by the WHO. Above all, the red futures glasses are used for prevention, particularly primary and secondary prevention. The other futures glasses serve to promote health in the widest sense – salutogenesis. This is the term used to describe the opposite of pathogenic medicine, which concentrates on sickness, and is instead "primordial" prevention, which means the concentration on promoting the health and well-being that comes before actual primary prevention.

Table 5.2 Stages of prevention

Stage	In medicine	In companies
Salutogenesis (primordial prevention)	■ Strengthen and promote health (salutogenesis)	■ Improve success ■ Increase viability
Primary prevention (healthy phase)	■ Prevent or delay the illness ■ Prophylaxis ■ Inoculation	■ Prevent the crisis (reduce the surprise itself) ■ *Implement preventive strategies*

Table 5.2 (cont'd)

Stage	In medicine	In companies
Secondary prevention (preclinical phase)	■ Recognize the illness at an early stage (screening) ■ Keep the illness at a minor level ■ Early healing and therapy	■ Recognize the crisis at an early stage ■ *Implement acute strategies*
Tertiary prevention (manifest phase)	■ Reduce the consequences of the illness ■ Late healing and therapy ■ Rehabilitation ■ Relapse prevention	■ Reduce the consequences of the crisis ■ *Implement acute strategies* ■ Turnaround and recapitalization/reorganization

Note: Stages 2 to 4 according to Caplan, 1964.

■ **The red futures glasses are intended to enable the development of eventual strategies, which are divided into preventive strategies and acute strategies.**

Preventive strategies are implemented before the surprise occurs as a kind of inoculation. This includes, for example, purchasing the software *Foldershare* through Microsoft, which is apparently only intended to safeguard the previously purchased and promoted software *Groove*. Both software packages are used to synchronize datasets between distant users on a peer-to-peer principle, that is, without a server. The situation was similar with Gillette, who entered into cooperation with Palomar, a developer of laser razors potentially threatening Gillette's market. Acute strategies are strategies that are planned, but only implemented when needed (the surprise occurs). These include, for example, crisis PR plans, which responsible, foresighted companies have ready.

States, organizations and individuals who have already once experienced a significant strategic surprise are often later protected against this discontinuity and prepared for it. The earthquake that hit Tokyo in 1923 claimed 142,000 lives. According to acknowledged forecasts, the next serious quake will "only" claim 11,000 lives. It is natural that people primarily learn from experience and only in second place from foresight.

■ *It wasn't raining when Noah built the ark.* (Howard Ruff)

Learning from experience can however strengthen our attempts at foresight so that we are constantly better prepared for surprises. However, a world that is changing at an ever-increasing speed becomes increasingly unpredictable, with the result that progress in anticipating surprises can ultimately become steps backwards in the level of protection.

System sciences would also connect the red futures glasses with the term sensitivity analysis, which measures the sensitivity of a system (a futures strategy in this case) regarding the changes of individual parameters and, based on that, enables the system to be made more robust.

You initiate necessary changes at an early stage

Psychologists assume that real personal changes mostly take place in crises. Even when the yellow futures glasses show a highly attractive vision, the red futures glasses still need to support the willingness to change.

> *People don't change because they see the light – they change because they feel the heat.* (Anon.)

As a rule, people need to get into situations outside their previous spectrum of experience in order to change their behavior. Discontinuities or potential surprises can help to simulate the crisis situation necessary for positive change and thus also create the willingness to change. It is known that many entrepreneurs and managers deliberately and regularly paint a dramatic picture of potential threat (not necessarily the surprise) to keep their employees attentive and, to a degree, in a state of alert. The fact that dictators almost always build up pictures of the enemy and threats, and that this is a popular way of keeping power for politicians of all parties, doesn't mean that entrepreneurs and managers act in an equally reprehensible way. After all, dictators usually construct the threats, whereas for entrepreneurs the threat needs to be real for them to achieve attention and effect within their teams.

You perceive more future opportunities

One of the most important benefits of the red futures glasses appears paradoxical at first sight. By thinking of improbable yet possible futures, you inevitably form the foundation for opportunity development. You can also use the green futures glasses to analyze the surprises imagined with the red futures glasses and see opportunities in them. If you recognize that a competitor could introduce a new business model, then you don't have to think too far to also use this possibility as a future opportunity for yourself.

> The mental preconditions for new paths, new solutions and new decisions frequently develop with the red futures glasses.

Scenarios of surprising developments serve, among other purposes, to generate options.[21] If the mind is forced to imagine improbable, not obvious futures, it more easily develops alternative strategies, which also prove to be helpful and often particularly promising in the future assumed to be probable. Imagine if all planes had to stay on the ground, all trains in the stations, all automobiles in the garage. How would you then do business? It becomes clear, that all travel budgets are to a large extent communication budgets and vice-versa and that a lot of physical business travel could be easily replaced by videophones, videoconferences and even the good old telephone.

> *If you don't do what you are afraid of, fear will control your life.*
> (Glenn Ford)

You improve your risk management

Corporate risk management has become matter of course, since it has become required by law in many countries in recent years. However, before risks can be managed, they have to be recognized. Risks can be surmised long before they are recognizable enough to be managed using prognostics, meaning signs or so-called weak signals.[22]

Risk management and the red futures glasses are therefore related but not identical. The red futures glasses are primarily for surprises in the future, be they positive or negative. Risk management is more defensive towards changes in the future, even if the risk managers always correctly claim that risks also contain opportunities.

Core concepts of the red futures glasses

The red futures glasses are concerned with discontinuities and surprises. The search for them is often started by surprise questions. The following illustration shows that surprises challenge your assumptions about the future and that you make your futures strategy more substantiated, solid and robust by working on them.

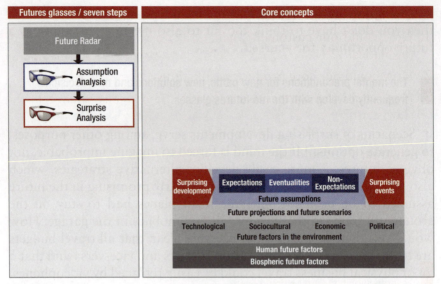

Figure 5.1 The core concepts of the red futures glasses

Surprise questions

When working with the red futures glasses, surprises are intended to divert your attention to those potential surprises that would have the greatest consequences.

> You use surprise questions to determine the essential knowledge requirements on possible and powerful surprises in your environment.

The surprise questions are as individual as the business models of companies and life drafts of people. The simplest approach to finding the right surprise questions is to orient yourself to the determining factors and fields of observation you have already selected for the blue futures glasses and for which you have made assumptions about the future. These were changes in:

- the behavior of your customers
- relevant technologies
- market dynamics and competition
- laws and regulations
- natural basic resources.

The following surprises could result for example:

1. How could our customers' demand for our services suddenly fall dramatically?
2. How could our core product be substituted by a new technology?
3. How could the competitive situation dramatically change in the short-term?
4. How could the legal and regulatory framework change in such a way that we would be severely affected by it?
5. What could happen in nature and the environment that would affect the existence of our business?

As the examples show, the important thing is to place the effect of a surprise in the foreground.

> It is more important to know where and how you are vulnerable, than to know exactly which surprises could occur.

Surprises

Surprises are different from the blue futures glasses' non-expectations in that their possible occurrence usually doesn't even come into the decision-makers' field of vision with projective thinking. The non-expectation has been consciously considered and then assigned a low degree of expected probability. With the blue futures glasses you would typically consider an increase or decrease in the market size in the form of two extreme projections and then develop a conviction (assumption about the future).

> The idea that the market could be destroyed by a known or unknown substitute technology is one that the managers of many companies have to force themselves to consider with the red futures glasses.

The blue futures glasses are used to look at more continual developments with gradual changes or functions (curves), the red futures glasses for more discontinuous developments and functions. Different attitudes and tools are needed for these two ways of thinking. We define surprises as follows:

> A surprise is a projection or a scenario of an event or a development in the environment with a low probability but potentially severe effects.

The definition makes it clear that surprises are also imagined in the external form of projections or scenarios, similar to the core concepts of the blue futures glasses (see Chapter 4).

A surprise is surprising because it causes a speed of change in the environment that is too much for your reaction speed. Something can be surprising because you:

- had never imagined it
- considered it be to virtually impossible
- had expected it earlier
- had expected it later.

Surprises can be either event-like or process-like, as Table 5.3 shows. This differentiation, which is fundamental for practical work, is unfortunately rarely made in the literature on wild cards.

Table 5.3 Two types of surprises		
Criterion	**Event-like surprises**	**Process-like surprises**
Definition	■ Surprise which suddenly occurs in the form of an event in the environment	■ Surprise which gradually occurs and which leads to an alternative future of the environment
Examples	■ The production problems at Airbus became known in 2006 ■ Tsunami on December 26, 2004 ■ Attacks on September 11, 2001 ■ Fall of the Berlin Wall on November 9, 1989 ■ Reactor accident in Chernobyl on April 26, 1986 ■ See also the examples in the Case studies section	■ A music market which needs no sound storage medium ■ An employment market in which the working hours become longer again (trend reversal in 2003, the signs of which had been apparent almost ten years earlier)
Effect	■ Fast and potentially permanent imbalance	■ Slow and generally permanent change of balance
Early perception possibility	■ More or less impossible to perceive at an early stage due to a lack of or only minimal prognostics (weak signals)	■ Basically possible to perceive at an early stage due to recognizable prognostics (weak signals)
Reaction time	■ Hardly available	■ Available
Typical method	■ Wild card analysis (disruptive event analysis) ■ Creative techniques ■ Analogies	■ Scenario analysis of alternative futures (additional to the blue futures glasses)

Event-like surprises (wild cards)

The earlier example of the *Battle of Dorking* describes the scenario of an event-like surprise. Events can trigger surprising events. The fall of the Berlin Wall, for example, was the turning point for numerous trends, from atomic armament to the EU's taxation and finance policies. The development of the World Wide Web, that is, a user-friendly internet surface, was a turnaround in the development of the sale of automobiles or the stock market or commodity exchange. However, we consider the further development of the internet into an html-based World Wide Web as a breakthrough or expected event, as the communicative simplification of the internet corresponded to the typical progression of computer technology.

Process-like surprises (alternative futures)

Thinking about alternative futures corresponds to process-like surprises. In contrast to the event-like surprises, the initial flop of the New Economy or the reversal of the reduction of working hours that had been going on for a century were more process-like surprises. Through signs thrown up in advance, weak signals or prognosticons, process-like discontinuities open the possibility of early perception and anticipation. Ten years before the failed strike for the 35-hour working week in East Germany in 2003, the first companies had already in fact lengthened working hours. So-called scenarios (in the narrowest sense) are used as a thought-instrument for process-like surprises. The strengths of scenario methods come to the fore with the red futures glasses.

As Table 5.3 shows, suddenness is not as important as you would probably first think with the term surprise. The internet didn't suddenly appear: something like the internet had already been foreseen in several studies in 1964 and the Arpanet, conceived of in 1962 and realized in 1969, was an obvious precursor. Numerous industries, companies and individuals were nevertheless surprised that (and to what extent) the internet revolutionized markets and the world within a few years.

Figure 5.2 shows a scenario cube, a structure for eight scenarios of surprising developments or alternative futures for the banking market. The scenario cube is defined by three axes and corresponding surprise questions (here the same as the assumption questions), to which the extreme answers are given on both ends of a scale. The structure corresponds to the projections of the blue futures glasses (see Figure 4.3).

1. *E-finance intensity axis:* What percentage of people use e-finance as the primary way to carry out their banking? Is it likely, after attacks on the internet, to be only a few – twenty percent – or ninety percent, meaning almost everyone?

2. *Advice market axis:* To what extent will financial advice be paid for separately in future? Will this be natural or will advice become purely a sales instrument again?

3. *Provider market axis:* How strongly will the financial services market be fragmented on the provider side? Will there be only a few large financial services providers or will practically every company – regardless of sector – offer financial services?

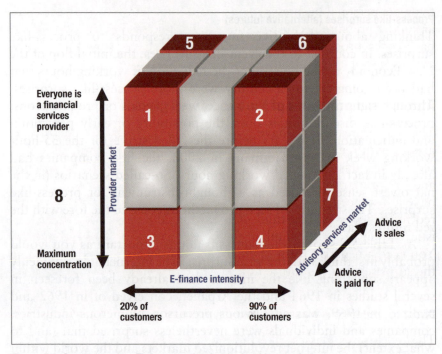

Figure 5.2 Scenario cube: Eight scenarios for the banking market

Very improbable yet imaginable scenarios of the future have appeared through the triple combination of the extremes. Thus the rear top-right combination,

(a) ninety percent e-finance intensity,
(b) advice is sold and
(c) everyone is a financial services provider,

is a scenario which could be referred to as "the death of the classical bank", for in this scenario only a very few data centers would be operated which offer their services to providers from different sectors. The low level of personal advice is concentrated on the most valuable products and solutions and continues to be paid for primarily through commission. The trio at the bottom front left,

(a) twenty percent e-finance intensity,
(b) paid for advice and
(c) maximum concentration,

on the other hand, shows a scenario that could be described as "boom of corporate financial advisors", for in this future, financial services remain a personal business which is paid for separately. However, fees are under pressure because of the high volume so that the costs of the back-office processes need to be radically reduced through volume advantages of corporations.

Attitude and principles of the red futures glasses

The red futures glasses have a lot in common with the blue futures glasses with regard to the required attitude and their principles. The red futures glasses also look at the world from a macro perspective and are primarily externally oriented towards the environment. You have a distanced, passive and observing view of the future. With the red futures glasses, you think in a calculatedly pessimistic and fatalistic way in order to simulate the consequences of possible futures. You need a negative form of creativity in order to be able to imagine the surprises that the future holds in store for you.

Direct the red futures glasses to your environment

The red futures glasses, like the blue ones, are only concerned with your environment and the environment of your company. You yourself cannot play a role in the surprises as the requirement for passivity shows (see "How creatable are futures?" in Chapter 3 and page 74). Unfortunately a lot of practitioners talk about scenarios when they mean their own options for designing and acting, which according to most experts is not very useful.

> The red futures glasses should not be confused with the planning question "what can go wrong" and also not with the notion of "risk".

Surprises also need to be differentiated from the term "risk". The original Italian word risk means danger and hazard. In French (risquer) it means even more clearly that you bring yourself or something into danger or jeopardy. Risk therefore requires actively doing something, taking a risk. Generally they are risks from normal business operations or the risks from additional activities beyond this normal business. But it is always a conscious, active act that causes the risks. The word threat has a somewhat different meaning – a danger that you can also be exposed to through your mere existence.

Think in a discontinuous way

When people think about the future of their environment, they generally do so with a projective approach. They extrapolate present developments. This thinking is typical of the blue futures glasses. However, most of the strategically relevant discontinuities cannot be foreseen with the known statistical or economic model forecasts, because the change cannot be explained as a causal-logical law of the past or because the "third variable" causing the change cannot be quantified.

▪ Surprises are difficult to see with popular projective thinking.

The red futures glasses require a much more discontinuous way of thinking, which we really have to force our brain to do. How could things happen in a completely different way? What if our assumptions about the future are completely wrong? What would need to happen to shake the foundations of our futures strategy? What would need to happen to catapult us to success within a short time? These and similar questions help us to see the surprising, unexpected and improbable.

Look for improbabilities

In contrast to the blue futures glasses of assumption analysis, the surprising future doesn't require thinking in probabilities, but thinking in improbabilities. As surprises are the only certain thing about the future, you must assume that the basic assumptions about the future will prove to be wrong and that the future will be different to what you imagined.

▪ *The most surprising future would be one which held no surprises.* (Herman Kahn)

Particularly large and seemingly improbable surprises demand an expanded perspective and a good portion of overcoming usual thought patterns. A lengthy breakdown of the internet sounds both unimaginable and initially not very dramatic. However, anyone who gets nervous because he left his cell phone at home or is unable to call up e-mails for a day can easily imagine what a global catastrophe a breakdown of the internet would cause. Today's internet is based on thirteen root servers, all of which are in the USA. The USA could therefore theoretically be able to "switch off" most of the internet.

Keep surprises on the agenda

Many people tend to push the improbable aside. They are used to looking for probabilities (with the blue futures glasses) and then concentrating on them. The red futures glasses are intended to literally force you to look at the future's improbabilities. After all, they are on the increase. You need to resist your colleagues' and employees' requests to concentrate on "realistic things".

This is, however, easier said than done, for if you point to possible surprises, you will almost always be looked at critically, mistrustfully, at best pityingly. From an emotional point of view, it stands to reason you would prematurely end the use of the futures glasses or even to completely do without them. At this point, it is helpful to make yourself aware of the meaning of the red futures glasses, using the case studies described earlier in this chapter so that you find the courage to hold hard and prevail.

> *It's a crying shame that the idiots are so self-assured and the clever people are so full of doubt.* (Bertrand Russell)

Spread possible stress more evenly in future

Being less surprised by the future also means anticipating the future stress that results from a surprise occurring and thus bringing that stress into the present. You reduce the painful, sometimes even deadly stress peaks and spread the stress as evenly as possible over your lifetime.

> The red futures glasses cause stress. But it is better to have a little more stress on a permanent basis than for it to become unexpectedly deadly.

Electricity costs are reduced using a similar principle. The very expensive peaks are reduced by avoiding all equipment being switched on at the same time and instead distributing their electricity intake.

The more is known about a potential surprise, the less threatening it is. The solutions and eventual strategies that can be used to face up to potential surprises become obvious.[23]

Don't regard surprises as being only negative

Although we have chosen red as the color for surprises, that doesn't mean they have to be something threatening and dangerous. The manufacturers of re-sealable plastic bags were surprised when the regulation that all air passengers had to use such bags for liquids they wanted to take on board was unexpectedly introduced. The regulation didn't exactly lead to a boom, but it certainly wasn't negative for the manufacturers of re-sealable plastic bags.

> A surprise is seldom negative for everyone. Something that is negative for one person always has something positive for someone else and vice-versa.

The surprising breakthrough in economic nuclear fusion reactors with a positive energy balance would be welcome for example. Humanity's energy problems and the earth's climate problems would be solved very quickly. This breakthrough would not however be very welcome to those whose power stations became superfluous thanks to nuclear fusion power stations. Petersen[24] describes a negative example of a wild card that also has positive side effects: a rapidly declining sperm concentration would also help to reduce population density.

A crisis is often a harbinger of something better. In the 14th century, the Black Death killed half of the central European population. As there were not enough workers after it, the farmers were able to enforce higher wages and lower leases on the lords.

Don't expect orientation from surprises

Classic scenario methods are based on the future being basically unpredictable. Using generally three to five scenarios of equally probable or equally improbable futures, they try to show the ways the future could possibly happen. The requirement is then to devise the futures strategy in such a way that all scenarios can be coped with well. As there are no perspectives of the future of the environment other than the drafts of alternative futures in classical scenario methods, the scenarios are also supposed to provide a certain orientation function.

In the five futures glasses system, the *Eltville Model*, the blue futures glasses take on this role by consciously developing and constantly monitoring the assumption about probable and improbable futures. The red futures glasses therefore have no explicit orientation and thus need less consistency in their projections and scenarios (see below).

> In the *Eltville Model* of the five futures glasses, the blue futures glasses provide the orientation function.

Look for plausible surprises

Even if the surprises you can see with the red futures glasses are improbable, they still have to meet the plausibility requirement. Something is plausible if it is evident, comprehensible, believable and cohesive. Plausibility is the measure of the general *possibility* of a certain surprise occurring. The better a projection or a scenario of a potential surprise is described and based on sound arguments, the more plausible it appears.[25]

In 2005, a fourth tectonic plate was discovered under the bay of the Japanese city Tokyo that significantly increases the earthquake risk. If large parts of Tokyo fell victim to a massive earthquake, 11,000 dead and no less than 811 billion Euros of damage would be expected. This could lead to the withdrawal of Japanese capital from the financial markets that could then result in a financial crisis. Not even the best experts are in a position to confirm or exclude that this could happen; nevertheless this potential surprise needs to be assigned a certain degree of plausibility. Incidentally, it is assumed with ninety percent certainty that Tokyo will suffer a severe quake (7 on the Richter scale) in the next fifty years.[26]

We intuitively tend to confuse plausibility with probability. The likelihood of there being no more evil in the world within the next few weeks is neither probable nor plausible. A breathtaking story would need to be provided to make such a surprise seem believable. It is also not very probable that humans will get evidence of the existence of intelligent extraterrestrial life, but we consider this projection to be much more plausible than the development of a thoroughly good world. After all, a new planet is currently discovered every two weeks on average.

> Surprises need to be challenging yet plausible and imaginable to be taken seriously.

The more imagination a surprise demands, the greater the resistance to occupying oneself with it. Ridiculousness kills. All overly bold scenarios run the risk that management will cancel the whole process. Beyond a certain level of challenge, healthy skepticism is needed: after all, for financial reasons alone, it is impossible and nonsensical to prepare yourself for extremely implausible and improbable surprises. The value of a surprise therefore initially increases with the level of challenge and then rapidly decreases.

The number of possible surprises is increasing

It is becoming increasingly difficult to recognize and understand the possible surprises and their effects. Their number is heading towards never ending. This effect is the result of a range of developments:

Increasing complexity
We make the world ever more complex. Attempts (with some success) to make it simpler don't change that fact. Surprises are by definition a characteristic of a complex system. A complicated system, a circuit board for example, generally does not behave in a surprising way. But a computer is already a complex system where hidden changes in software (often automatically downloaded) mean that it doesn't always behave in the same way with the same input. If people who independently make more or less good decisions are then involved, we are faced with a complex adaptive system, like a market or a society for example. Such systems are never exactly predictable or, put another way, they constantly produce surprises.

Increasing number of factors
A further aspect of complexity, and thus a driver of implicit surprises, is to be found in the increase of the active and passive elements in the system. More people, more companies, more organizations and more computers make it increasingly difficult to keep an overview of all essential factors let alone to recognize and understand their interconnected effects.

Increasing cross linkages
The increasing cross linkages of the actors, both in terms of informa-

tion and the mutual dependencies and attractions form ever more possible causes of surprises. They are the drivers of the abovementioned complexity. Before the discovery of the internet, there was no possibility of its crashing or of new, purely internet-based competition developing. It was equally unimaginable that the likelihood of a country being attacked would dramatically increase within a few days through the publication of an internet page.

The number of potential surprises increases with the speed of change and with the complexity of the world.

Chain reactions and accumulations

Surprises trigger chain reactions that are hard to predict or understand. Accumulations of surprises have a similar effect, such as the last child murder in a series, which finally leads to protective measures. The effect tunnel, meaning the totality of changes caused over time by a surprise, can never be fully taken in. René Thom's catastrophe theory[27] initially promised a solution. It was supposed to be a method that would enable us to understand and calculate discontinuous developments as well as continuous developments. The trigger and the course of chain reactions were supposed to be as easy to calculate as trends. Unfortunately, the mathematical model never really worked.

The relevance comes from the potential effects

At first glance, we often don't see the effects a potential surprise would have. As it is generally something relatively new, then you haven't thought through the surprise itself or its effects. The stronger the effects, the greater the relevance of the surprise and the more urgently you need to immunize yourself against it.

You need to prepare yourself for the effects of the surprise, not for the surprise itself.

Although this may sound obvious, it is not so easy to implement it in practice. It is easier when you take a shortcut and first ask yourself which central factors your success depends on and then completely or partially simulate the loss of these factors. For people as life entrepreneurs, for companies and for almost all organizations, turnover and profit contribution are central parameters. The quickest and simplest discontinuity analysis is therefore to ask yourself and then answer the "5–50" question:

What will we do, if we permanently lose fifty percent of our contribution margin in the next five weeks?

> **If you know the worst imaginable effects, then the surprise causing them is insignificant.**

If a fifty percent slump is normal in your business, assume sixty or even eighty percent. Everything you do to survive this blanket discontinuity would also protect you against all other imaginable surprises.

Take the necessary time

The effects of surprises are regularly over- or underestimated. Always remain skeptical and cautious if someone can tell after only two seconds that something will have dramatic consequences or that a surprise can be neglected. Even if a surprise appears very simple, its consequences and its interactions can nevertheless be very complex and significant.

See your vulnerabilities in flexibility sacrifices

The surprise analysis would never end if you didn't limit it to the most important potential surprises. Figure 5.3 helps to determine those strategy elements for which eventual strategies should be developed.

> *It isn't the strongest or the most intelligent who survive, but those who are most prepared to adapt.* (Charles Darwin)

The relevant observation objects are to be found in the first column. The strategy elements that can be determined short-term are listed in the first line. An example would be your pricing model that you can change very quickly in the strategy perspective. You and your company are as flexible as a motorboat in this regard.

Below this, the strategy elements that must be determined long-term are listed. These are elements such as real estate, your information technology and, in particular, your corporate culture, where you can only change direction or even turn around very slowly like a tanker. Changing a corporate culture usually takes several years. All other strategy elements are listed in the third area.

Observation object	Time frame	High readiness to assume risk	Risk-aware strategy	High need for security
Strategy elements with short-term commitment	Today		Preventive eventual strategies not necessary	Implementation of preventive eventual strategies
	Future	Reaction as and if needed	Reaction as and if needed	Implementation of acute eventual strategies
Strategy Elements with long-term commitment	Today		■ Implementation of preventive eventual strategies ■ Avoidance of long-term commitment ■ Full exploitation of flexibilization possibilities	■ Implementation of all preventive eventual strategies if possible ■ Minimize long-term commitments
	Future	Reaction as and if needed	Implementation of acute eventual strategies	Implementation of acute eventual strategies
All strategy elements	Today		Installation of an early perception system	Installation of an early perception system
	Future		Continuous early perception	Continuous early perception

Figure 5.3 Focal points of the surprise analysis

> You are most vulnerable in the areas where you have made the greatest flexibility sacrifices in the interests of efficiency.

The second column differentiates the point in time when action is needed: what needs to be done today and what will need to be done in the future. The third column describes a strategy with a very high risk, in which high strategic risks are accepted. This strategy is difficult to follow in most companies for legal reasons alone. The column at the extreme right describes a security-oriented strategy, which can, however, be just as dangerous: as everyone knows, someone who wants to protect himself against all risks destroys every opportunity. The risk-aware strategy column shows the ideal situation in which you protect yourself against existential risks yet show sufficient entrepreneurial responsibility and readiness to take a risk to reach and maintain a good competitive market position.

The risk-aware strategy concentrates on the strategy elements that need to be determined long-term, as the greatest flexibility sacrifices have been made here in the interests of competitiveness. The less flexible your company is, the more foresight is needed.

■ **Flexibility replaces foresight.**

The imaginable surprises therefore need to be examined as to how far they would be fundamentally affected by the strategy elements that need to be determined long-term. If your IT system could become obsolete due to a discontinuous market development, for example, then it is advisable to develop an eventual strategy. The IT system could be modernized as a preventive step or the justification for an alternative system could be proposed as an acute strategy.

■ **Flexibility is only a hygiene factor, not a success factor.**

This model enables you to check all strategy elements that need to be determined long-term and thus make your futures strategy more robust in the face of surprising future developments.

Stake out the area of possibilities with extremes

In practice, it is neither possible nor necessary to conceive of and think through all possible surprises. In most cases it is enough to take a number of scenarios of extreme futures into consideration. The management team of a bank for example, could imagine that there could be a future within a foreseeable period of time in which ninety percent of all private clients carry out their banking online, advice can still not be charged for separately and almost every company also additionally offers financial services. In this imaginably difficult scenario, there is practically no room for the classical bank. If the management team finds eventual strategies that are suitable for ensuring the survival of the bank in this scenario, then it would at the same time protect itself against an unclear number of other scenarios.

■ **A few extreme projections and scenarios can sufficiently determine the area of possibilities.**

The fact that a few scenarios can stake out the area for surprises does not however mean that two or five scenarios are sufficient, as is practiced by many scenario methodologists. For your practical work we recommend including at least eight scenarios of alternative futures (surprising developments) and about a dozen surprising events in discontinuity analysis.

Reduce the effect of filters and barriers

Despite a systematic approach and rationality, strong psychological factors have an influence with the red futures glasses. The term *groupthink*[28] describes the phenomenon where, particularly, management teams that work well together tend to agree too quickly on a uniform opinion and way of thinking. This can quickly become deadly in an increasingly fast and complex world.

The ability to be able to even recognize potential surprises is dependent on several factors, how much someone basically knows, how well his reality assumptions reproduce the reality perceived by others, what he likes and what he doesn't like, how intelligent he is, how many languages and symbols he understands, and his current physical and mental state. All of these are causes of perception, awareness, imagination and action barriers, which are detrimental to the early perception of potential surprises (see Figure 5.4).

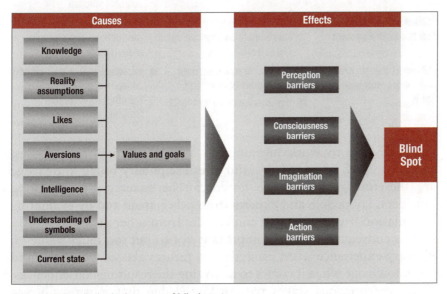

Figure 5.4 Psychological causes of blind spots

The effect of the filters mentioned can be reduced at an early stage by knowing of their existence and reminding others within a team that you could be wrong.

> *The first lesson from philosophy is that we all might be wrong.*
> (William Durant)

Arrange for insider and outsider knowledge

The view of the experts within your own organization is not enough to recognize surprises in the future. Four types of knowledge, as shown in Table 5.4, are necessary for the red futures glasses of a potential surprise.

Table 5.4 Competences for the red futures glasses

Level	Key question	Required competence
Recognizing the surprise	■ Which surprising things could happen?	■ Knowledge from mostly extrinsic fields
Character of the surprise	■ How exactly does the surprise work?	■ Knowledge about the mechanisms and characteristics of the potential surprise
Effect of the surprise on the entire system	■ How will the system and the environment be changed by this surprise?	■ Knowledge about the mechanisms and principles of systems in general
Effect of the surprise on the person looking at it	■ Which consequences does the surprise have for us? ■ How can we best react to it?	■ Knowledge about the market concerned, the company or the other object of the analysis

To be able to work meaningfully with the red futures glasses, specialist depth of knowledge and interdisciplinary broad knowledge are therefore required. The latter can be ensured by consulting outsiders, lay people and experts from other areas and by evaluating information from media and conferences from other areas.

It is consequently hugely important not to put too much value on industry experience when using the red futures glasses, you only need this knowledge when it comes to analyzing the resulting consequences. The three previous stages require knowledge that is generally not available in your company.

Take a pragmatic approach in the scenarios

In addition to looking at surprising events – the wild cards – it is also advisable to identify and analyze surprising developments. Scenario methods are a useful tool for this.

There are innumerable scenario methods covering a conceivably broad spectrum of philosophies and techniques. We will discuss two extreme schools here: the *intuitive school* and the *mathematical school*.

The intuitive school of scenario methods[29] places the focus on the degree of challenge and the general effect of a scenario on its user. Plausibility is ensured by a largely evident, comprehensible, believable and cohesive description and a simple design. At the same time, this degree of plausibility also leads to a weak form of consistency, meaning lack of contradiction of projections within the scenario. The intuitive school consciously places no value on mathematically based consistency.

The mathematical school of scenario methods on the other hand, considers that real consistency, that is, complete lack of contradiction, can only be guaranteed in the analysis of a system such as a market if:

1. each element of the system being examined is included with its descriptors (quantifiable characteristics)
2. all relationships between all elements are displayed
3. the quality, strength and direction of all relationships are captured
4. and all possible developments of all elements are taken into consideration.

This is the only way to develop non-contradictory scenarios of the future,[30] which are the only type to be qualitatively acceptable. This type of consistency can, of course, only be achieved by extensive and precise computer modeling and calculation.

Neuhaus says of the mathematical school's attitude that "the main thing is the calculations are correct," and that of the intuitive school "the main thing is that it fits in the mental models of management". He terms the representative of the two directions the "scenario grammarians" and the "scenario pragmatists".[31]

> Both extremes, calculating scenarios and the simple inventing of scenarios, cannot be optimally used in practice.

1. The simple conceived scenarios of the intuitive school with their intuitive-logical[32] basis may be able to provoke mental models and

accelerate learning,[33] but they have little or no methodical fundament with which to counter the critical minds of most managers and are therefore quickly dismissed as charlatanism, however inspiring or useful they may be.

2. The calculation of scenarios in the mathematical school also has its disadvantages. First, not even the present is as consistent as we would like to make the future. Second, scenario mathematics comes from the 1970s' view of the world, when many people believed that we only needed better computers to be able to better control the future. The fact that improbable futures are calculated in the scenarios does not change the fundamental criticism. Third, the effort involved in creating mathematical consistency is generally much too high when comparing its low or non-existent marginal utility in practice with more simple methods. After all, more simple methods also lead to usable scenarios. And fourth, the question of "ownership" and acceptance of scenarios from the computer is raised, where self-discovery by the user is considered to be particularly valuable.[34]

> For your practical work, we recommend following the intuitive school whilst at the same time observing the principles of the mathematical school (without mathematical modeling).

You have already recognized the possible developments of your environment or your markets with the blue futures glasses. You have also already analyzed and evaluated extreme projections and scenarios.

If you know your market, you can do without complex simulations. You don't need experienced market experts. Complex models and calculations are only worth doing if you are examining an unknown market or object, because they systematize getting to know the unknown market.

Methodology checklists

The red futures glasses primarily focus on those futures that have not yet been analyzed as non-expectations with the blue futures glasses. The event-like surprises (wild cards) are therefore more important here than classic scenarios. This section provides you with a checklist for your work in your company and one for you as a life entrepreneur. The methods checklist is aimed at future management experts.

Procedure for companies

1. **Get your futures team together.**
2. **Determine your surprise questions** using the description and examples on page 102.
3. **Develop projections and scenarios of surprising events** with one of the following methods and techniques:
   (a) *Answer the surprise questions intuitively*, in order to discover the really obvious surprises without too much effort. This can probably lead to sufficiently good results. After all, to emphasize it again, the point is not to think of particularly imaginative surprises, but to identify essential vulnerabilities.
   (b) *Reverse your assumptions about the future*. Formulate the opposite of each of your assumptions about the future and describe this future as a process that takes place relatively suddenly. If your assumption about the future is that your market will grow by five to eight percent annually, then the resulting potential surprise is that your market declines by twenty to thirty percent within one year. If your assumption about the future is that personal advice will continue to be the domain of human beings, then you would need to develop the surprise from that, that a breakthrough in artificial intelligence or simply an innovative software process could deal with half the cases at no charge and with no help from a human being.
   (c) Use *future factors* (future trends, technologies and issues), as listed in the checklist in Table 4.4. Answers to your surprise questions can be derived from almost every future factor. As will be shown with the green futures glasses, you can use three intensities of future factors analysis (see Methodology checklists in Chapter 6).
   (d) *Evaluate wild card catalogs*. Good sources are the books *Ungezähmte Zukunft (The Future as Wild Card)* by Karlheinz Steinmüller and *Out Of The Blue* by John Petersen. You will need however, to specify and adapt the wild cards mentioned there to your own requirements.
   (e) *Ask "prophets" and lateral thinkers*. They can be found both inside and outside of your industry. Good sources are authors of articles, blogs and books with unusual theses. Ask them your surprise questions.
   (f) *Review your opportunity panorama and your vision candidates*. Check which opportunities and vision candidates you

don't want to use and imagine your competitors doing so very successfully.

(g) *Employ "enemies"*. Get several people to think up damaging actions against your company. This can be done as simple brainstorming or as a research project. This aggressive method will enable you to increase the probability of recognizing negative surprises at an early stage.

(h) *Play war games.*[35] In the case studies section of this chapter, two examples for the use of war games are described. What was previously referred to as role play or simulation is now called war games, at least in the environment of dynamic competitor analysis. The blind spots in management's attention can be significantly reduced using this instrument. In view of the notorious lack of time, we recommend carrying out the following three moves:
- Put yourself in the position of each of three competitors, either real or imaginary. Which actions could these competitors take against you?
- How could you react to each of these attacks to suffer no disadvantage or even gain an advantage?
- How would the competitors now react to each of your actions?

4. **Develop scenarios of surprising developments or alternative futures.** Force yourself and the members of your futures team to think of alternative futures which you cannot see with the blue futures glasses and which therefore do not appear in your assumption panorama. An example can be found from page 105 onwards (the scenario cube).

   (a) Identify three assumption questions from the assumption analysis with the blue futures glasses to which you would assign the highest degree of uncertainty.

   (b) Determine two extreme answers to each of them.

   (c) Combine the extreme answers to eight scenarios of alternative futures using the scenario cube model.

   (d) Describe the scenarios as plausibly as possible in the form of projections.

   (e) Ensure an acceptable degree of lack of contradiction by using a matrix to check each statement in your scenario for compatibility with each of the other statements and correct them as necessary.

5. **Add the standard surprise "4–40"**: *What will we do if we permanently lose forty percent of our profit contribution within four weeks?*

6. **Determine the potential effects on your (provisional) futures strategy.** You primarily wear the red futures glasses to protect your vision, mission and guidelines against the unpredictable future in the form of event-like and process-like surprises. If you only have twenty to thirty surprises on your list, then you can do this for each individual surprise. If you have significantly more, then you should initially carry out an intuitive assessment of the assumed strength of the effects. As with the blue futures glasses, you should do this using a Delphi survey of the members of your futures teams. Figure 5.5 shows the basic thought structure for the effects analysis.

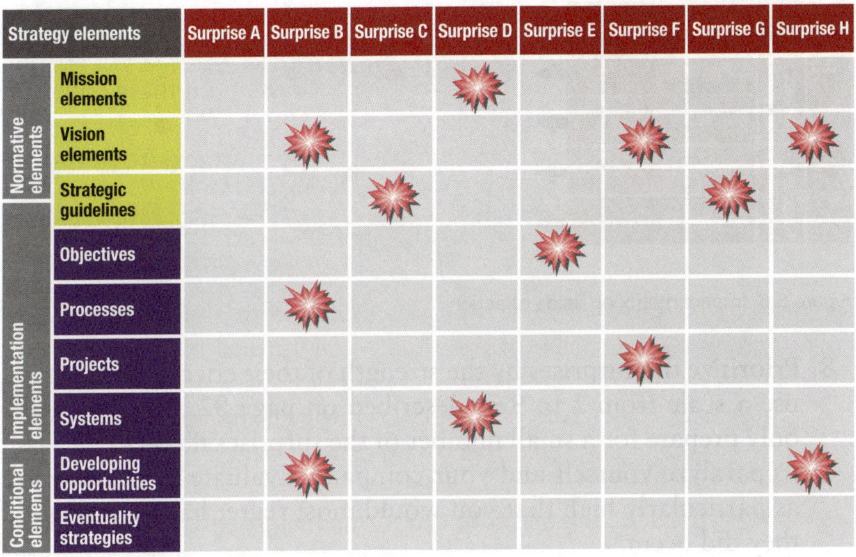

	Strategy elements	Surprise A	Surprise B	Surprise C	Surprise D	Surprise E	Surprise F	Surprise G	Surprise H
Normative elements	Mission elements				💥				
	Vision elements		💥				💥		💥
	Strategic guidelines			💥				💥	
Implementation elements	Objectives					💥			
	Processes		💥						
	Projects						💥		
	Systems				💥				
Conditional elements	Developing opportunities		💥						💥
	Eventuality strategies								

Figure 5.5 Impact matrix on futures strategy

7. **Alternatively: Determine the potential effects on your current company.** If you are only concerned with safeguarding your current situation, then you should relate the effects of the surprises to your current company, not to your provisional futures strategy. You do this by linking the surprises to the major fields of action like marketing and sales, products and solutions or systems and processes. (For further reading about fields of action see Chapter 6, Table 6.3).

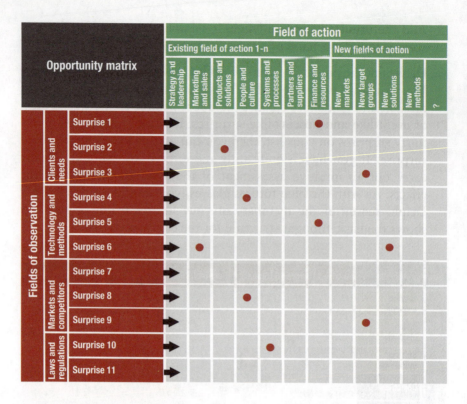

Figure 5.6 Impact matrix on fields of action

8. **Prioritize the surprises** by the strength of their effects. Once again, use a scale from 1 to 9 as described on page 82. You can really only prepare for a small number of the surprises if you don't want to paralyze yourself and your company. Evaluate those surprises as particularly high that you would most regret having ignored if they did occur.

■ The degree of potential regret is decisive for evaluating surprises.

9. **Draw up a surprise panorama.** Whereas your assumption panorama (blue futures glasses) refers to probabilities, you use the red futures glasses to draw up a surprise panorama, meaning a tabular overview of the recognized possible surprises and their effects, evaluated on their strength.

10. **Improve your vision, your mission and your guidelines.** Every effect that can become an existential threat needs to be countered with an appropriate change in or improvement to your prelimi-

nary futures strategy. Guidelines for developing eventual strategies can be found in Chapter 8, Table 8.3 in the description of the violet futures glasses. The green futures glasses can also be helpful in this task.

Procedure for life entrepreneurs

For your personal life enterprise, you can focus the red futures glasses on a few essential steps that you should make a note of in writing:

1. Ask your surprise questions.
   (a) In your personal life, questions regarding health, family and relationships in particular should be added to the job and company related questions mentioned in the Core concepts section. If you work with your hands, what would happen if you had to do without them? If you rely on your voice: what would happen if it disappeared for a lengthy period of time?
   (b) Also ask the standard question for your life enterprise: What would you do if you could suddenly and permanently no longer carry out your profession?
2. Describe the imaginable surprises in a few sentences. If you would like to take more time, then you can use the methods for companies described above.
3. Determine the potential effects on your
   (a) professional activities
   (b) family and social relationships
   (c) psychological and mental constitution
   (d) material wealth
   (e) life environment.
4. When you use the red futures glasses again after development of your vision, use them to improve it. Guidelines for developing eventual strategies can be found in Chapter 8, Table 8.3 in the description of the violet futures glasses.

Checklist of methods and techniques

The methods checklist for future management professionals provides you with references on the methods and techniques you can use to improve your work with the red futures glasses.

Professional checklist:
Methods for the red futures glasses and suggested literature
(see Bibliography)

Developing surprise questions (analogous to the blue futures glasses)
- Structure analysis (Geschka and Reibnitz, 1981; Godet, 1994; Gausemeier et al., 1996)
- Critical success factors (Rockart, 1979)
- Comprehensive situation mapping (CSM) (Georgantzas and Acar, 1995)
- Surprise question / Delphi (Mićić, 2006)

Developing projections / scenarios of surprising events
- Assumption reversal in the assumption panorama (Mićić, 2005)
- Futures wheel / mind mapping (Glenn and Gordon, 2003; Buzan, 2006)
- Historical analogies (Armstrong, 2001)
- Intuitive approaches (Glenn, 2003) and creative imagery (May, 1996)

Developing projections / scenarios of surprising developments
- As for surprising events
- Scenarios (Schwartz, 1996; de Geus, 1988; van der Heijden, 1996; Godet, 1994; von Reibnitz, 1991; Gausemeier et al., 1996) and others
- Cross impact analysis (Glenn and Gordon, 2003)
- Simulations (Rausch and Catanzaro, 2003)
- Games (Rausch and Catanzaro, 2003)
- Role play / war gaming (Armstrong, 2001)
- Evaluating speculative literature and art (May, 1996)
- Scenario cube (Mićić, 2004)

Identifying potential effects
- Cross impact analysis (Glenn and Gordon, 2003) with the surprises and vision elements
- Futures wheel / mind mapping (Glenn and Gordon, 2003; Buzan, 2006)
- Disruptive event analysis (von Reibnitz, 1991)
- Strategic conversation (van der Heijden, 1996)
- Delphi (Helmer, 1983)

Developing eventual strategies
- Green futures glasses methods
- See also violet futures glasses

Presenting results
- Text, structured or prosaic
- Diagrams, charts and mind maps
- Drawings
- Films and animations
- Acting

6 Your green futures glasses: Which future opportunities do you have?

After the windjammer captain has substantiated assumptions on the future development of the ocean and the weather together with his crew, by wearing the blue futures glasses, and after he has imagined possible surprises, he asks himself which interesting destinations it would be worth heading for. Fertile islands and countries can be reached and conquered, even if you have never been there before and only know about them from hearsay or your imagination. Fertile countries are green, as green as the green futures glasses.

The future is made of future opportunities. Opportunities are advantageous possibilities to act or to create something. They are the material from which you form your decision options and your futures strategy. Future opportunities are based on your assessment of future (market) developments, that is, on the assumption panorama you developed in the assumption analysis and on the conceived possible surprises.

> The blue futures glasses form the foundation, the red futures glasses make it solid, and the green futures glasses form the bricks.

The goal of opportunity development with the green futures glasses is to develop as many future opportunities as possible through more or less systematic and unlimited creative thinking. There are two main areas of focus, which can be expressed in two questions:

1. Which future opportunities do we have in the sense of long-term design options for our strategic direction?
2. Which future opportunities do we have in the sense of short to medium-term design options to achieve our strategic vision?

The windjammer captain doesn't ask himself only about possible destinations, but also which possibilities he has to reach the destination determined as the vision. As the five futures glasses should be seen not only as a process, but also as a loop and as a control circuit, the green futures glasses can also be used after the yellow futures glasses.

Your green futures glasses: Overview

Table 6.1 summarizes the characteristics of the green futures glasses.

Table 6.1 Overview of the green futures glasses

Objective: To get to know your possible courses of action.

Work step and key question:
- Opportunity development
- Which future opportunities do we have?

Purpose:
- You can act earlier and achieve more.
- You have a better view of what the competition could do.
- You transform threats into opportunities.
- You can handle future developments in a better way.
- You form components for your futures strategy.
- You improve motivation and confidence.

Attitude and principles:
- Use future opportunities to form the basis for your competitiveness.
- Believe in improvement.
- Stimulate your subconscious.
- Look through the green futures glasses with the eyes of a beginner.
- Prohibit any form of criticism with the green futures glasses.
- Prefer advantage-opportunities over catching-up-opportunities.
- Look for opportunities at an early stage.
- Big opportunities hold big risks and vice-versa.
- Don't look for opportunities that are new to the world.
- Recognize which opportunities are not being used.
- Be more honorable than the fast followers.
- Make your future opportunities as simple as possible.
- Balance feasibility and competitive advantage.
- You can only determine the value of an opportunity imprecisely.
- Carefully select which future opportunities you want to leave to the competition.
- Determine the chances of success of an opportunity based on the balance of pro and contra arguments.
- Think about your later cautiousness at an early stage.
- Foster modest and sensible expectations.

Core concepts:
- Opportunity questions
- Future opportunities
- Threats transformed into future opportunities

> **Table 6.1 (cont'd)**
>
> **Typical methods:**
> - Effects analyses
> - Creativity methods
> - Morphologies
> - Empathy
>
> **Procedure:**
> 1. Carry out the opportunity development with your futures team.
> 2. Determine the fields of action.
> 3. Make your opportunity requirement precise by using clear opportunity questions.
> 4. Develop future opportunities from assumptions about the future.
> 5. Develop future opportunities from individual future factors.
> 6. Recognize opportunities through inquiry.
> 7. Recognize opportunities through analogies.
> 8. Recognize opportunities through empathy.
> 9. Categorize your future opportunities.
> 10. Form an opportunity panorama.
> 11. Evaluate your future opportunities.
>
> **Results:**
> An opportunity panorama will develop which, depending on the chosen intensity, includes between 50 and 500 opportunities and is systematically evaluated.

Case studies on the green futures glasses

The examples in this section attest to the variety and significance of the green futures glasses.

Toyota recognizes the hybrid motor as an opportunity

You have to start digging the well before you develop a thirst. With this in mind, Toyota developed scenarios on the future of the automobile industry at the beginning of the 1990s. The Toyota management reinforced its assumption about the future that it would be impossible to fulfill the upcoming strict emission regulations in states such as California using traditional drive technology.

Whereas other automobile manufacturers occupied themselves with improving tried and tested concepts, Toyota recognized a future opportunity in the idea of the hybrid motor, which had already been filed for a patent in 1896 by Ferdinand Porsche and realized in 1902. None of the mass producers had developed the hybrid motor to the stage of readiness for production, although this drive concept promised great future opportunities in view of trends such as climate change, which had been foreseeable for a long time, and the notorious shortage of oil.

In 1997, the Toyota Prius became the first mass-produced car with hybrid drive. It achieved fuel savings of up to thirty percent. Toyota is now considered to be the world leader in hybrid technology and has been able to transfer the technical knowledge to the luxury segment by fitting Lexus brand automobiles with hybrid drive.

E-mail for everyone

In the middle of the 1990s, Sabeer Bhatia and Jack Smith made the assumption about the future that everyone would be able to have their own private e-mail address in the foreseeable future. As they always had problems with their employer's firewalls when they wanted to exchange data, they developed the idea of an e-mail account that could be called up from any computer anywhere in the world via an internet browser. This early perceived opportunity led to the founding of the company Hotmail, which specialized in personal electronic mailboxes. In 1998, they sold their company to Microsoft for 400 million dollars.

Puma sportswear as everyday wear

The success of the sports goods manufacturer Puma is in large part due to its early perception of future opportunities. Puma recognized earlier than its competitors Adidas or Nike, that sportswear is increasingly being worn as normal everyday clothing.[1]

Reinhold Würth recognizes the potential of his company

When Reinhold Würth took over his father's screw wholesale business at the age of 21, it was a regional trading company with a few initial international contacts. The product focus was on wholesale trade in screws. Reinhold Würth reports,[2] that when looking at the adhesive manufacturers, he always had the feeling that every dollar they earned in turnover was one less dollar for his turnover. He was only able to explain and understand the connection when he asked himself what it was his customers actually paid him for. The initial answer was "for fixation", meaning attaching something movable to something immovable. Later, more comprehensively, it was "for connecting". It was this perspective, according to Würth, which opened his eyes to the unimaginable potential in his company. He therefore transformed his company step by step from a product trader to a provider of connection as a function. The company was able to expand its field of activities without departing from its core competence by concentrating on this function. The Würth Group became one of the first suppliers of adhesives for use in automobiles. Today, the company has 55,000 employees in 83 countries.

From pesticides to insurances

A pesticide manufacturer thinks in terms of tons. Tons of pesticides are often the measure of performance and size in this business. If however, you ask one of his customers, a farmer, which effect he *really* pays the pesticide manufacturer for, then he will quickly hit upon the fact that he is not really concerned with pesticides and pest destruction. It will occur to him that he buys output increase and output security. Let's imagine that the farmer comes up with the idea of only paying the pesticide manufacturer for the effect. The latter already delivers the solution, he distributes the pesticide directly to the field, but he still charges for kilograms and tons of pesticide. The farmer however now offers him twenty percent of the additional revenue achieved thanks to the pesticide and also an insurance premium of another five percent.

If the pesticide manufacturer declined, the farmer would keep looking for another supplier until he found one who agreed to the deal. As soon as the pesticide manufacturer agrees, his business life changes dramatically. His activity previously centered on tons of pesticide, the more the better. From now on however, his aim is to use as little pesticide as possible.

When the pesticide expert thinks a little further, he realizes that he can also achieve the effect of his pesticide with other means. He searches for and finds biotechnology and nanotechnology solutions and includes fertilizers. Finally, he realizes that he had always been in the insurance business; he just hadn't seen it that way. Sensibly, he doesn't build up any new capacity, but buys in the biotechnology, nanotechnology and insurance. He comes to the ultimate question as to why he should continue producing pesticide when he could buy it on the world market. In this way, the pesticide manufacturer transforms himself into a specialist for high revenue and safe harvests, who orchestrates the solutions of various suppliers, such as optimized seeds, pesticides, fertilizers and insurances, in the best possible way. The result is as expected – he sells his pesticide production, which was previously his life's work and pride and joy, convinced of making the right decision.

What happened? Just because a customer and a supplier thought their business through to the conclusion and saw the essentials, their world changed forever.

Future opportunity "personal fabricator"

The Replicator in the science-fiction series *Star Trek* is slowly starting to appear on the horizon as a real option. In the futures scenario, you told the Replicator what you wanted and the machine produced it atom by atom. This future opportunity, which today still sounds very futuristic, could find its way into real applications. This is the idea behind "fabbing". In future everyone will be able to own a personal fabricator (PF) in the same way they have a personal computer (PC). The computer models of products will be downloaded from the internet, allowing the physical product to be produced at home. This could be realized with the successors of today's 3D printers, as produced by the US company 3D-Systems for example, which enable complex CAD (computer-aided design) models to be printed at the local workplace. They are currently limited to a few materials and are therefore primarily used in product development. Numerous companies are researching possibilities for the use of further and new materials. Boeing is one of the pioneers of "additive fabrication", as which the concept is also known.

Vision candidates for banks to illuminate imaginable future opportunities

The green futures glasses form the strategic options for the captain of the ship. With them he sees the potential destinations, the vision candidates from which he must later choose using the yellow futures glasses. The vision candidates illuminate the possibilities for creating one's own future. Table 6.2 roughly describes a selection of potential strategic vision candidates for banks. With a little imagination, the models behind the fictive names can be recognized.

Table 6.2 A few vision candidates for banks in 2020

Bank vision	Short description
Bank "Ryanaldi"	Consistent, totally simple banking with no frills. Customers need certain core services and pay a very low price for these and nothing else.
Bank "CIT"	Completely dedicated to the needs of private customers. Products, services and advice are standardized to the smallest degree. Third party products are stringently integrated into its own service offer.
Bank "Coach"	Characterized primarily through relationship competence. The close relationship between consultant and client demands effort but leads to long-lasting loyalty and follow-on business. The consultants and the clients grow old together.
Bank "MCK"	Specializes in highly professional advice to entrepreneurs and companies with a close affinity to classical management consultancy.
Bank "MCD"	The focus is on an easy to understand range of services, transparent costs and uncomplicated processing. Standard options make selection easy. Banking is easygoing, affordable and enjoyable.
Bank "POS"	The bank is where the customers are, at the point of sale, where you like to drop by once a week. In addition to financial products and advice, a varying range of products is offered.
Bank "Tiffany's"	Only the very up-market clientele of wealthy private clients is served. Exclusivity and discretion and high-quality standards ensure client relations over several generations.
Bank "Community"	The community is most important. The bank is the platform for communal problem solving and for the provision of important services, which are not only of a financial nature. Only members have access.
Bank "3M"	Permanently looking for innovative solutions, with no limits to its fields of activity. New opportunities are taken advantage of, markets developed and managed in independent entrepreneurial units.
Bank "3I"	The participation bank invests in independent fields of activity and manages them in a holding organization with strategic sovereignty.
Bank "Brainpool"	The project bank carries out a wide variety of projects with a highly qualified team and sees its core competence in the business intelligence and performance capability of its employees

Purpose of the green futures glasses

Future opportunities are life options for people and companies: they fulfill a number of existentially important functions.

You can see more of the possible future

The green futures glasses help you to illuminate future possibilities in the same way that you illuminate a dark room to better become aware of its dimensions and characteristics. The blue futures glasses described in Chapter 4 are intended to make it easier for you to see the probable future. The red futures glasses help you to see conceivable surprises. However, as the probable future and the surprising future form a subset of the possible future, the green futures glasses help to improve the results of the blue ones. Everything that could be possible in the future is also determined by what the seven billion futures creators on earth see as being possible.

> *Desires are premonitions of the capabilities that lie within us, harbingers of what we will be able to achieve.*
> (Johann Wolfgang von Goethe)

The perspective of the green futures glasses is different to that of the blue and red ones; with the green futures glasses you are not concerned with the environment but with yourself. It is not about the sea and the weather, but about selectable destinations and possible sailing strategies.

You increase your probability of success

Someone who can choose is freer and generally also happier. The more paths there are open to you, the greater the probability there will be some among them that suit you and/or lead more easily and quickly to success. It doesn't matter whether the success is material or more immaterial. It is also irrelevant in this respect whether we are talking about life management or about the management of a large corporation.

People kill themselves if they see no further opportunity to lead a life worth living. If none of the options recognizable to the suicide are worth living, or at least acceptable, he will put an end to his life. If however, the person weary of life can be shown additional opportunities, which he couldn't see before although they were imaginable and recognizable, his suicide can possibly be prevented.

> *We can see future opportunities as quanta of vitality for people and for companies.*

The more future opportunities you see for your company to achieve competitive advantages, the wider its opportunity horizon[3] will be, the more successful and secure it can become.[4] Every additional perceived opportunity increases the value of the company,[5] as the achievement of a high market position in an existing market, entry into an existing, not yet served market, or the development of completely new markets becomes more probable with every opportunity regardless of its type.[6]

> *Nothing is more dangerous than an idea, if it is the only one we have.* (Émile Chartier)

There is a saying that if you have two possibilities, then you should choose the third. The assumption is that there are usually more alternatives than we see at the moment we make a decision. The more decision options you are able to recognize, the better your decision will probably be, potentially at least. The green futures glasses therefore make it easier for you to think an issue through better and more deeply and to recognize more future opportunities from it, in the sense of options for courses of action, before you make a decision.[7]

You can act earlier and achieve more

Recognizing a future opportunity actually has nothing to do with forecasting (blue futures glasses), it is nevertheless an act of anticipation. One could assume that opportunities existed before they were discovered,[8] that they therefore belong to the possible but not yet imagined future. Octave Uzanne for example, described the idea for Sony's Walkman in 1894 in a book about the end of books.

> Recognizing an opportunity earlier means thinking a thought that would anyway be thought by someone at some point in the future.

Actively seizing an opportunity therefore means doing something that would be done anyway at some point in the future. As our lifespan is limited, the green futures glasses help us to live a life richer in experiences and success, and in a company they simply lead to greater success.

You have a better view of what the competition could do

With the green futures glasses you pre-empt the competition (and, basically, yourself as well)[9] and can cause, achieve and enjoy success earlier. The green futures glasses therefore also fulfill a small part of the function of the red futures glasses, as they point to possible surprises. As future opportunities, as already described, are sometimes literally in the air, using directed and systematic opportunity development enables you to see more of what your competitors are currently thinking and planning or will think and plan in the future.

You transform threats into opportunities

We often talk about opportunities and risks or opportunities and threats in connection with the future. On a purely semantic level, we are concerned with risks when we actively do something and enter into risky situations in doing so, and with threats when we passively experience changes in our environment and our current position is endangered. Both threats and risks can be transformed into opportunities when perceived early enough with the green futures glasses.

> If you perceive a threat at an early stage, you have the opportunity to avert it more easily than if you perceived it later.

Threats tend to become bigger over time so that it becomes increasingly difficult to avert or master them. As we saw when discussing the red futures glasses, there are several possibilities for turning a threat into an opportunity. Even when it is actually too late, the green futures glasses help through imagination to see more opportunities, so that threats become the seed for opportunities. Colloquial language also expresses the final possibility: it was probably good for something. Following this view, the aging of many modern societies could also be seen as an opportunity to rethink existing attitudes towards health, life, age, wisdom and death.[10]

With the green futures glasses you can also transform the risks you take into opportunities. Someone who is aware of risks at an early stage has a greater opportunity to avoid, reduce or use them as a stimulus for a better strategy. The green futures glasses, in addition to the red ones, are therefore an instrument for the early recognition of risks that you can then analyze and manage as part of your company's risk management.

You can better handle future developments

If you recognize, and therefore have, more possibilities for creating something, you can cope much better with the often challenging developments which the future promises to bring. Someone who sees more future opportunities faces the future with more optimism, or at least more composure. On the other hand, someone who has virtually no alternative to his current life concept will see the future rather as a threat.

> More future opportunities mean more flexibility and more flexibility means more future security.

You form components for your futures strategy

Future opportunities are the material from which good decisions and good futures strategies are made. Future opportunities are therefore the raw materials that you can transform into vision elements, goals, projects, processes, guidelines and systems.[11] Here again, the more options you have, the better the result will fundamentally be.

You improve motivation and confidence

Someone who sees more future opportunities, has greater success opportunities in the future and recognizes the possibility for positive courses of action even in threats, will no doubt look with more confidence towards the future and also be more motivated in view of the success which can be achieved. Opportunities give you more energy,[12] for yourself and your company. The worst atmosphere is to be found in companies, organizations and families where the members can hardly see any more future opportunities.

> *Where there is no hope in the future, there is no power in the present.* (John Maxwell)

If you can show your employees that your company, despite possible threats, still has more valuable future opportunities than you can cope with together, then you will have an optimistic and motivated team. There is a good reason why it is said that the prospect of a better future makes it easier to bear difficulties in the present.

Core concepts of the green futures glasses

The green futures glasses have two core concepts: the opportunity questions and the future opportunities. The future opportunities build on the assumptions about the future as shown in Figure 6.1.

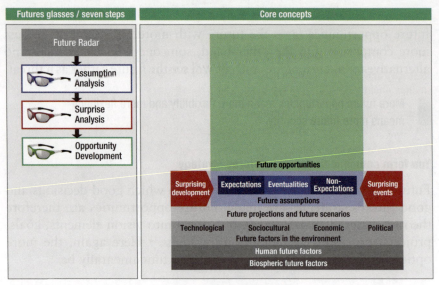

Figure 6.1 The green futures glasses and their core concepts

Opportunity questions

Opportunity questions determine the search fields to be placed in the foreground depending on the task in question. They direct the search for future opportunities towards fields of action that are important to you and your company. After all, many good ideas don't appear in workshops and creative meetings, but in the most unlikely places at unexpected times.

> With opportunity questions, you can find out what you need to know about possible advantageous action in your fields of action.

With the help of the opportunity questions, you want to determine exactly why you want to recognize future opportunities. In the story of the windjammer captain (see Chapter 3), these would be questions on possible destinations, sailing strategies and optional courses of action concerning the ship itself for example.

Opportunity questions refer to fields of action. These describe approximate categories of development factors as ingredients or elements that are necessary for the existence and success of a company. One or more opportunity questions can be assigned to each field of action, as the examples in Table 6.3 show.

Table 6.3 Fields of action and opportunity questions

Field of action	Examples of opportunity questions
Strategy and management	■ Which mission are we setting ourselves? ■ How are we positioning ourselves?
Markets and business areas	■ Which markets can we develop? ■ Which business areas can we expand?
Marketing, sales and acquisition	■ How can we win new customers? ■ How can we retain customers?
Products and solutions	■ How can we improve our products and services? ■ Which new products and services can we develop and offer?
People and culture	■ How can we attract the best talents in the market? ■ How will we become the best team in the industry? ■ How can we create a culture in which we can achieve high performance with fun and fulfillment?
Systems and processes	■ How can we become highly efficient through more output? ■ How can we become highly efficient through using fewer resources?
Partners and suppliers	■ Which new partners can provide competitive advantages for us? ■ How can we make our network into a success factor?
Finances and resources	■ How can we ensure financing that is flexible and carries acceptable capital costs?

Future opportunities

The definitions of futures opportunities discussed in practice and in the literature swing between three understandings. The first sees an opportunity as a favorable attribute of the environment,[13] whereas the second sees in it an advantageous attribute in the sense of a precondition for success.[14] We prefer the third definition:

■ An opportunity is an advantageous possibility for action.[15]

This definition includes the other two definitions as preconditions. An opportunity is therefore always a possibility to do something: "We will enter the Chinese market" or "We will start a logistics company". Ideally the opportunity is beneficial to the environment and thus beneficial to you.

As this list shows, a future opportunity can appear in several forms:

1. as the consequence of an expected or not expected future

2. as a threat which becomes an opportunity through early recognition

3. as an option for creating the future, meaning as a vision candidate, goal candidate or another possible action (Table 6.2 above shows a range of vision candidates, which are a special form of future opportunities).

You can even transform threats into future opportunities conceptually. After all, there is always more than one way of facing up to a threat. The threat "new competitors appear from other markets" can, for example, become the opportunity, "face the threat of competitors appearing from other markets by buying one of them".

We use the term *future* opportunity, because it also includes opportunities that will only be able to be perceived in the distant future. Innovation is often used as a synonym for opportunity. However, we see innovation more as a process of transforming opportunities into tangible reality.[16] The term "idea" doesn't exactly explain the meaning of opportunity either, because an idea is not only limited to the thought of a possible action. An opportunity is part of the term idea.

Table 6.4 shows the morphology (overview of types) of future opportunities. To describe a futures opportunity, you can use one or more characteristics for each element. In this way, an opportunity such as this develops: *We (actor) develop (action) a software (field of action), which independently (result) makes investment decisions using artificial intelligence (source and means).*

Table 6.4 Structure of future opportunities

Element	Characteristic	
Source	■ Future factor ■ Future projection	■ Surprise ■ Other
Actor	■ Me ■ We (Team) ■ We (Organization)	
Field of action	■ Strategy and leadership ■ Markets and business areas ■ Marketing, sales and acquisition ■ Products and solutions ■ People and culture ■ Systems and processes ■ Partners and suppliers ■ Finances and resources	

Table 6.4 (cont'd)

Element	Characteristic	
Action	■ Form ■ Change ■ Improve ■ End ■ Eliminate	■ Integrate ■ Introduce ■ Copy ■ Choose ■ Multiply etc.
Medium	■ Strategy ■ Guideline	■ Technology ■ Method
Result	■ Different ■ New	■ Better ■ No longer

Attitude and principles of the green futures glasses

The green futures glasses for opportunity development require a special type of thinking. The green futures glasses look at the future from the micro perspective of your own world. The view is directed inwardly at the futures you can create. You see yourself being involved and actively intervening. The attitude of the green futures glasses is in principle optimistic, creative, imaginative, progressive and transformative, as the green futures glasses are ultimately supposed to illuminate the possibilities of the future.

Use future opportunities to form the basis for your competitiveness

From a business point of view, future opportunities are the building blocks of competitiveness. Someone who recognizes a higher number of future opportunities creates the basis of competitiveness. Someone who actually implements them, achieves competitiveness, which in turn creates the basis for further future opportunities. The potential contribution of a future opportunity towards strengthening or increasing competitiveness, which one could also call competitive fitness, should be one of the few primary quality criteria in evaluating and selecting future opportunities,[17] at least in a business context. In a private context, the "happiness contribution" of an opportunity can be the criterion. When implemented early, a future opportunity contributes to competitiveness, if it can only be understood or copied with difficulty by the competition.[18] Something that everyone can quickly imitate is really not a great contribution to competitiveness. You can improve your competitiveness by strengthening strengths or compensating for weaknesses.

Believe in improvement

The blue futures glasses require realism. Having illusions about the future development of the world and the market makes no sense. The green futures glasses require an optimistic view so that you illuminate the creatable future as far and as wide as possible.

Our present is much better in many of the ways that we imagined the future would be. A generation ago, our rivers were latrines; nowadays people can enjoy swimming in them again in many areas. The forests haven't experienced mass destruction. The younger generation doesn't have a "no future attitude" and hasn't sunk into a drugs swamp. The third World War hasn't broken out yet.

It is generally known that a pessimistic and cynical attitude towards future possibilities tends to self-fulfillment. Someone who believes that the future will be worse than the present will undertake little or nothing to improve his situation and that of the world. The green futures glasses therefore require a fundamentally optimistic attitude, even if it is only calculated optimism.

Stimulate your subconscious

Future opportunities generally emerge like weeds, completely unplanned, often unwanted and rarely targeted. Many great ideas didn't occur to brilliant inventors and companies as part of systematic opportunity development, but when taking a walk, or a bath or when dreaming. It is nevertheless sensible to systematically look for future opportunities for two reasons: first, in today's rapidly changing markets, we cannot wait for brilliant inspirations without losing ground, and second, we stimulate our subconscious by looking at the future so that we can perceive better future opportunities intuitively and almost "accidentally" when out walking or when dreaming.

Look through the green futures glasses with the eyes of a beginner

In the assumption analysis with the blue futures glasses, it was advantageous to be particularly qualified and have a lot of experience. Experience is a success factor in that case: the more experienced the future manager, the better. In opportunity development, the opposite is true. The more experience someone has, the less able he is to imagine new futures. Experience becomes a success divisor: the more knowledge someone has about a subject, the weaker the results of opportunity development will probably be. The Chinese say that there are millions of possibilities in the mind of a beginner, but only very few in the mind of an expert. Psychologists call it negative transfer. We apply experiences, methods and principles we know from one area to another area and handicap ourselves in this way. In the case of the green futures glasses, the negative transfer takes place from the world of the past to the changed world of the future.

> *I have learnt to use the word "impossible" with great care.*
> (Wernher von Braun)

The more detached your view of the present, the more opportunities and the more creative the possibilities you can discover. The challenge for you in opportunity development is to regard your company and your market or field from a distance.

Prohibit any form of criticism with the green futures glasses

Almost everything of importance concerning the necessity of separating creativity and criticism has already been said and written in connection with innovation and brainstorming. Creativity and criticism are known to neutralize each other. It's a pity that the practice is so weak despite all this knowledge.

> **In the green futures glasses, criticism is punishable damage to your ability to exist.**

Future opportunities are difficult to recognize because they demand a lot of tolerance and imagination in their early stages. Critical thinking is highly valued in our society. After all, we shouldn't believe everything that is put in front of us. It might seduce us! Yet when we need to form something new, lifelong training in being critical does enormous damage to us. Managers who believe in the positivistic knowledge paradigm, in which only the things that can be proven or refuted count, tend to find it an imposition, or at least a major challenge, to accept ideas that they find absurd without criticism or comment. They only feel at ease with facts and admire themselves for their ability to be critical. Scientists traditionally belong to this group.

We have witnessed how even experienced management consultants have failed to keep up the creative mode, despite appropriate instructions and repeated reminders. The desire to pick at other people's ideas was uncontrollable.

> Every silly child can tread on a beetle, but a thousand scientists cannot build one.

The development of an idea, and in this case of an opportunity, is an amazing creative feat. The literal crushing of a tender shoot of an idea, on the other hand, requires only minimum intellectual capacity and creates damage that cannot be assessed and is potentially huge. A small opportunity, which can be destroyed simply by someone rolling their eyes, is sometimes worth millions or even billions.

At exactly the moment in which an idea seems strange, absurd or unimaginable to you, a new successful era could be in the making. Looking through the green futures glasses is not a competition in being right; it is about the widest possible illumination of future opportunities and options.

> The limits of thoughts are the limits of success.

Prefer advantage-opportunities over catching-up-opportunities

As a basic rule of competitive strategy, strengthening your strengths is a greater contribution to improving competitiveness than compensating for weaknesses. The company's energy, that is, money, time and intellect, should accordingly be invested in further developing potential in existing strengths. The precondition is, however, that the current market or the market to be served in future would reward a strengthening of your strengths. If your customers do not value shorter delivery times, then every attempt at achieving them makes no sense. If your error rate, which customers react very sensitively to, is worse than the competition, large opportunities could consist of finding good ways of catching up. However, it would not necessarily be correct to talk of future opportunities in this case.

Look for opportunities at an early stage

A future opportunity is the more valuable the earlier it is perceived.[19] The earliest perception is the first invention, discovery or imagined future opportunity (see Figure 6.2).

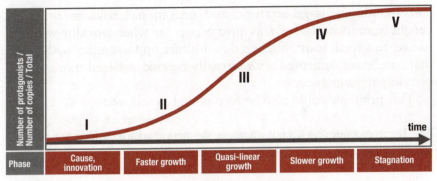

Figure 6.2 S-Curve as a thought model for futures developments

The diffusion of an opportunity that has been perceived follows an S-curve (also known as logistical function or diffusion function). It first spreads slowly into the minds of a few people, then increasingly quickly into the minds of ever more people, then increasingly slowly into the minds of ever more people, and finally it spreads no further. If it is forgotten or its carriers die, then the diffusion of the knowledge and the opportunity actually falls. Dawkins' concept of memetics[20] describes the evolutionary mechanisms of such diffusion processes.

■ **The earlier an opportunity is perceived, the bigger it is.**

The earlier an opportunity is recognized in the diffusion process, the bigger the accessible benefit to the person perceiving it. The reasoning behind this obvious principle is, that in an early stage, the number of potential beneficiaries of the opportunity is relatively high, the effort involved in using the opportunity comparatively low and the number of competitors low or even zero.

Big opportunities hold big risks and vice-versa

This widely known principle is often overlooked, ignored or thrust aside despite being so obvious. There is rarely an opportunity with which a company can make a huge profit in a short time with little effort. The apparent ease of Red Bull's success is extremely rare. After all, there is no investment that brings ten or even twenty percent interest with no risk either. Generally, obviously good opportunities are perceived and exploited very quickly by everyone on the market. What remains are the vast majority of opportunities, which involve correspondingly large strategic and operational risks in order to benefit from them. Naively, as most people are when working with the future, this truth is often ignored and future opportunities wished for that can be implemented with virtually no risk, yet lead more or less certainly to huge success.

This principle could also be formulated as follows:

> **The more innovative the opportunity is, the more change it requires and causes, the greater the risk involved in its implementation.**

The exceptions to this principle are rare and limited to those cases in which an innovation solves really urgent problems or fulfills major wishes with no great effort.

The financial risk is the probability of failure multiplied by the financial means at stake. This results in a possible financial loss as a result of an unsuccessful attempt to seize the opportunity.

> **The strategic risk is the probability of failure multiplied by the necessary flexibility sacrifice.**

This arithmetically undeterminable formula aims to make clear that using an opportunity for improving efficiency often reduces flexibility and a company's ability to survive, because it is more committed and tied through more efficient production equipment for example. This disadvantage increases through the risk of failure in implementing the opportunity.

Classical business studies only calculate and reward efficiency. This calculation is half-blind where flexibility is concerned, so that reducing it is rarely taken into account as a disadvantage and risk. Strategic risk finally turns into financial risk, although often years later.

Don't look for opportunities that are completely new to the world

Benjamin Franklin once said that it's no great feat to see an opportunity. The difficult thing is to be the first. This may be true in many areas of life. In connection with business and life management it is easy to misunderstand. It often wasn't the inventors and discoverers who became happy and/or rich with the opportunity they discovered.

> The person who finds happiness through an opportunity is not the person who first imagines or discovers it, but the person who first puts it to use.

To think of an opportunity as a possibility for action is the first step. To actually make use of an opportunity is quite obviously the second, indispensable step. It is therefore not very profitable to be satisfied only with those opportunities that you believe the world has never seen. You can seldom really know if an opportunity is new or not.

Experience of life and the S-curve described above show that over a period of a year, for example, only a small part of the future is really imagined for the first time. We could say that, in every year, the future is five percent innovation and ninety-five percent diffusion of innovation. Correspondingly, as Goethe once said, almost everything is already here.

> *Every clever idea has already been imagined, you just have to try to think it again at the right time.* (Johann Wolfgang von Goethe)

It is sensible to assume that the future opportunities you can *recognize* when observing your environment already exist, and that the opportunities you can *conceive* of have already been imagined by someone else. In creative opportunity development, a future opportunity is therefore sufficiently new if you haven't yet implemented it in your life or your company.

Recognize the danger of not seizing opportunities

Innumerable managers have been dismissed and numerous companies failed because they seized a future opportunity and failed in doing so. It is obviously a "management mistake" to start a project which in the end creates losses or even costs the company its existence. If they had behaved conservatively and kept quiet and only done things that carried minimum risks, and of course minimum opportunities, they would have acted in a better way in the eyes of the employees, the public and even the shareholders. If the company had failed in that case, it would have been the market's fault not the management's. A certain positive suspicion that failure to take risks is poor policy only starts to grow when a competitor becomes more successful by using a future opportunity. Although even in such situations, the stakeholder can be convinced that the jobs and the company's existence should not be placed at risk for such a risky strategy. It would be claimed that the competition was just lucky; it could have turned out completely differently. That, as the opportunity-averse would say, has nothing to do with responsible company management.

This is convincing until other competitors also use the future opportunity concerned and you have a hard time explaining your opportunity-averse strategy. The most obvious rational and emotional way through this minefield is the popular "fast followers" strategy. One could throw into the argument that the most important thing is not being the first, but being the first to do it right (see above). But seizing opportunities is not necessarily high-risk pioneering. Make sure that the non-use of opportunities becomes recognized in your company.

■ Anyone who wants to exclude all risks also destroys all opportunities.

Be more honorable than the "fast followers"

Anyone who is only concerned with making or maximizing profits, may find a suitable strategy in copying – or to put it in a nicer way, in systematic imitation or "fast followership". Systematic imitation can of course lead to success, as numerous cases have proved.[21] Yet no economy and no company can thrive mainly through imitation.

In 2005, the Chinese began to copy whole small European cities, from Great Britain initially. They copied complete bar concepts, even the names and recipes of the cocktails on the bar menu. At the end of 2006, it became known that they are not only building buses that look similar to European-built buses, but also barely differentiable copies of small cars such as the Smart (by CMEC) or the BMW X5, for which the dealer then even supplies the BMW emblem which can be exchanged for the emblem of the Chinese manufacturer.[22] The around 100 Chinese automobile manufacturers won't work that way forever. The same process that happened in Japan thirty years earlier will take place. The Japanese began by copying and nowadays are technologically world leaders in numerous areas.

■ Copying alone only results in temporary success.

Copying may promise success but not honor, glory or pride. As you are reading a book like this, you are obviously not only interested in mammon. Honor, glory and pride will also be essential categories for your employees, which cannot be served simply by copying.

Make your future opportunity as simple as possible

Both practice and theory insist that future opportunities should be as simple as possible.[23] The obvious opportunities where you ask yourself why you hadn't seen them before are those that represent the greatest value. The simplicity of an opportunity is generally, but not necessarily, equal to its feasibility. Schiller appropriately said that simplicity is the result of maturity. An opportunity can be simple in principle, but a great challenge in implementation, as was and is the case with the simplification of telephone call rates. The opportunity is simple and obvious, but its implementation demands a lot of resources and a lot of patience on the part of the provider.

Balance feasibility and competitive advantage

It applies time and again: if it were simple, everyone could do it. Simple is not the same as easy, as the above example with the telephone rates shows. Everything that the competition can also immediately do or that can be directly copied or creatively adapted is not really a great future opportunity.

> The easier it is to implement the opportunity, the less competitive advantage it probably offers.

A certain degree of challenge in implementation both at the management level and the action level is a precondition for a good future opportunity.

You can only determine the value of an opportunity imprecisely

Experience shows that only five to ten percent of opportunities that you can imagine are suitable as components of your futures strategy. The value of an opportunity can be determined by classical value analysis, meaning by comparing the estimated future value with the estimated future effort, taking minimum requirements into consideration.

In a business context, the nominal value of an opportunity is assessed by its contribution to the improvement in competitiveness. In most cases, it is impossible to measure the exact nominal value of an opportunity as a capital value or cash value from discounted future revenue. The expected long-term revenue from replacing combustion engines with hybrid engines cannot even be measured without determining numerous uncertain auxiliary conditions, although we are talking about technically and economically easily calculable objects. It is generally accepted that customer and competitor behavior or yet to be discovered technologies make such estimates uncertain and risky. On the other hand, it is this uncertainty that is the reason for the prospect of above-average success and profit.

The expenditure involved in exploiting an opportunity is measured in money, time or effort, be it in the form of absolute values or relative values such as opportunity costs, that is, the unrealized revenue from other opportunities. In addition to the effort, the absolute amount of investment and the amortization period are of relevance. Even if the opportunity under investigation promises huge success, the investment amount can be a limiting factor if it cannot be financed or if doing so would place too much of a strain on your liquidity. The amortization period states how long the capital will be tied up and thus, how high the capital costs are which need to be considered. The material value, or net value, is therefore the nominal value minus the real expenditure. The investment amount is often a knockout criterion.

> The most effective evaluation method is to test it with limited effort and expenditure under ideal conditions.

The Walkman, Post-it-Notes, or television would never have existed without trial and error. However, it is impossible to test 150 opportunities in a reasonable period of time. You are likely to be able to test only five or ten. A practical test is therefore best suited to a third stage of evaluation. It provides quick and reliable feedback. If your opportunity is deemed to be a failure, then ensure that it fails as early as possible.

The same models can be used in a private or idealistic context, only the terms need to be redefined. Increasing competitiveness for you as a private person could mean increasing your feeling of happiness; for a charity it could be a contribution towards fulfilling its mission.

Carefully select which future opportunities you want to leave to the competition

Future opportunities are never lost. If you don't use them, someone else will – often your competitors. If seizing a future opportunity makes even the slightest sense, then sooner or later someone will realize it. Taking this circumstance into account when quickly rejecting a future opportunity is unfortunately not self-evident. You should therefore always initially develop future opportunities without thinking of whether they are the right opportunities for you or your company, or whether they are too uncomfortable or politically not realizable. Accept all future opportunities – your competition could be more open-minded and less constrained.

Determine an opportunity's chances of success based on the balance of pro and contra arguments

In order to evaluate whether you will succeed in seizing a future opportunity, you should prepare a pro and contra list and weight the arguments if necessary. The difference between the two lists – the balance – shows the prospects of success. We are not talking about probabilities of success here, because according to the definition of the blue and green futures glasses, the criterion of probability should only be used when you yourself have virtually no influence on what you are looking at. The prospect of success in realizing a future opportunity is, of course, determined by external criteria, too, which can only be influenced with difficulty or not at all, but to the same if not greater extent by our own activities, potential and capabilities.

Think about your later cautiousness at an early stage

When concerned with seizing a particularly innovative future opportunity, most management or specialist teams become overcautious again. At the beginning, thinking "way out of the box" is demanded; the thought horizons can't be wide enough. However, when it comes to evaluating the future opportunity, very conservative aspects are drawn on in practice: a manageable risk, at the price of an equally manageable value, of course; a clear contribution to increased competitiveness; short-term realization and an acceptable level of investment are popular criteria. The most innovative and audacious future opportunities are regularly killed by these criteria. Take this conservative attitude into account at an early stage. Against this background, it only makes sense to invest a lot of time and money in very distant futures in exceptional cases. It nevertheless makes sense to illuminate the future widely and broadly: this is the only way to ensure a high level of innovation despite the cautiousness that later appears.

Foster modest and sensible expectations

A frequent error with the green futures glasses is to expect patentable inventions, discoveries at Nobel Prize level and adventurous departures. All of these may happen. However, such things are rare, and shouldn't be the primary goal of opportunity development. As explained in the above principles, everything you haven't yet realized and that would obviously be advantageous is a future opportunity for you. If the future opportunity has the additional honor of being new for your market or even new for the world, then be pleased about this fortunate but rare circumstance.

> Modest demands and expectations are always a good principle in future management.

Be realistic and think back ten years. Which revolutionary future opportunity have you, your company or anyone in your market recognized and realized in the last ten or twenty years? What you come up with as an answer to this question is the maximum you should strive for. More than that is rarely doable.

Methodology checklists

This section provides you with step-by-step guidelines for your practical work with the green futures glasses. The first checklist shows what you need to do as a manager in a company. The second, shorter checklist shows the process for a life entrepreneur. The third checklist is aimed at future management experts.

Procedure for companies

1. **Carry out opportunity development with your management team.**
2. **Determine the fields of action** for which you want to develop and find opportunities. Table 6.3 shows examples you can choose from.
3. **Make your opportunity requirement more precise through clear opportunity questions.** Table 6.3 also provides a number of examples for this. The opportunity questions set the agenda for your work with the green futures glasses. The following questions help you to find your opportunity questions:
    (a) What in our business are the critical success factors that we need to become even better at?
    (b) What is hindering our current development most, such that new opportunities in that area are particularly valuable?

(c) For which questions about our future strategic action would we pay a million Euros each to have them answered?

4. **Develop future opportunities from assumptions about the future.** The task of the green futures glasses is identifying the opportunities resulting from the blue futures glasses' assumptions about the future, including the threats and the consequences. The assumptions about the future-opportunity matrix make the thought process, the interlinking of assumptions and fields of action clear. In addition to the fields of action in your existing business, there are those for recognizing new areas of business. The opportunity questions are asked in the fields of action (see Figure 6.3). Which opportunities do you have if that is what happens (expectations), if it doesn't happen that way (non-expectations) or if it happens one way or the other (eventualities)? As an example: the projection "the desire for simplicity and convenience has grown considerably" in the "systems and processes" field of action in the opportunity matrix, would suggest carrying out a "make it simple" project in order to consistently simplify all structures and processes and make them more effective. The opportunity to train employees to recognize possibilities for simplification and additionally, to make simplicity an element of the corporate culture would be perceived in the "people and culture" field of action. The opportunity to radically reduce the number of basic products and increase the degree of modularization would logically then arise in the "products and services" field of action.

5. **Develop future opportunities from individual future factors.** Every future trend, every technology and every issue is a quantum of energy for change and therefore an important source of future opportunities. You only have to think long enough to recognize valuable opportunities in each of the future factors listed in the checklist in Table 4.4. Use the future factors opportunity matrix to structure your thinking (see Figure 6.4). You can take three approaches to recognizing the future opportunities.
    (a) You can proceed on an extensive basis and "surf" over the numerous future factors. Your creativity thus results from the breadth.
    (b) You can proceed on an intensive basis and consider *one* future factor at a time. Your creativity thus results from the depth of your observation.

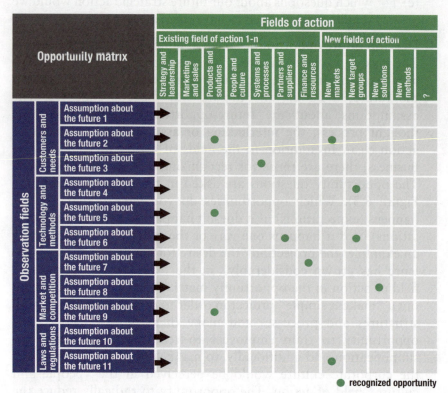

Figure 6.3 Developing opportunities from assumptions

(c) You can take a combined approach and, either planned or arbitrarily, consider two, three or four future factors at once and let yourself be inspired to creative opportunities by the combinations.

6. **Recognize opportunities by asking questions.** Don't just ask your management team your opportunity questions. Also include employees, customers, experts, consultants and partners. They often have more than enough ideas, enabling you to save a lot of methodological creative work.

7. **Recognize opportunities by using analogies.**

(a) *Recognize opportunities from historical analogies* to the current situation of your market or company. Opportunities for what you could do yourself in the present or the future can be derived from analyzing the strategies of earlier actors with similar challenges. Which opportunities did they or could they have used?

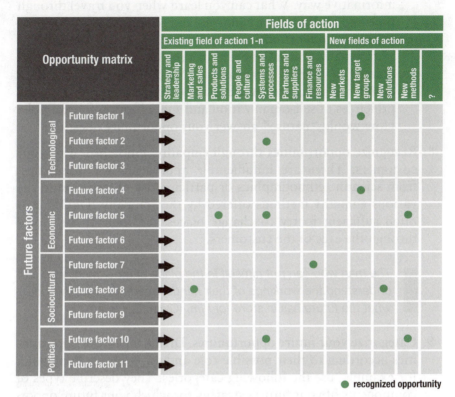

Figure 6.4 Developing opportunities from future factors

(b) *Recognize opportunities from science-fiction analogies.* Very few technologies or imaginable scenarios of humans living together have not been the subject of a novel, a film or science fiction at some point. These works in particular, which place such importance on plausibility and a solid foundation, are often a treasure trove of ideas and real future opportunities.

(c) *Recognize opportunities from industry analogies.* Technologies, business models or management concepts that "suddenly" revolutionize a whole industry have often been the norm for years or even decades in other industries, particularly in strategically related industries with similar promises of effects, products and solutions, target groups, strategies or structures. What can you learn from such relatives?

(d) *Recognize opportunities from geographic analogies.* Cultures and markets in other countries and regions have often developed differently than your home country in an interesting and informative way. What can you learn when you travel through time and look at other countries and regions?

(e) *Recognize opportunities from nature analogies*. Nature has traditionally not only helped to provide innovations in technology, in bionics for example. Nature can also provide a number of stimuli for strategy and corporate organization, the principles of self-organization and specialization for example. How would "nature" answer your opportunity question?

8. **Recognize opportunities through empathy**. Empathize with your customers. There are innumerable approaches for doing this, from scientific ethnographics or participatory observation to the various empathy methods offered by the company IDEO.[24] It is often sufficient to try to change places and look at the world through the eyes of the customers.

> *The man who can put himself in the place of other men, who can understand the workings of their minds, need never worry about what the future has in store for him.* (Owen D. Young)

9. **Categorize your future opportunities**. Divide the future opportunities according to their possible role and importance. You could, for example, use the following categories. They describe types of components of your futures strategy for which your future opportunity could be used, namely for potential:
   (a) Vision elements
   (b) Mission elements
   (c) Strategic guidelines
   (d) Goals
   (e) Projects
   (f) Processes
   (g) Systems
   (h) Eventual strategies.

10. **Develop an opportunity panorama**. By this we mean a tabular overview of the future opportunities, in which you should note the following information:
    (a) fields of action
    (b) opportunity questions
    (c) future opportunities
    (d) arguments for and against each individual opportunity
    (e) evaluations of the individual participants

(f) joint evaluation (average values)

(g) degree of contentiousness of the future opportunities (distributions in the form of standard deviations).

11. **Evaluate your future opportunities.** The most important evaluation criteria are usually the suitability of the future opportunity to answer the opportunity questions asked and the contribution of the future opportunity in increasing competitiveness. Additional evaluation criteria can be found in the principles section, page 141 ff. If you want to make the evaluation more sound then you can make an additional effort and form a pro and contra list for each future opportunity as described in the methodology for the blue futures glasses.

Procedure for life entrepreneurs

If you want to occupy yourself intensively with the green futures glasses, you can in principle apply the same methodology as for companies.

> Based on Rockefeller's words, we can say that it makes more sense to think about your future opportunities for one day, than to work hard for one month.

As part of a simplified procedure for your personal use, you should at least carry out the following steps and note the results in writing.

1. Ask your opportunity questions.

2. Make a note of the answers that spontaneously occur to you in response to your opportunity questions.

3. Determine which future opportunities follow from your assumptions about the future (if you have formulated any in writing).

4. Determine which future opportunities you can recognize from the future factors in the checklist in Table 4.4.

5. Determine which future opportunities your friends, colleagues and family members see as answers to your opportunity questions.

6. Evaluate the future opportunities according to the degree to which they contribute to your professional satisfaction or your professional success.

7. Manage your opportunity panorama as a kind of accounting system for future opportunities.

Checklist of methods and techniques

The method checklist for future management professionals shows a comprehensive overview of methods and techniques for the individual work steps of the green futures glasses.

> **Professional checklist:**
> **Methods for the green futures glasses and literature recommendations**
> (see Bibliography)
>
> **Developing opportunity questions**
> - Opportunity questions / Delphi (Mićić, 2006)
> - Gap analysis (Kreikebaum, 1997)
>
> **Developing opportunities from assumptions about the future**
> - Brainstorming/-writing (May, 1996)
> - Futures wheel / mind mapping (Glenn and Gordon, 2003; Buzan, 2006)
> - Micro–macro matrix (Krystek and Müller-Stewens, 1993)
> - Opportunity matrix (Mićić, 2005)
>
> **Developing opportunities from future factors**
> - Futures wheel / mind mapping (Glenn and Gordon, 2003; Buzan, 2006)
> - Micro–macro matrix (Krystek and Müller-Stewens, 1993)
> - Trend-impact analysis (Gordon, 2003b)
> - Opportunity matrix (Mićić, 2005)
>
> **Developing opportunities through analysis and simulation**
> - Structure analysis (Geschka and Reibnitz, 1981; Godet, 1994; Gausemeier et al., 1996)
> - Comprehensive situation mapping (CSM) (Georgantzas and Acar, 1995)
> - S-curve analysis (Pengg, 2003)
> - Causal layered analysis (Inayatullah, 2003)
>
> **Developing opportunities through creative methods**
> - Morphologies (Glenn and Gordon, 2003)
> - Field anomaly relaxation (Coyle, 2003; Rhyne, 1981)
> - Historical analogies (Armstrong, 2001)
> - Industry analogies (Mićić, 2003)
> - Precursor analysis (May, 1996)
> - Evaluation of speculative literature and art (May, 1996)
> - Meta opportunity (Mićić, 2003)
> - Empathy (Kelley, 2001)
> - Intuition (Glenn, 2003)

Professional checklist (cont'd)

Evaluating opportunities
- Analytic hierarchy process (Saaty, 1996)
- Cost–benefit analysis (May, 1996)
- Risk analysis (May, 1996)
- S-curve analysis (Pengg, 2003)
- Opportunity panorama (Mićić, 2005)

Presenting results
- Mind mapping (Buzan, 2006)
- Opportunity panorama (Mićić, 2005)

7 Your yellow futures glasses: Which future do you want to form?

By putting on the yellow futures glasses, the windjammer captain and his crew decide on one of the possible destinations that they perceived with the green futures glasses. The color of the yellow futures glasses is derived from the metaphor "sail towards the sun" or towards the island with the most beautiful (yellow) beach. Through the yellow futures glasses you see the future that you want to have realized at a given point in time. It is the strategic vision of your life or your company, which you put together from the future opportunities you recognized with the green futures glasses.

> Many empirical studies have shown that outstanding successes started with a more or less clear picture of the desired future. [1]

As will be explained in more detail in the core concepts section, the yellow futures glasses lead to decisions about the mission (meaning your long-term basic task), the strategic vision (meaning the long-term goal picture) and the strategic guidelines, the agreed rules that need to be observed as part of the mission and on the way to the strategic vision. What these elements of a futures strategy have in common is their normative function, the decision for a certain direction. We particularly emphasize the vision in this book, as it is of most importance in practice.

Vision was a buzzword. Most professionally managed companies have a document with the word vision in the title. The title is generally followed by a few well-formulated, nice-sounding sentences about quality, growth, profitability and fairness. The yellow futures glasses, however, are concerned with something else, with a clear decision on a direction for the future.

Many are tired of this understanding of vision, yet there is no way around the fact that vision will never be outdated. Much of this vision terminology is now tired, yet there is no way around the realization that vision is not subject to the tides of management literature and will at some point go out of fashion in the same way as everything which is "lean". Every person and every organization always has some form of vision. The question is, whether the vision is in harmony with those of your colleagues.

In daily use, the word vision unfortunately often has an aftertaste of something not quite serious, dreamy, fantastic, or pathological. The former German chancellor Helmut Schmidt is alleged to have said, "Anyone with visions should see a doctor."[2] If vision means the same as hallucination, then this is valid. But through the yellow futures glasses we see a strategic vision, not rose-tinted dreams, illusions and utopias. Every company, every organization, every country, every family, and finally, every individual can be significantly more successful with a strategic vision as a fascinating, jointly desired and achievable picture of the future than without it. You could even say that more or less nothing is more important for the success of an individual or an organization than having a clear and motivating vision of where he, she or it is headed.

> *If life has no vision which we strive for, long for and want to realize, then there is no motivation to make a lot of effort.* (Erich Fromm)

Have you ever put together a puzzle made up of 1,000 pieces? Together with several other people perhaps? That is probably even more fun. But would you come up with the idea of asking a team to put together a puzzle and not give them a template to work by? That would be highly inefficient to say the least, if not totally impossible. Yet that is exactly what a manager does if he doesn't give his team a strategic vision in the sense of a template for the puzzle of daily business. By doing so, he does without one of the strongest, if not *the* strongest, management tools. Only a strategic vision can form the orienting picture and the template for the numerous small decisions in daily business.

With the yellow futures glasses, you decide which future you want to realize for your life or your organization. You evaluate the future opportunities you recognized with the green futures glasses according to how far their implementation is advisable in view of future environment developments and your priorities. A vision is not concerned with the usually nice and pretty sentences often to be found under the heading "vision".

> **The vision is the concrete picture of a fascinating, jointly desired and achievable future of your life or organization.**

A strategic vision needs to impart a picture of what your life and work should look like in five, eight, ten or more years. The more pictographic it is, the more easily you and your colleagues will remember it and also realize it. There are fewer misunderstandings and more orientation and thus more efficiency. A strategic vision therefore contributes not only to more successful business development, but also to a great extent to cost optimization.

A strategic vision can be considered to be good if it motivates and enthuses people and provides them with orientation and if they can identify with it. It is supposed to enable mental focus through its "lighthouse function".

In addition to the strategic vision as the core term of the yellow futures glasses, they are also used to develop the mission and the strategic guidelines.

Your yellow futures glasses: Overview

Table 7.1 summarizes the characteristics of the yellow futures glasses.

Table 7.1 Overview of the yellow futures glasses

Objective: To determine the desired future and orientation.

Work step and key question:

- Vision development
- Which fascinating future do we want to realize long-term?

Purpose:

- You can manage your company as a complex adaptive system more easily.
- You provide orientation for yourself and your team.
- You determine and form the future you want to have.
- You increase your efficiency and reduce your costs.
- You activate your performance potential.
- You can set better goals.
- You decide more easily what is important and right.
- You recognize threats and opportunities earlier.
- You impart confidence in difficult times.
- You differentiate yourself from the competition.
- You become more successful overall.

Attitude and principles:

- Use the yellow futures glasses for decisions.
- Benefit from self-fulfillment.
- Align your vision to your assumptions about the future.
- Develop the strategic vision from future opportunities.
- Describe the situation you want in the future.

Table 7.1 (cont'd)

Attitude and principles (cont'd)
- You can live without a vision, your organization cannot.
- Form your vision as a picture.
- Developing your vision is your task, not someone else's.
- Believe in self-responsibility.
- Believe that the future can be deliberately created.
- Ignite and promote passion for the vision.
- Strengthen the common vision through coherence of the individual visions.
- Acquire as many supporters as possible for your vision.
- Form harmony with the whole.
- See a homeopathic amount of challenge as ideal.
- Have the courage to set a conservative vision.
- Orient your vision on achievable competences and resources.
- Make your vision compatible with your history.
- Don't overload your customers with innovations.
- Make your vision as precise as necessary, as complex as required and as flexible as possible.
- Form the necessary differentiation with vision candidates.
- The higher the organizational level, the more general your results for the yellow futures glasses will be.
- Your strategic vision is a periodic prototype.
- What is decisive is not the achievement of your vision, but its effect on the present.

Core concepts:
- Vision questions
- Mission (mission elements)
- Vision (vision elements)
- Strategic guidelines

Typical methods:
- Conception methods (morphologies etc.)
- Decision methods (analytic hierarchy process etc.)

Procedure:
1. Develop the vision with your futures team.
2. First use the blue futures glasses to make yourself aware of your assumptions about the future.
3. Determine the time horizon of your vision.
4. Determine the vision questions.
5. Develop or check your mission.
6. Develop vision candidates.
7. Evaluate your vision candidates.
8. Determine the core of your strategic vision.

Table 7.1 (cont'd)

Procedure (cont'd)
9. Develop your strategic vision further.
10. Determine your strategic guidelines.
11. Make sure that your vision is consistent.
12. Check your vision using the assumptions about the future.
13. Check your vision using the surprises.
14. Carry out a value reconciliation.
15. Discuss the strategic vision (together with the mission and guidelines) with employees and other people.
16. Summarize the core of your vision in one sentence.
17. Visualize your vision.
18. Implement the strategic vision.

Results:
A comprehensive and structured vision develops which can also be visualized in drawings or pictures. The strategic vision is embedded in a clear mission and framed by the strategic guidelines.

Case studies on the yellow futures glasses

Visions, the desired futures, have determined the way of the world over the millennia. Moses showed the way to the promised land, the Carolingians and Carl the Great, Napoleon, Hitler and numerous others had a vision of a great empire, Theodor Herzl had the vision of a "Jewish state", Mao Zedong wanted to make the great leap forward (see below), Martin Luther wanted a future, in which people would live by the word of God, Karl Marx wanted to let everyone contribute to society according to their abilities and live according to their needs on a democratic basis, John F. Kennedy wanted to see Americans on the moon, Apple wanted to democratize the computer and Ronald Reagan wanted Gorbachev to tear down the Berlin Wall. Many of these examples remind us that visionary power can be used both positively and negatively, constructively and destructively. They show the power that someone can have, if he knows what he wants and can communicate it attractively.

Mao Zedong's great leap forward

In 1958, the Chinese leader Mao Zedong developed the vision of the "great leap forward". He wanted to enlarge China's agricultural and industrial sectors at the same time in a huge feat of strength. He wanted to overtake Britain's steel production within 15 years. Chinese production was supposed to double in the first year alone. Mao wanted to overtake output without importing capitalist values, in much the same way as in the former German Democratic Republic, where the idea was to beat the West without following its ways. Chinese steel was to be produced in small, decentralized furnaces. Agricultural work was neglected for this purpose, woods were deforested, and in some cases the farmers' furniture was even burned and used to heat the steel furnaces. As Mao was not interested in the opinion of experts and placed all his faith in the farmers' collectives, expert evaluations, which said that only substandard steel could be produced in this way, had no effect on him. The same thing happened with Mao's assumption on how agricultural productivity could be increased. Critics were discredited at best. It took steel production six years to achieve the export value it had before the pronouncement of the great leap forward. Because of this concentration on steel production, agriculture and food production was neglected. According to official Chinese statistics, the result was 14 million deaths from starvation. Neutral sources claim 20 to 43 million deaths!

Hermann Sörgel's vision of Atlantropa

In the 1920s, the publisher of the magazine *Baukunst* had the vision of separating the Mediterranean from the Atlantic at Gibraltar and reducing the sea level in the Mediterranean by 200 meters over 150 years through simple condensation. Hermann Sörgel assumed that an additional land area the size of France and Belgium would develop in this way. This would weld together the neighboring countries and create employment for 150 years, Sörgel claimed. The reservoirs would additionally solve Europe's energy problems. A new continent of Africa and Europe would develop, which Sörgel called Atlantropa. Prohibited from publishing by the Nazis, Sörgel extended his vision to Africa after the Second World War. Large reservoirs were supposed to develop as part of a huge project forming dry land that would change the climate in Africa and make the deserts reclaimable. The writer John Knottel made a novel out of this vision and financed an advertising film for Atlantropa. The problem was, that this vision can probably never be realized, even from today's point of view.

What good things can you do with 50 billion dollars?

What would be the best way to increase global prosperity, particularly in the developing countries, if 50 billion US-dollars were available for the purpose? In 2004, Björn Lomborg, a lecturer at the Copenhagen Business School, organized the Copenhagen Consensus, an initiative to develop a basis for the decision on the most effective measures to solve global problems and increase prosperity for humankind.

With the participation of a panel of eight globally acknowledged economic experts, including three Nobel Prize winners, a ranking of possible measures was set up. In the sense of the green futures glasses, the possible measures were future opportunities. According to the evaluation, the curing and control of AIDS heads the list. By 2010, around 28 million cases could be prevented (from the perspective of 2004). The costs for achieving this would be around 27 billion dollars and the benefit would be around 40 times as high. It is surprising that climate protection measures, such as the Kyoto Protocol, were given a relatively low evaluation. The reason is that the costs for reducing greenhouse gases are over-proportionally high. The possible (economic) benefit on the other hand is relatively low, at least compared with the potential benefit arising from solving other problems such as diseases and undernourishment. It is not possible to solve all the world's problems at the same time. The Copenhagen Consensus was supposed to provide governments and other international organizations with an orientation for most effective action. In the sense of a vision, the Copenhagen Consensus prioritizes future opportunities and thus describes, in a certain sense, a strategic vision for humanity.

Björn Lomborg is totally convincing in face-to-face conversations and in his presentation. Yet the question remains whether assigning a low priority to the climate protection problem doesn't mean giving up on the planet. Death cannot be calculated in an economic sense.

Lou Gerstner's non-vision and vision after all for IBM

Lou Gerstner was CEO of IBM from 1993 to 2002. IBM was in one of the deepest crises in its history when he took over the job. The core business of mainframe computers was largely obsolete and provided no basis for future business in the future. During this period, Gerstner is often quoted as having said: "The last thing IBM needs now is a vision." In fact, he had already decided on a vision, even if he didn't call it one. In the same speech in which he decisively rejected a vision, he drew one of the most challenging strategic visions in recent decades. The giant IBM was supposed to develop from a manufacturer of mainframe computers into an IT-integrator and concentrate more on services. He directed all activities towards achieving this vision and thus created one of the most remarkable turnarounds in economic history. When he stepped down as CEO in 2002, IBM was making almost forty-five percent of its turnover with services.[3] In 1993, it had only been around fifteen percent.[4] This example shows how differently the concept of vision can be understood.

> *You cannot change things by fighting against existing reality. In order to change something, you have to build a new model which makes the old model obsolete.* (Buckminster Fuller)

A software vision

The management of a small software company, at that time really only a startup with not much turnover and even less capital, motivated its employees with a, for its time, fascinating strategic product vision, stated as follows: "a software solution which understands the meaning of the written word, links information from various sources, draws conclusions from these links and communicates with man in his language."

Changing strategic visions for Daimler-Benz

Edzard Reuter, Chairman of the Board of Daimler-Benz AG from 1987 to 1995, held the assumption about the future (blue futures glasses) that the automobile would no longer contribute the necessary growth rates and that it was necessary to enter several technology fields to balance out the risks and opportunities in various markets. Reuter followed the vision of the "integrated technology corporation". Daimler-Benz AG logically, partly before Edzard Reuter was Chairman of the Board, bought up companies such as AEG, Dornier, MTU, MBB and, on Jürgen Schrempp's initiative, also Fokker. In 1995, the year that Reuter handed over to Schrempp, Daimler-Benz AG made losses of around three billion Euros. The losses were only alleviated by the success of one of the strongest, if not the strongest, automobile brand in the world, Mercedes.

With Jürgen Schrempp, Chairman of the Board from 1995 to 2005, the automobile moved back into the focus of management attention. However, Schrempp also developed an ambitious vision, namely that of the "World Inc.", which would be a real global player with a very wide product range benefiting from maximum synergy potentials. This vision was based on the assumption about the future (blue futures glasses) that only very few automobile manufacturers would be able to survive. Jürgen Schrempp and his co-decision-makers merged Daimler-Benz AG with the Chrysler Corporation in 1998 to form DaimlerChrysler AG. Schrempp additionally acquired a significant share in Mitsubishi and a minority share in Hyundai. Schrempp's statement that he would first lead the company together with the then Chairman of the Board of Chrysler, Robert Eaton, then lead "the firm" alone indicated the kinds of motives that play a role in such decisions. The economist Herbert Giersch called mergers an expression of the intellectual poverty of management. Measured by the stock market value of the company, this strategic vision was an almost unparalleled financial disaster. The stock value of the total company fell to around one third: Chrysler lost 40,000 jobs after the merger – although shareholder value was supposed to be the real driving force. Management of a company is, of course, not the same as building a house that can be planned to the smallest detail and where anything other than success is a failure. But the destruction of two-thirds of the company's value at a time when the stock markets experienced enormous growth isn't just bad luck.

This example shows the power that can radiate from a strategic vision. At the same time it shows that a vision must not be a foolhardy adventure. The conservative vision can be the best one. Further discussion on this example can be found on page 197 in the section on the principles of the yellow futures glasses.

Trier 2020

Shortly after the millennium, the city of Trier, probably Germany's oldest city and with a population of approximately 100,000, developed a strategic vision with our support. This didn't happen in the usual way, with external advisory opinion and work at the specialist level, but in direct and permanent cooperation with the mayor, Helmut Schröer, his departmental heads and heads of important offices, such as Johannes Weinand, Head of the Office of City Development, and a number of representatives of society, culture and business.

The strategic vision was extensively developed on the basis of the *Eltville Model* with all five futures glasses. It was broken down into goals for the next two years and then into projects. It was the basis for long and medium-term finance and investment planning, for land utilization planning and for the operative sub-plans. In this way, a high level of congruency and consistency was achieved in the municipal decisions, plans and activities. Table 7.2 shows a rough summary of the vision elements.

Table 7.2 Strategic vision "Trier 2020"	
Field of action	**Vision element for 2020**
People and environment	■ 100,000 people live in our city, with a balanced age and employment structure. ■ Trier and the Trier suburbs are an attractive place to live for families with children. ■ Trier is a city with high landscape quality. ■ Downtown Trier is the social, cultural and economic focal point. ■ The traffic infrastructure is developed based on requirements. ■ Trier offers a wealth of cultural experiences.
Business	■ As one of Germany's oldest cities, Trier is known internationally. ■ Trier is a highly attractive European scientific and academic location. ■ Trier is a competence center for business traffic and logistics. ■ Trier has a high percentage of companies and households operating in a sustainable way.
Citizens and administration	■ A joint culture and business area is being developed with the nearby regional centre. ■ The administration is managed and organized like a commercial enterprise. ■ The citizens show unique social engagement. ■ The city is part of a cooperative regional authority. ■ The municipal budget is balanced.

From trading company to personal X-manager

This case study has been modified to avoid jeopardizing the interests of the company. A trading company for automobile accessories, which operates on a European basis, was faced with extreme competitive pressure in the classical trade sector. Instead of just concentrating on the efficiency of the existing business, the management looked for a new strategic vision to both promote differentiation from the competition and open a new, positive and energizing perspective for the employees. From a series of vision candidates, the management finally selected the vision to become a personal X-manager in the existing product area (X stands for a specific need). Increasing complexity and the resulting need for simplification created the basis for the choice of this customer-focused strategy. The vision very quickly led to a euphoric mood, which still holds up today, and successively to a radical restructuring of the company with the corresponding strengthening of its revenue basis.

Purpose of the yellow futures glasses

Through the yellow futures glasses you see the long-term vision of your company. Viewed not only rationally and economically, but also emotionally, the yellow futures glasses have a number of positive effects. With the vision, the mission and the strategic guidelines are also determined.

You can manage your company as a complex adaptive system more easily

A strategic vision that is aligned to assumed developments, clearly formulated and known to most employees, has a greater effect on the success of the company than any other measures that you could carry out with a comparable level of investment. A complex adaptive system, like a company or any other organization, cannot be managed effectively by projects, programs and measures alone. All your activities must at least in essence lead to a common picture in the future. It makes no sense to improve the organization, production, marketing, employee satisfaction or customer satisfaction in isolation without knowing in which direction the company is supposed to be developing. Only a long-term picture in the sense of a strategic vision provides the necessary orientation. The vision creates congruence, coherence and harmony of goals, which medium and short-term actions need in order to be effective. Strategic corporate planning is literally meaningless without a strategic vision. A necessarily detailed and adequately flexible strategic vision is the most effective practical step in strategic planning, both in life and in a company.

If a person has a vision, he strides forward more quickly and, in the end, more happily. If a team has a clear common vision, it gets high on the future to be created together.

> If the people in a company have a clear vision, it is easier to manage, more profitable and more secure for the future.

You provide orientation for yourself and your team

A good strategic vision works like a beacon. It creates the foundation for all strategic and operative decisions. In the same way that drawing metal pins to a magnetic object is easier than pushing them towards the object through opposing poled forces, it is easier to lead people with a strategic vision than to manage them long-term with small targets or even instructions. That's why it's called leadership and not "pushership".

> Leading people is what is needed, not "pushing people".

A strategic vision helps to intelligently concentrate your employees' and colleagues' creativity and energy on effective approaches, meaning the most important goals and projects. One way of increasing innovative power is to focus the innovators on a smaller target. With a strategic vision, you select such smaller targets and at the same time ignite enthusiasm in those who want to travel the road with you. Ideally, this applies to every single person in your organization. The developer will predominantly work on those solutions and products that lead to the vision, the accountant will perceive options in the balance sheet such that they are helpful to the vision, the salesperson will include your strategic vision as a quality characteristic in his presentations and give the customer the feeling that your company will perform even better in future, and the departmental head will plan and manage his department in a way that contributes as much as possible to the strategic vision. Such a total harmony is of course theoretical. It requires a lot of involvement, reflection and communication. The actions in your company will be more harmonious with a vision than without, where it will be much more prone to conflict.

Nowadays, we have more possibilities than ever, but we have many fewer factors under our own control. In many cases, fear and helplessness are the result. A good strategic vision integrates and reduces complexity (which has to be extended by the red futures glasses). The simplicity and holistic approach of a strategic vision provide orientation in daily life and business.

A strategic vision creates clarity as to whether colleagues or employees want to follow you. Long conflicts are often resolved by simply going separate ways, which has finally been made possible through a clear commitment to or against a certain direction.

You determine and form the future you want to have

Developing and realizing a strategic vision is one of your most valuable rights. Mind creates matter. Developing a strategic vision means mentally exchanging cause and effect. You imagine the future effects in order to be able to set the causes now. The human mind is the cause of most of the relevant effects in our world, be it your own home or climate change. The Roman emperor Marcus Aurelius knew it, numerous philosophers knew it and all cultures probably knew and know it. Our life is the result of what we think and feel. We needed modern knowledge in order to understand the background of sport training methods and to understand what mental training really means. Anyone who can imagine taking the next hurdle, jumping over the eight-meter marker or beating a top football team has at least created the precondition for actually achieving it. A strategic vision is therefore mental training for individuals, companies or even countries.

■ *It is the mind which builds the body.* (Friedrich Schiller)

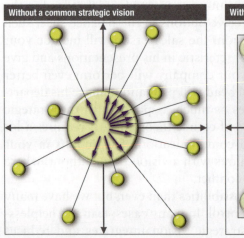
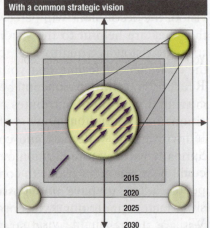

Figure 7.1 The effects of a strategic vision

The sociologist and futures researcher Fred Polak[5] has dedicated his life to the question of how much importance the sum of all individual visions in a country has for the future of this country. His work can be essentially summarized in the thesis that a country and, therefore, basically every group of people and every individual person tend to form the future they expect. If there is no vision seen with the yellow futures glasses, then the blue futures glasses are used. If one expects a negative development, then the belief of the people strengthens the probability of it occurring.

You increase your efficiency and reduce your costs

The allegory of the puzzle used at the start of the chapter makes it clear that the yellow futures glasses provide the integrating template for many daily activities and decisions. In this way, you can even achieve something not usually associated with the term "vision", namely a relative reduction in costs. Under certain preconditions that will be described later, a strategic vision can become the most powerful cost-reduction tool in an organization. This thesis can unfortunately not be proved, as you cannot manage the same company in the same situation once with a vision and once without a vision. Sadly, we have no access to parallel worlds. We can only draw on arguments and comparisons as indices. It nevertheless seems plausible to more or less every observer, that a strategic vision makes an organization significantly more efficient.

> The vision focuses the attention and activities of the management and all employees and thus leads to efficiency and cost reduction.

You activate your performance potential

Reinhold Würth, who has turned a two-man company into a global company with 55,000 employees since 1954, has always given his company a continuously adapted, challenging vision. As he explains himself, he did so to maintain his company in a state of becoming, in Spring and in youth, for as long as possible because companies commonly span the stages of becoming, being and decaying. The people in his company should always be aware that in a competitive situation, every moment of standing still means a step backward. Without a challenging vision, the employees, particularly the more than 29,000 salesmen, could have easily become complacent about the company's success and changed down a gear or two.

> The strategic vision creates a demanding but realizable future perspective and activates the employees to the highest possible performance.

Without a vision of a desired future, people, companies, cities, regions and countries cannot be as successful as actually possible. The yellow futures glasses help to achieve these potentials.

You can set better goals

Without a clear long-term vision, it is difficult to set goals and take the measures necessary for achieving them. We can only do something in the present, but we need to derive what we do today from the desired future.

> *Without a specific image of the future, we can neither live, nor plan, nor find orientation in the present.* (Horst W. Opaschowski)

You can lay your strategic vision over the current situation of your life or your company like a template and then check where there is a gap between expectation and reality. That's where action is needed. In practice, the metaphorical template is a table with three columns: "target", "actual" and "solution".

You decide more easily what is important and right

A strategic vision enables the mental focusing on the twenty percent of goals, projects, programs and actions that bring eighty percent of the results. It therefore directs concentration of mental, financial and time-based resources to what is essential in and for the future.

> The yellow futures glasses of the vision direct your attention and thus your future development.

Justus von Liebig discovered the principle of mineral fertilizer: namely, that every plant at any given time is only lacking one factor to make it grow – the minimum factor. There is no point in adding other factors; only the minimum factor or the bottleneck factor enables the next stage of development. Wolfgang Mewes, with his bottleneck strategy, has transferred this principle, which is in fact the foundation of production planning and control, to people and companies.[6] What is totally clear in the case of plants, needs, however, to first be created by people and companies: namely the vision. Only when you know the desired future can you know what the bottleneck is towards achieving this vision. Without a vision there is no real bottleneck. If you don't know in which direction you want to develop your company, then you cannot determine what the biggest hindrance on the path to it is.

A strategic vision helps you to make the right decisions in the present. Everyone in your company can check whether or not certain decisions, opportunities, ideas or questions are helpful for achieving the vision.

You recognize threats and opportunities earlier

Without a strategic vision, you evaluate trends and future technologies with regard to their effect on your *present*. With a strategic vision, you have the possibility of checking the effects of these future developments not only on your present but also on your future.

> A strategic vision is like a probe into the future, with which you can recognize and evaluate opportunities and threats of future environmental changes much earlier.

Future strategies need, particularly nowadays, constant revision and adaptation to changes that have occurred or are expected. With a strategic vision, you have the ability to introduce changes before the necessity of doing so is generally recognized in the market and by competitors. You can therefore act before most of the others have even suspected the necessity. Time is used as a strategic instrument: someone who can see the coming realities of a business before his competitors gains a vital advantage.

You impart confidence in difficult times

> *Someone who knows "why" can cope with almost every kind of "how".* (Viktor Frankl)

The psychiatrist Viktor Emil Frankl wrote that about his experiences in a concentration camp. How can you give people courage? How can you give someone contemplating suicide a new zest for life? By showing them in a believable way that the future can be better and probably will be better than the present. A believable strategic vision makes it easier to bear and accept many a difficulty and inconvenience in the present in the interest of a better future. It is obvious that any dishonest, empty promises of better times to come will become apparent after a short time and thus achieve the opposite of the desired effect.

If a company is facing a crisis that threatens its very existence, then a strategic vision is the second most important measure. The first is to ensure the continuance of the company through adequate financial liquidity. But the second task must be to give the people in the company a clear direction again, so that they can find a way out of the crisis as quickly and efficiently as possible.

You differentiate yourself from the competition

It is amazing how little the knowledge of the effects of a strategic vision is used in practice. More or less every company has, of course, written down a few polished, lofty sentences that are then called the vision, but a strategic vision in the sense we are using it here is the exception. This is exactly the reason why using the many positive effects of a strategic vision is an opportunity for differentiation.

The differentiation from the competition is even greater if you put your strategic vision together from several vision candidates (see Table 6.2) and in this way develop a truly unique picture of a fascinating, jointly desired and achievable future.

You become more successful overall

The results of systematic studies on the question as to who is more successful in life and in the marketplace, people and companies with a strategic vision or those without one, agree with commonsense judgment. Success is far from being the same as financial profit, yet if we were just for a moment to measure success by this criterion, then a study by Collins and Porras[7] at Stanford University clearly shows that a strategic vision leads to greater success. They observed eighteen companies with a strategic vision and compared them in a long-term study with eighteen companies in the same industry sector that were primarily focused on short-term profit. The number of studies that came to the same result mitigates the skepticism concerning the explanatory power of such studies. The visionary companies were significantly more successful, particularly when compared on long-term profit.

> *When the utopian oases dry out, a desert of banality and helplessness develops.* (Jürgen Habermas)

Core concepts of the yellow futures glasses

The yellow futures glasses are used to develop not only the strategic vision, but also the mission and the strategic guidelines. The focus is placed on the strategic vision, because it usually makes the biggest difference to the present compared to the mission and the strategic guidelines, although the mission is the more comprehensive concept. If however, you change the fundamental task of your company, then the mission becomes the focal point. All the core concepts of the yellow futures glasses are based on one or more future opportunities (see Figure 7.2). Generally, only a few future opportunities are rated so highly that they play a role in the yellow futures glasses.

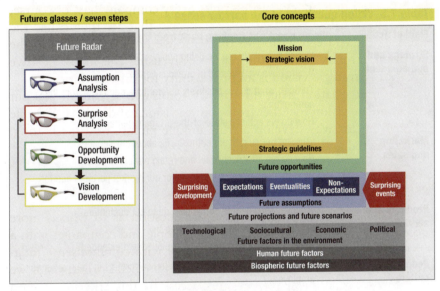

Figure 7.2 The yellow futures glasses and their core concepts

Vision questions

There are in fact vision questions, mission questions and guideline questions. For the sake of simplicity, we are summarizing them all under the term vision questions, in the same way that we call the work step of the yellow futures glasses *vision development*, although the mission and the guidelines are also developed in the process.

> With vision questions, you determine the essential need for decision about the desired future.

We are concerned with three questions, which look simple at first sight:

1. Vision: What do we want our company to look like in 20XX?
2. Mission: What should our company be there for in the future?
3. Guidelines: How do we want to decide and act in future?

Examples of deeper vision questions in the narrow sense are shown in Table 7.3. If your vision encompasses several business areas (within one mission) then most questions will need to be answered separately for each business area.

Table 7.3 Vision questions in the narrow sense

Field of action	Vision questions (looking back from the desired future)
Strategy and management	- In which markets are we doing business? - Where have we invested in previous years? - Through what do we positively differentiate ourselves from the competition? - How do we achieve state-of-the-art management?
Marketing and sales	- Why are our customers enthusiastic about our services? - How do we effectively gain and retain our customers? - Why are we a likeable company for our market partners and for the public?
Products and services	- Which special benefit do we provide to our customers? - What is praised about our services? - Which competences have we developed and extended?
People and culture	- How do we manage to attract the top performers in the market as employees? - Which culture are we proud of?
Systems and processes	- What makes us efficient and effective? - How have we maintained a high degree of flexibility? - In what kind of environment do we work?
Partners and suppliers	- How do we work well with our suppliers? - How do we work well with which partners?
Finance and resources	- How have we financed our qualitative and quantitative growth?

Strategic vision (vision elements)

We define strategic vision as follows:

> A strategic vision is the concrete picture of a fascinating, jointly desired and achievable future.

A one-sentence summary of a strategic vision could be as follows: *In 2018, we are the fastest developer of individual cosmetic products in Europe.* Several vision elements (parts of the vision), which are complex and visionary long-term goals, are put together to make a vision.

> The strategic vision, together with the mission and the strategic guidelines, forms the anticipatory foundation for the future of an organization.

Accordingly, the vision is the totality of the vision elements that are based on future opportunities. Before John F. Kennedy, to give an over-used example, could formulate the vision in 1961 of sending a man to the moon by the end of the decade and bringing him back again, the opportunity needed to be recognized that this was a fundamentally possible and useful course of action, which would also bring a number of moral and military advantages. Before you can formulate the vision of being the world market leader in your business, you must at some point have recognized opportunities to achieve this position.

Table 7.3 makes clear that a strategic vision cannot be just a few polished sentences. It shows a basic structure and a number of typical key questions for the development of a strategic vision.

Mission (mission elements)

The mission creates the framework for the vision. Whereas the mission describes the game, the vision describes the kind of player you want to have become and how far you want to have come at a given point in time. The mission is the "eternal assignment" of your company, a general requirement of what your company is supposed to achieve in its environment. The mission is therefore the "raison d'être", its reason for being and its general purpose. The vision on the other hand is the future that you want to form within the framework of your mission. Your vision could be to fulfill your mission in a particularly excellent way. If you define your company's mission as "a provider of high quality foodstuffs", then this does not provide the answer to the question as to whether you are looking for aggressive global market domination or value-led and growth-independent sustainable business with appropriate revenues. We define mission as follows:

> A mission is the general long-term purpose that an organization fulfills for its customers (in the widest sense).

The mission is the totality of the mission elements that, as with the vision, develop from opportunities. A one-sentence summary of a mission could be as follows: *We reduce the financial consequences of accidents* (an insurance company) or *We are responsible for measuring and settling accounts for water and energy.*

The mission of an individual person is rarely so clear. Fortunately, not many people want to dedicate their whole life to a single purpose. If however, we concentrate on the professional part of a person's life, then a person's mission can be just as focused as a company's. We formulate our professional mission as *Help leaders to see more of the future than their competitors.*

Strategic guidelines

The guidelines form the safety fences for the future. They do not determine where you or your company want to go, which would be the vision, but they determine the rules and principles according to which you want to act on your way to your vision. We define strategic guidelines as follows:

> Strategic guidelines are rules and principles on strategic values and behavior.

We invest five percent of our turnover in research and development is a strategic guideline. Guidelines can be set:

(a) at a normative-strategic level (together with the vision and mission)

(b) at a cultural-strategic level, and

(c) at an operational-strategic level (together with goals, projects, processes and systems).

The yellow futures glasses are primarily concerned with (a) and also with (b). The guidelines at the operational-strategic level are more a violet futures glasses issue.

Attitude and principles of the yellow futures glasses

The yellow futures glasses for the desired future are of little importance in the classical understanding of futures research, but are however essential for practicable future management. The yellow futures glasses provide a normative image of the actor's desired future and thus look at the world with an inward orientation from the micro perspective. You are an active, intervening part of what is happening. The yellow futures glasses are of a hybrid nature; they are characterized by an optimistic and at the same time critical view, by intuition and analysis, by experience and progressive imagination.

Use the yellow futures glasses for decisions

The yellow futures glasses are characterized by decisions. A strategic vision, the most important result of looking through the yellow futures glasses, is the result of a very thorough prioritization of the development options and a final decision for the direction to be followed. In the same way that the captain of the windjammer uses the yellow futures glasses to decide on one of the possible destinations, you should follow a certain direction in your life or with your company and, what is much more difficult, decide for that one direction and against many others. As Stephen Covey has said, the point of the yellow futures glasses is to decide which mountain you want to climb and not how you want to climb it.

> *If someone doesn't know which harbor he wants to sail to, then there is no such thing as a favorable wind.* (Lucius Seneca)

A good strategic vision can certainly be free of adventures and simply describe a concrete image of a fascinating, jointly desired and achievable future to be strived for together. But a vision that doesn't include a real decision and direction, that contains many possible options and directions, is about as useful as a road sign that points to the way to Rome in three different directions.

It is therefore essential that your mission, your strategic vision and your strategic guidelines are clear commitments and decisions for or against the opportunities and options perceived with the green futures glasses. Only then will a clear image develop which provides orientation for the people in your family, your organization or your company. Only then can the yellow futures glasses function as a template for the daily puzzle of activities and decisions.[8]

Benefit from self-fulfillment

"Every strong image becomes reality" according to Antoine de Saint-

Exupéry. Buddha, Marcus Aurelius and many others pointed out that life is a product of thoughts. This connection has been proved in many psychological experiments since the 1970s. Expectations of success or failure influence performance. The social psychologist Jens Förster discovered[9] that blond female students get worse results in intelligence test if they are told jokes about blonds first. If women have to state their gender before solving mathematical tasks, their results are worse. The same thing happens with men when their language competence is called for. If a task (in the experiment concerned, the plaiting of thin wire to make a fly screen) is described as "embroidery", then women generally work more quickly than men, but also less carefully. If the work is described as a technical task, the effect is exactly the opposite. Men then work more quickly, but also more carelessly. Förster summarizes the results as follows: "Positive conditioning has an advantageous effect on speed and creativity. Negative pre-attitudes however increase accuracy, self-discipline and the ability to analyze." Show yourself and the people you manage a challenging but achievable future perspective in order to increase their achievement potential.

Align your vision to your assumptions about the future

In the first step, the officers on the ship made assumptions about the development of the sea and the weather. They noted what, according to their estimate, will happen, what will not happen and what they considered could not be estimated. Their decision for a strategic vision will be based on these assumptions about the future. They will use the yellow futures glasses to determine their strategic vision against the background of their conclusions with the blue futures glasses. You need to align your vision to your assumptions about the future in the same way, in order to be able to describe those desired futures that not only correspond to your values and desires, but also fit the conditions and mechanisms of the probably assumed future.

Develop the strategic vision from future opportunities

The windjammer captain first used the green futures glasses with his crew to think of possible options, before using the yellow futures glasses to make a decision on the vision to be chosen.

The genesis of a vision could be compared to the development of a pearl. The mussel needs an impulse to be able to form a pearl over several decades. There is still no agreement whether it is a grain of dust, a grain of sand or some other impulse. In the same way, the opportunity perceived with the green futures glasses provides the impulse for the development of a vision. Further opportunities provide the material for further vision elements. A strategic vision generally consists of a whole bundle of opportunities.

> The green futures glasses provide the options from which the yellow futures glasses select.

Describe the desired future situation

Apart from very rare exceptions, all experts in the area of futures work interpret the vision as a future situation in the sense of a later state of one's self. The yellow futures glasses demand an egocentric perspective.

A future situation can be realized and then again needs another vision. A small minority of people understand the vision as something ongoing, as an activity or as a system of values. The latter can without a doubt be the foundation of a vision, but not the vision itself. It is possible to reconcile the definitions if we understand the vision as a means to achieve an emotional purpose. We aspire to a vision because we assume that it will form a desired state of emotions. It can be feelings of power, satisfaction or ecstasy that we want to experience with consecutive visions. In the business context, which we are concentrating on here, the strategic vision is understood as the desired state of one's own life or the company.

> We are not talking about "visions". The vision is always singular.

You can live without a vision, your company cannot

Many people consider the concept of a vision as the cause of unhappiness. Do we really have to strive for a different, supposedly better reality? Doesn't the disappointment of not having achieved something more than make up for the happiness at what we did achieve? What is so wrong with not making ambitious goals and plans and just enjoying life? Isn't the artist who, encompassed in his work, lives and looks for happiness in the here and now, a good model? Why shouldn't we draw our happiness from our achievements?

There are no doubt advantages in living as a person without a vision. You don't have to bear the tension created by the perceived difference between a desired future and lived reality. You don't have to set out on journeys with unknown courses and surprising events. You can save your mind and soul from exertion. You are free of regret and sadness about things not achieved. And finally, you don't have to make a painful choice on the direction, which, in view of the increasing complexity and number of options available, is becoming ever more difficult.

Billions of people prove every day that they can live without a real strategic vision – many of them very happily. If we stay with our definition of the vision as a fascinating (jointly) desired and achievable future, and don't just regard it as an image of a state of happiness, then we can conclude that a person does not really need a strategic vision to be happy.

Nevertheless, many feel the need not to leave the mountain they will climb to chance, but to form better realities and to describe a vision of this reality that is worth pursuing. And some of them make their happiness complete by even enjoying the pursuit of the vision.

Companies risk death if they are not regularly provided with a challenging task (mission), a direction in which they should develop (vision) and guidelines according to which they should behave.

> People continue to live and can be very happy even if they don't have a vision. Companies, as a collective of people, on the other hand, are constituted by a mission, a vision and strategic guidelines.

Design your vision as a picture

We need to be able to visualize a strategic vision. When looking through the yellow futures glasses, we are usually first concerned with words, because most people cannot draw that quickly or that accurately. But as soon as the future we are striving for has been described clearly, then it should be translated into pictures as soon as possible for several reasons:

1. As is generally known, pictures can be imparted more simply and quickly.
2. Pictures make understanding more precise, increase coherence and reduce misunderstandings.
3. Pictures are a precondition for the realization of a vision: only a picture in your mind creates the necessary emotional attraction to the vision or clearly shows its rejection.

4. Pictures are easier to remember, enabling your vision to be more apparent and therefore more effective in your and your employees' thoughts and actions.

> The word vision comes from the Latin *videre* (to see).

The illustrations in Figure 7.3 are taken from a total of twelve illustrations with which a Swiss company visualized its strategic vision for its employees. According to the Managing Director, even the cleaning staff in this company know in which direction it is headed.

> A vision should be written in the future present[10] or at least in the future perfect,[11] as if the vision were already reality.

The tense in which the vision is written can support the pictorial image, even without visualization. Both tenses, the future present and the future perfect, enable the present to be seen as if it were the past of the future. In the future perfect for example, it could be: *In 20XX we will have acquired 140 successful and enthusiastic licensing partners.* The same fact, stated in the present would be: *2020: We have 140 successful and enthusiastic licensing partners.* Whereas the formulation in the future perfect sounds more rational, the same statement in the present can easily form an impression of megalomania in others.

Developing your vision is your task, not someone else's

What is the task of the management of any organization if not the formulation and further development of the vision? If you do not determine the values and priorities in your company, which are intended to become your company's reality, then there is no vision vacuum. What actually happens is that the visions of the most influential employees fit together to make a virtual vision, which is rarely the best and most meaningful vision for your company. If the vision creates the reality, then it means that a reality is created that you probably do not want.

> If you don't determine the strategic vision, others will do it for you.

All kinds of things are nowadays supposed to be the responsibility of the person at the top. However, there is virtually nothing more obviously the task of top management than the yellow futures glasses,

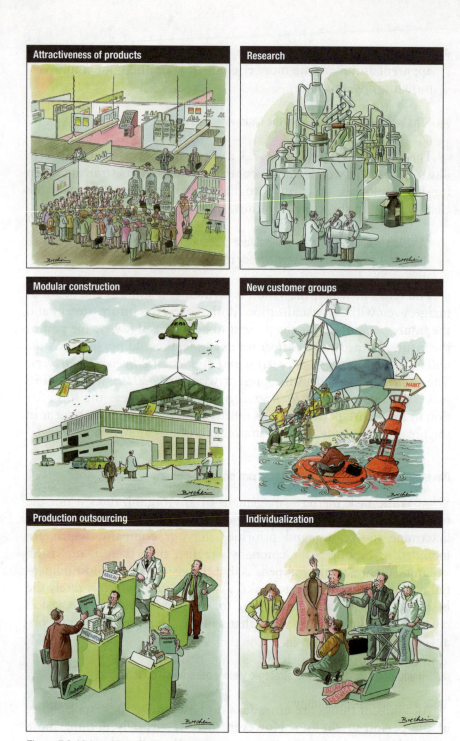

Figure 7.3 Videre: Visualization of a strategic vision

that is, the mission, the strategic guidelines and the strategic vision. It is not enough for support to be provided from the top, the strategic vision has to come from the top.[12]

There are a number of approaches that suggest involving as many employees as possible in the development of the vision. In some cases, procedures are called for which take one or two years before the vision is even formulated. In view of our experience in practice, we consider this to be of little value, to put it mildly. Such projects have serious disadvantages:

- If the vision is developed by several hundred or even several thousand people and is supposed to do justice to all of them, it will be neither particularly original nor unique. The end result of such a mammoth process is a democratically developed vision with no real differentiation to the competition. It could have been developed almost as well by chance.

- Only a minute percentage of all company managements are willing to invest in such comprehensive projects, particularly as the vision needs to be periodically maintained and updated. Effective strategic visions are too rare to have such huge hurdles put in front of them.

- The supposed advantage of such a big project, namely the support by as many people as possible, cannot be achieved. Only a minute percentage will really become enthusiastic about a vision that is a multiple compromise.

- Our experience shows that the wisdom or intelligence of the crowd cannot carry out a competitor analysis or develop a concept for strategic differentiation. Democracy doesn't develop a vision worthy of the name.

> The wisdom of the crowd is highly suitable for solidifying a strategic vision, but not for developing one.

What needs to be done is to develop the strategic vision as a draft from a solid foundation and only then enter into a wide-based dialog during the course of which much will be added, changed or deleted.

Believe in self-responsibility

Can everyone really take responsibility for his or her own situation? Do we form our own reality? Can people really live according to

Sprenger's "self-responsibility principle"?[13] Friedrich Schiller wrote that the mind creates the body, and the Roman emperor Marcus Aurelius philosophized that our life is the product of our thoughts. Critics cynically argue that you cannot tell the rape victim, the abused child or the African brutally attacked in the street by skinheads that you always create your own situation. Are Schiller, Aurelius and Sprenger charlatans? This argument, which at first sounds convincing, uses a minute exception to prove the invalidity of the whole thing. Let's take this as an opportunity to reinforce the rule of self-responsibility:

> **Whenever no one else is clearly responsible for the current situation, then it is generally correct and usually valuable to assume that you are responsible for your situation yourself.**

Consider the consequences. Someone who doesn't believe in self-responsibility can vociferously complain and call for those who are responsible to please save him. It's the others' fault, he cannot do anything himself and therefore *doesn't have to* do anything. Someone who does believe in self-responsibility on the other hand, will always first ask what he can do to change the undesirable situation, however difficult that may be in a given case. With this attitude there would be a whole lot fewer economic and social problems in the world. In the real world, we may not have created the person smelling of garlic sitting next to us in the crowded and hot train compartment, but we do have the possibility of moving to the corridor. If we stay in the compartment, then seating comfort is obviously more important to us than fresh air.

The critics of the can-do-belief doubt that mind can move matter, with which they attack an ancient and, to our mind fundamental, principle of how the world works. Almost every serious philosophical school of thought is constructivist. The fact that the mind sometimes creates realities it didn't want doesn't change the fact that, as proposed by Hegel, the idea comes first and then its execution. It basically remains true that we shape our reality ourselves. Children, people who are sick or helpless, victims of crime or accidents are exceptions that do not change the basic rule. The question should always be, who made the current situation if we didn't? If there is clearly someone else who is responsible, then we did not shape our own reality. If however, this other clearly responsible person does not exist, we must be responsible ourselves.

Believe that the future can be deliberately created

Can we really shape the future? If we believe the guidebooks for success, then it seems that every vision and every goal is achievable as long as you use the right strategy and method. With good reason, there is some opposition to this can-do-delusion, as Michael Mary puts it.[14] A number of questions need to be asked:

- Will we be happier if we formulate our vision?
- Will we be happier if we achieve it?
- Is it at all possible to consciously set and achieve a vision?
- Can we achieve everything we resolve to do?

The "high priests of achievability"[15] spread the good word in books, videos, audios, seminars and lectures, that everyone chooses his own reality, everyone can be successful, and everyone can change his situation. The absoluteness of these theses alone, makes it impossible for them to be suitable to describe complex reality. But they are not completely wrong, even if some of the critics of the high priests of achievability are quick to form this impression. A simple differentiation throws light on the situation:

> Every person and organization has the notional *possibility* for a clearly positive change within a foreseeable period. But the statistical *probability* is relatively low from the perspective of the individual.

In principle, every smoker *can* stop smoking. However, only some of them will quit. As a principle, almost everyone *could* earn one million Euros per year, but only a very small number will *actually* do so. Is it therefore fundamentally wrong to develop and teach strategies for a healthy life without cigarettes or for achieving a high income? Perhaps every step in the direction of the goal should be considered a success.

Let's temporarily adopt a utilitarist attitude: whoever heals is right or, put another way, if it is of benefit, it is meaningful. With this assumption, we try to increase the probability of success through calculated optimism. The probability of something considered for the totality of people and companies can be enhanced for the individual if he believes in his success. And vice-versa, the probability can be reduced to around zero if everyone assumes there is no point in setting goals because they will not be achieved anyway. Those who correctly criticize the "delusion of achievability", but at the same time give the impression that almost nothing is deliberately achievable, turn their message into a self-fulfilling prophecy. Those who don't make the slight differentiation between possibility and probability and thus talk about sure strategies, which almost definitely lead to success if you just really want it, are firstly charlatans, and secondly responsible for the unhappiness of many people who curse and despise themselves if they are not as successful as they wish.

In summary, we arrive at the not surprising, but at least realistic, estimation that neither the "high priests of achievability" nor those who dispute achievability are completely right. People can shape their lives according to their own will, but within certain limits. Nevertheless:

> It is useful to think about limits at the end of the thought process, not at the beginning.

Ignite and promote passion for the vision

The power of the view through the yellow futures glasses is determined by the enthusiasm with which the members of the team or the organization support you. The vision needs to be shared,[16] the people need to take ownership of it,[17] it needs to speak their language[18] and thus be anchored in their hearts.[19] Mission, vision and passion are often talked about in the same breath.

It is usual in many large companies to outline ten-year horizons and then call them "Vision20XX" and so on. The contents of such elaborations are often not more than sober presentations of business areas, turnover and profit figures. There is no sign of passion and fascination. And the leaders of small and very small companies also unfortunately lapse into always wanting more and write such nonsense as "our number one goal is growth" as their vision. Growth cannot be a goal because it describes a process and a material result of having achieved a vision and the only people likely to become enthusiastic about growth are the owners.

> A strategic vision should be equally attractive for heart and mind.

Peter Senge[20] describes seven attitudes that employees can adopt towards a vision:

1. Commitment
2. Participation
3. Genuine consent
4. Formal consent
5. Reluctant consent
6. Non-consent
7. Apathy

Senge doesn't even approach the term passion. His caution is justified. People rarely develop passion for a vision which is not their own and which they have not completely made their own. Apathy is the exact opposite of passion and therefore correctly marks the other end of the scale. It is obvious that those companies in which all senior managers show real engagement with or even passion for a common vision, have huge cost and quality advantages compared to their competitors. How do you achieve the commitment of all senior managers for the company's strategic vision? The principle is simple: it needs to be the vision of all senior managers.

Strengthen the joint vision through coherence of the individual visions

Everyone has at least some idea of what his life, his family, his company, his city, his country or the world would ideally be like to make him happier. Even if the view through the yellow futures glasses of the desired future is not concrete and clear enough, not systematically developed, not coordinated with others and not safeguarded against surprises, this doesn't change the fact that almost everyone has a vague idea of his desired future, even if it is only that he knows what he doesn't want or no longer wants. There is always a latent vision of your company, formed by the common elements of the individual visions.

> Love at first sight happens extremely rarely with a strategic vision. A team gradually falls in love with the vision.

External impulses can inspire, enrich and provide ideas. Yet people tend to recognize the real vision in themselves. You experience the contact with your inner vision by the level of response or harmony with a potential vision, or vision candidate as we call it. It has to be said that a vision candidate that has been developed by an external party is not necessarily inferior to the one developed by yourself.

People can become just as enthusiastic about a vision that is suggested by someone else and that they experience as being in harmony with their inner vision as for a vision they developed themselves. Strangely enough, the categorical rejection of someone else's vision can lead to your own vision if you establish it as an enemy to be beaten. This is the case to a certain extent with Microsoft for Apple and Coca-Cola for Pepsi-Cola.

The reason that so many people wander apparently aimlessly through life is probably that they cannot yet link their desires to practical action, or doubt the feasibility of their ideas and notions, or cannot decide between several alternatives. The reason that so many companies get by without a real strategic vision is, in our view, because they believe the vision can be dealt with in a few polished sentences. In this way, the task of developing a vision is marked off as completed much to early.

> The strategic vision of a team and an organization is to a certain extent always a compromise.

A common ground is what makes a vision valuable. The coherence factor – the alignment of the individual visions – determines the strength of a vision. Every person, and the vast majority of management teams, has a vague idea of the direction in which the company should develop. However, there are as many different visions and thus as many potential visions (vision candidates) as there are members in the team. The team's vision is therefore initially the intersection of the individual visions (the congruence) which, experience shows, is generally relatively low if not worked on. The main purpose of the yellow futures glasses in your company is therefore to harmonize the existing vision candidates of the most important individuals.

We have often experienced people leaving a company once they realized that they were not able to support the new vision. They then decide to follow a different vision, in the best cases their own. Clarification processes thus take place, which are advantageous for all concerned when it comes down to it. Coherence can therefore also be established through a parting of the ways.

The blessings of coherence do not come free however. The more coherence has to be achieved among many people, the greater the danger that the resulting compromise is nothing special any more.

Acquire as many supporters as possible for your vision

All the various advantages of your strategic vision can only be used to their full potential if the vision has conquered the hearts and minds of the senior people in your company. It is obvious that a vision will be stronger the more supporters it has.[21] It would however be wrong to deduce from this that every employee needs to be an enthusiastic supporter of the vision. That's not necessary even in small companies and organizations. Although in most cases it's nice to know that even the cleaning staff know the direction in which the company is headed, there is a certain danger in too much widespread detailed knowledge about the vision. Competitors will get to know it.

Management at every level and the critical experts need to know the entire company's strategic vision in detail. Beyond that, the minimum requirement is that employees know the sub-vision for their area and see a meaningful connection to the whole company. The bigger the company is and the more varied its business areas, the more decentralized the development and maintenance of the strategic vision of each unit will need to be.

The developers of the strategic vision, the members of the management team, also need to be its ambassadors. They need to feel burning in them the fire that they want to ignite in their employees. They need to invite people to discuss the draft of the strategic vision in order to be able to use that collective wisdom and see the desired future even more clearly and make it more robust against potential surprises.

If you work in one of the numerous companies that know a lot about managing the future in theory, but where it plays an insignificant role in reality, then moving the employees will be a particular challenge anyway. In such a case, it would be bold to believe that all relevant people will accept, understand and enthusiastically support the strategic vision right from the beginning. The concept of a spiral is useful at this point: convincing people requires going through a number of loops, during the course of which the positive effects increase.

Form harmony with the whole

The yellow futures glasses require an egocentric view in the sense that you place your organization or your company in the focus of your considerations. As is generally known, in a free, humane world based on the division of labor and a social market economy, personal advantage can only be legally and legitimately achieved by making sure that what you do is useful to certain people and at least does not interfere with other people.

Kant's categorical imperative is just one version of the universal social rule: behave unto others, as you would like them to behave unto you.

Be aware therefore of your responsibility for the whole in whatever you think and do. To a certain extent, a good vision should also serve the common good.[22] Make sure that you see a future through the yellow futures glasses that is in harmony with the values and needs of your environment and is not unnecessarily directed against others. You cannot, of course, go easy on your competitors, but being better for the customers, and in this way "winning", is not the same thing as directly harming the competition with no benefit for the customers or the world. Create alterocentric benefit to achieve egocentric advantages.

The usual egocentric visions whose core is becoming the greatest or richest can only be achieved if you previously offered alterocentric benefit. The image of market leadership is therefore less desirable than the picture of having 100,000 enthusiastic customers.

See a homeopathic amount of challenge as ideal

The word vision awakens the naive longing for revolution in many people. Many consider only the foolhardy, adventurous and highly innovative to be truly visionary; thinking of the widest future horizons in the most vivid colors and deciding to make it reality. Herman Sörgel's vision of Atlantropa (see page 165) falls into this category.

> The personal longing for a quick, positive revolution of our own life, for breaking out of an unwanted part of it, is often transferred to the adult playground called the company.

We long for bold adventures in far off markets, but with a guarantee of success of course. It is naive to want to satisfy this longing in a company for a number of reasons:

1. A management team's jointly desired vision cannot be completely new in its essence or it would not find sufficient support, when it comes to radically changing the entire company.

2. A drastic repositioning of the company is not done except in an emergency. Chronically poor profits or critical threats to the company's existence seen in the assumptions about the future are the triggers for a total turn in the strategy, which is rather rare.

3. Only a small percentage of the forays away from the core business into new worlds, developed out of pure pressure to grow or out of thirst for adventure, were successful in the long run.

4. The yellow futures glasses are primarily concerned with decisions on strategic direction. New products, let alone new technologies, are generally not created or developed in a futures project or vision project. This would be equivalent to wanting to direct the repair of a Swiss watch on the ground from a helicopter. Detailed developments cannot be done at a strategic and visionary level. It is however possible to make fundamental discoveries and developments as part of a targeted innovation process which can be considered further at the strategic level.

We have worked with numerous practitioners on the term *vision* and researched the majority of literature on its definition. The majority of practitioners and futures experts agree that a vision is a challenging, but not necessarily surprising or very bold image of the desired future. Illuminating the future with all its unlimited possibilities is more the task of the green futures glasses not the yellow ones; they should lead to a meaningful and justifiable strategic vision.

The best strategic vision is probably somewhere near your current business. In contrast to the widespread desire for sensation, the vision is not better the more it leads away from your company's current competence. The strategies of Nokia (from rubber boots to cell phones), Mannesmann (from pipes to cell phone networks) and Preussag (from mining to the tourism company TUI), which are often mentioned in this context as allegedly bold strategies, are the exception, not the rule. This kind of dramatic change is never made without good reason.

> **Bold visions are generally called for by people who have never had the responsibility of managing a company at their own risk.**

As already mentioned in the context of the green futures glasses, a too ambitious vision is generally an entrepreneurially irresponsible undertaking, which demands too much of the employees, the organization, the finances and finally the customers, and causes a break point which threatens the company. Ideally, a good vision is therefore compatible with your current business,[23] particularly with the effects and functions you provide for your customers.

> The value of a strategic vision increases a little as it moves away from your current business, but then falls again dramatically with every additional step away.

A homeopathic amount of innovation is what creates the value, but innovation quickly leads to a dissipation of energy. Ansoff's early theory has been proved by practice. The risk and effort increase exponentially, not linearly, the further the vision moves away from your business. You should only move out of the environment of your current business if your current company concept, meaning your mission and the way you are fulfilling it, is existentially called into question.

According to Mihaly Csikszentmihalyi,[24] the feeling of happiness he called "flow" develops on the borderline between routine and challenge. It is said that goals and visions should be within our sights but beyond the reach of our mind (see Figure 7.4). There is a lot to be said for this image, we can see it, we can imagine it, but we do not yet know in detail what the road that will take us there looks like. A vision that demands too little of people is just as worthless as one that demands too much of people. The vision endangers the company's existence in both cases. If it demands too little, it doesn't activate the competitive performance potential, if it demands too much, people don't give it the required support.

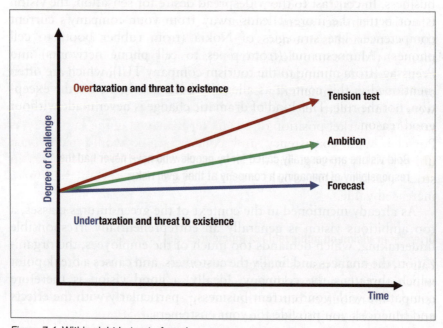

Figure 7.4 Within sight but out of reach

In practice, we observe that every team creates exactly the level of challenge that it feels capable of implementing. That is what we mean by a homeopathic degree of challenge. The more future-competent the team is, the more innovative and challenging the strategic vision can and will be. You can recognize the right degree of challenge by the fact that not only your management team but also all other employees see a big challenge, but one which can be mastered. The frequent fear of thinking too far or not far enough into the future is almost always shown to be unfounded.

Have the courage to set a conservative vision

We arrive at an interesting mental exercise with the question of how Daimler would be performing now if Edzard Reuter and Jürgen Schrempp had managed their company in the same way as Wendelin Wiedeking managed Porsche and had invested the billions they wasted in diversification and mergers (see the case studies earlier in the chapter) in the further development and marketing of their automobiles.

■ The most conservative vision can be the best one.

The admittedly spectacular story of Daimler, alias Daimler-Chrysler then once again Daimler AG, in any case clearly shows that the great vision is not necessarily the best one. Let's imagine for a moment that the many lost billions had only been focused on making every Mercedes branded automobile constantly a little better, safer and more environmentally friendly. If this company and this brand were able to relatively well withstand the capers of the last twenty years, the market position of a Daimler managed in the same way as Porsche, with consistency and concentration, would have been unimaginably strong. In addition, the several billion of losses in stock market value would probably have been several billion in increased value.

Orient your vision on achievable competences and resources

False modesty is just as wrong as the naive desire for sensation. The maximum to be achieved in the future is not limited by current competences and resources but by those competences and resources which are achievable for you based on your current situation.

Make your vision compatible with your history

Your strategic vision should be plausible against the background of the history of your life or your company. A person who has been reticent all his life has a huge challenge in front of him if he wants to become a party animal. It is no different with companies. Not that the past should colonize your future, but the history of a person or a group of people is the time in which values, personality and behavior were formed. All of this cannot simply be discarded and other values, personal characteristics and patterns of behavior be installed like an operating system. If that were possible, then millions of therapists, counselors and change agents would be unemployed. The overzealous modernizers, mostly rather young, always tend to underestimate the importance of history. Significantly, that has always been the case throughout history.

▪ The future needs and has a past.

Don't overload your customers with innovations

This circumstance is also an argument in favor of not designing your strategic vision as innovatively as possible and not regarding only the sensational as the real future. The Smart, the very small automobile based on Nikolaus Hayek's Swatch idea, came onto the market with a highly innovative integrated concept. Being able to park cross-wise in parking spaces and on trains, special spaces in car parks and the modular variability of the automobile itself were just a few of the ideas with which a completely new concept of mobility was supposed to be realized. It was obviously too much for the target group, although most of the ideas were ten or more years old. The fact that such projects are always about egoisms and politics between the partners, in this case between Hayek and Daimler, doesn't change the fact that the actual idea failed due to lack of customer acceptance. On the contrary, it indicates that a lot of other preconditions for success need to be created in addition to the recognition of opportunity.

The VW Lupo, the world's first three-liter mass-produced automobile was introduced to the driving public in 1999. Production stopped due to lack of success in 2005. Even if there were design and production errors, what really killed it was that there were not enough buyers for such an ascetic automobile. Hormones defeated innovation and sense. The majority of drivers didn't start to revise their thinking until 2007. Climate research with dramatic forecasts triggered a new understanding. A majority could suddenly imagine driving a smaller automobile with less power and making fewer air trips to help protect the environment.

In summary, it is advisable not to overestimate your customers' receptiveness to innovations and not to demand too much of them through your own desire for great leaps in innovation.

Make your vision as precise as necessary, as complex as required and as flexible as possible

The yellow futures glasses as the perspective for decisions on direction require a clear picture of the desired future. It must be described or drawn so exactly that the designated recipients are provided with a clear and unambiguous statement of direction and can clearly imagine the situation desired for the future. The vision should basically only include the things that can actually and need to be decided about for the period in question. A vision focused on the most decisive things can be communicated much more easily. We will call this the necessary accuracy. Only a few key points of the strategic vision need to be described so unambiguously for its achievement to be unambiguously proved. Argumentative evidence is sufficient to be able not only to interpretatively recognize but also to mark that the vision has been achieved. Measurability in the narrowest sense is not required, because it generally leads to single indicators being emphasized too strongly.

No one can know if through your values and your life circumstances, your customers, your employees, your competitors and whoever or whatever, you will have created new realities for tomorrow which require a different mission, vision and guidelines when looking through the yellow futures glasses. In consideration of the fact that the future can essentially not be predicted, a strategic vision, together with the mission and the strategic guidelines, needs to be free from details and focused on the essentials. If this is not the case, then the direction chosen becomes a fixed rudder with no possibility for correction in the midst of the storm of changing environments and markets. You need to be free to be able to change your vision and adapt it to new realities. That does not however mean that you can send your employees off in different directions every few months. It means that you need to keep adjusting and polishing your vision, but keep to the basic general direction for as long as possible.

A radical about-turn, if it is really necessary is always better than stubbornly keeping to a path you have set out on. Flexibility replaces foresight (see also page 116). A too detailed image of the desired future is detrimental to the necessary flexibility.

Clear and measurable goals in the sense of detailed planning should only be set for time periods within which an internal or external paradigm change is considered unlikely. This planning time frame (violet futures glasses) is nowadays one to a maximum of three years. It is often the internal rather than the external paradigm changes that make a vision inopportune. If the management changes, then the old vision tends not to appeal to the new bosses. Even the same managers need to throw their doctrines and the knowledge they have acquired overboard more frequently, thus the vision is threatened by mental starvation in these cases as well.

As opposed to complicatedness, which makes a vision opaque and difficult, complexity is a basic requirement of a strategic vision.[25] The term complexity stands for something connected, all encompassing, interlinking and whole. The view through the yellow futures glasses needs to show a holistic image of the future. Depth can also be understood as a desirable characteristic of a vision, if it means that a vision can have depth and intellectual content in the same way as a good painting or picture.[26]

> **The simultaneous demand for precision, complexity and flexibility contains a number of trade-offs and conflicts, which can never be totally solved.**

In practice, systematic discourse is necessary, which needs to be carried out on several vision candidates (green futures glasses) in view of an estimation of probable futures (blue futures glasses) in order to identify a version of the vision that is agreed to by the team and meets the requirements of assumed future developments.

Form the necessary differentiation with vision candidates

If you ask any board member where the company will be in five or eight years then you usually get a familiar answer, even if the board has just come back from several days' workshop. More quality, better customer relations, new markets, new technologies, a more future-oriented corporate culture, more profit and, of course, growth and market leadership is what they are striving for. If you ask the competition, you hear ... the same! The vision of even very professionally managed companies is too often just a series of obvious statements on quality, growth, profit and market leadership. Too many entrepreneurs and most managers have this standard future in mind because they view success in primarily short-term, financially oriented terms.

> *The natural cause of profit is having a head start.*
> (Joseph Schumpeter)

If the vision is the same as the competition's, then you are depriving yourself at a very early stage of the opportunity for an easily achievable lead. It is then no surprise that the viability or, put another way, the profit margin and earnings will at best remain below their potential and in the worst case point the way to ruin. Everyone knows that, and yet companies' visions are still mostly unbelievably boring and interchangeable.

The purpose of all strategic work is to positively differentiate your company long-term. At the point at which the foundation for strategies is laid, namely in the strategic vision, uniqueness is a *conditio sine qua non*. Where should the foundation for sustainable success be created if not here?

Differentiation develops from concrete commitment and decisions. Your strategic vision will be unique and original if you connect two differentiating factors and take two quality assurance factors into consideration:

1. the variety of vision candidates (see the example of vision candidates for banks in Table 6.2)

2. the agreement of the management team in the sense of congruence of the vision candidates with the individual visions of the managers

3. the meaningfulness of the vision candidates with regard to the assumptions on future developments elaborated with the blue futures glasses

4. the robustness of vision candidates against the possible strategic surprises in the market.

> Working with vision candidates makes it possible to have several alternative vision drafts competing against each other for the team's emotional and rational agreement in a quasi-evolutionary process.

A vision candidate is the rough draft of a strategic vision. Anyone who wants to go into the future on a relatively sure footing needs to be able to imagine his company in more than one vision. As in evolution, the number and the variety of vision candidates and selection criteria are practically the guarantee for a rare, maybe even unique strategic vision.[27] A range of three to ten vision candidates makes it possible, or at least significantly easier to:

- be able to imagine significantly more different futures
- think of the possible directions in alternative strategic visions with a considerably wider horizon compared to the standard future
- really make a choice and a decision *against* many and *for* one strategic vision (or a combination of vision candidates)
- in this way find and define a strategic vision which is unique in your environment.

The higher the organizational level, the more general your results for the yellow futures glasses will be

Every task in future management is subject to this principle. If you only manage yourself, then it is very easy for you, if not also psychologically then at least methodologically. If you manage a team, then the vision will already be a compromise. A medium size company with one area of business already needs to consider dozens of interests and views of the world. Harley Davidson's five guidelines[28] could just as easily come from a small Mexican savings bank:

1. We speak the truth.
2. We keep our promises.
3. We are fair.
4. We respect the individual.
5. We promote curiosity.

They don't describe a vision, but cultural guidelines. In total, they could be a model, but quite obviously not a strategic vision.

The highest level of generality has been reached when someone wants to use the yellow futures glasses to provide a normative constitution for a corporation with a high number of business areas. A common vision is nowhere to be seen. This is shown by BASF's strategic guidelines:[29]

1. We earn a premium on our cost of capital.

2. We help our customers to be more successful. In order to grow profitably, we intend to be even more attuned to the needs of our customers in future and to apply the best business model for them and for us in each case.

3. We form the best team in the industry. The employees are the most important factor in BASF's success. It's down to them: their ability, their ideas, their experience and their enthusiasm.

4. We do business in a sustainable way for a future worth living in. By sustainable development we mean connecting economic success with environmental protection and social responsibility.

Your strategic vision is a periodic prototype

As the future cannot be predicted, every new day brings a changed view of the probable future seen with the blue futures glasses. A strategic vision therefore needs to be regularly monitored, corrected and expanded. Although a strategic vision should be as irrevocable as possible, a vision is generally so many years away from the present that a certain need for change is more or less incorporated from the beginning. Why do your earlier letters and texts sometimes appear alien to you? Because you have changed in the meantime, because you have learned and forgotten things in the force field between your interests and the environmental influences. Things become imaginable which were previously considered impossible and former hopes proved to be utopian.

The strategic vision, the strategic guidelines and, considerably less often the mission, need periodic prototyping in practice. A vision whose fundaments are brought into doubt spreads uncertainty and derision. Radical about-turns are rarely necessary. Partial changes are often sufficient for the vision to fulfill its function as an illuminating beacon again.

What is decisive is not the achievement of your vision, but its effect on the present

If the strategic vision is a periodic prototype, meaning that the beacon is regularly placed somewhere else, then the final achievement of the vision is not a suitable measurement of success. What is crucial is the effect the strategic vision unfolds on your present by providing you and your fellow colleagues or your employees with orientation and meaning. Even if you look at your reality ten years later and compare it with the vision you developed ten years earlier and discover very few similarities, the vision can still have completely fulfilled its purpose. There are two reasons for this that may seem a little strange at first sight:

1. We cannot act in the future, but only in the present. The quality of a vision therefore has to be measured by its effect on the present. If the vision has remained more or less constant over ten years, then that is a welcome state of affairs, but it is not a flaw or an error if the vision is a completely different one after ten years than it was at the beginning of the journey.

2. A vision needs to be in the distance, it needs to be within our sights, yet out of reach, it needs to signify a certain degree of challenge. The vision tends to continually lose its power of attraction the nearer we get to it, until it is finally not ten years away, but with the same wording only three years away. Its content might still be meaningful, but it will very likely have lost most of its degree of challenge. You therefore need to set a new vision long before you have achieved it, the fulfillment of the vision can thus not be the goal.

Methodology checklists

This section describes the steps involved in applying the yellow futures glasses and links the sections above with instructions for action. The detailed checklist for companies is followed by the easier checklist for life entrepreneurs. The method checklist is designed for future management experts.

Procedure for companies

1. **Carry out vision development with your team** after having looked through the blue and green futures glasses.

2. **Use the blue futures glasses to make yourself aware of your assumptions about the future.** Your vision needs to be in harmony with your assumptions about the future development of your environment.

3. **Determine the time horizon of your vision.** As already stated in the checklist for the blue futures glasses, you can use the following rule of thumb: the length of time required for the development of a field of business from the idea to first earnings, multiplied by two. In most cases, ten years is a good approach.

4. **Determine the vision questions** using the instructions and the examples in Table 7.3.
5. **Develop or review your mission** as described on page 179. Changes to the mission are only made if really necessary and generally only in exceptional cases. The mission determines the field in which the vision is developed. It is provisional in as far as it needs to be reviewed and consolidated at a later stage by the red futures glasses.
6. **Develop vision candidates.** The meaning of vision candidates is explained on page 200. Table 6.2 provides an example of vision candidates that could be used in retail banking. We would recommend that you do not follow the usual path and develop a single vision at the beginning, but first draw up different candidates. The section on the principles of the yellow futures glasses provides the necessary knowledge for vision development. If you would like to develop the vision candidates in a detailed structure, then morphology is a useful method. It is comparable to a menu that has three options each for starter, main course and dessert and thus provides a total of 27 possible menus.
    (a) Write your visions questions in the first column of a matrix. The other columns are headed option 1, 2, 3 and so on.
    (b) Make a note of the imaginable and meaningful vision elements (answer possibilities) for each vision question in the others.
    (c) Prioritize the alternatives in every line by dividing 100 points across the existing alternatives.
    (d) Now determine the vision candidates by identifying the combination of vision elements with the highest number of points by selecting one vision element from every line. Write the combinations in a list starting with the highest number.
    (e) Delete those vision candidates that contain meaningless or impossible combinations of vision elements, for example your company's highest efficiency and greatest flexibility.
    (f) Select between three and eight plausible and attractive vision candidates for further processing.
7. **Evaluate your vision candidates.** Various evaluation methods are available which are all essentially based on comparing vision candidates on the degree to which they meet certain criteria. Choose one of the following methods which are listed in ascending order of complexity:

(a) A simple discussion with pro and contra arguments recorded in writing
(b) Weighted pro and contra lists
(c) Scoring procedures using several criteria
(d) Paired comparison using several criteria also known as analytic hierarchy process according to Saaty.[30]

8. **Determine the core of your strategic vision.** The obvious core of your strategic vision is the vision candidate with the highest score. In practice, it is often combined with individual aspects and vision elements from vision candidates with a lower score. Although this may seem inconsistent at first sight, it does lead to further individualization of the strategic vision. In addition, subsequently including further additional aspects increases the acceptance of the vision by those decision-makers who would have preferred other vision candidates.

9. **Expand your strategic vision.** The vision questions in Table 7.3 show a possible structure for the content of a strategic vision.

10. **Determine your strategic guidelines.** Based on your evaluated future opportunities with guideline character, determine the rules and "strategic laws" you want to apply on your way to your strategic vision. Use the description on page 180 to help you.

11. **Make sure your vision is consistent.** The present is not without contradiction either: however, the statements in your strategic vision should not blatantly contradict each other. Draw up a matrix with which you can connect each vision element with the others, systematically identify contradictions and subsequently resolve them.

12. **Review your vision using the assumptions about the future.** Compare every sentence in the mission, vision and guidelines with your assumptions about the future. This works best with a matrix, in which the elements of the mission, the vision and the guidelines are entered in lines and linked with the assumptions about the future entered in columns (or vice-versa). This structure makes it easier for you to recognize potential conflicts and subsequently resolve them by changing the vision elements.

13. **Review your vision using the surprises.** You should use the same structure that you used to compare the vision elements with the assumptions about the future to align the surprises that you

identified with the red futures glasses. More information on the methodology of the red futures glasses can be found on pages 120 onwards.

14. **Carry out a values reconciliation.** You don't have to actually specifically go through this stage as your future team's values have flowed into the discussion and evaluation process anyway. The value aspect is only mentioned here for the sake of completeness.

15. **Discuss the strategic vision (with mission and guidelines) with employees and other people.** As already explained in the section on attitude and principles, the development of the vision is the management's job: at the same time, it is essential that the vision is carried and regularly reviewed in many hearts and minds.

16. **Summarize the core of your vision in one sentence.** This creates a mental anchor in the consciousness of all participants. Good examples – purely methodically, not necessarily filled with content – are the German President Horst Köhler's vision of a "country of ideas", Mao Zedong's "great leap forward", Herman Sörge's "Atlantropa" or Edzard Reutter's vision of Daimler-Benz as an "integrated technology corporation". It is not always possible to express such a complex futures image in one sentence or buzzword. It is never easy. The final alternative is then the format [company + year], IBM 2020 for example.

17. **Visualize your vision.** Make it easier for you and others to communicate about your vision and support the constant reminder of it using the examples on page 184 ff. Another alternative is to use photos and other pictures from specialized databases.

18. **Implement the strategic vision.** Use the strategic vision, the guidelines and the mission in daily business. They should then always form the preamble and the framework for major decisions.

Procedure for life entrepreneurs

The strategic vision is much easier for you as a life entrepreneur, at least as far as the methodology is concerned. If you are primarily interested in a life vision based on your career, then you can in principle follow the steps above. If you are concerned with a more general life vision, then you can develop it using a simple but important question: what more do I want to experience in my life? Figure 7.5 shows a structure that can be used to answer this vision question. The table of course contains examples from several fictional lives.

Year	2015	2020	2025	2030
Age	40	45	50	60 +
Job and finance	■ Start my own company ■ Have no debts ■ Achieve financial independence	■ Welcome 1,000 visitors to an exhibition of my sculptures ■ Start a radio station	■ Only work six months a year ■ Make a speech to 10,000 people ■ Become Chairman of the Board	■ Meet the head of Government ■ Become head of Government ■ Register a patent
Leisure time and pleasure	■ Be able to play the piano ■ Come across lions roaming free on a safari ■ Meet a hammerhead shark whilst diving	■ Buy and restore a sailing boat ■ Travel to Istanbul with the Orient-Express	■ Stay at the Luxor in Las Vegas ■ Sail round Cape Horn ■ Own a horse	■ Secretly climb Ayers Rock ■ Travel the Panamericana
Family, friends and society	■ Start a son and a daughter off on a fulfilled life ■ Have a rewarding personal relationship	■ Start a foundation to support starving children	■ Celebrate my silver wedding anniversary ■ Help to reintegrate ten homeless people	■ Celebrate my 80th birthday with my best friends A and B
Mind and knowledge	■ Travel through India ■ Learn to be quick-witted ■ Climb Mount Everest	■ See the earth from outer space ■ Achieve a black belt in karate	■ Write a book ■ Live for one month on each continent ■ See the Taj Mahal	■ Live with a group of primitive people for a month ■ Complete a degree in philosophy
Body and soul	■ Own a country manor ■ Achieve a BMI (body mass index) of 23	■ Take a year out ■ Conquer my illness	■ Run a marathon ■ Take part in/win an Iron-Man	■ Live in the sun all year round ■ Live to be 100

Figure 7.5 Personal life vision (examples)

The procedure suggested in the table will not necessarily result in a consistent picture of a desired future. It is more of a structured wish list than a strategic vision with real strategic life decisions. You thus give yourself the flexibility that a modern life in the present and foreseeable future requires.

> *Someone who knows nothing about the goal, cannot have the road to it and will keep going round in the same circle all his life.*
> (Christian Morgenstern)

The following steps provide a methodological happy medium between this very simple approach and the procedure for companies:

1. Ask your vision questions. You can derive them from the life areas in the illustration.

2. Proceed with developing your vision candidates using the morphological matrix as described above for companies.

3. Determine three vision candidates that appear most attractive to you.

4. Evaluate your vision candidates using paired comparison, using the following two criteria for example:
   (a) How attracted am I to it?
   (b) How well does this vision candidate fit with my assumptions about the future (blue futures glasses)?

5. Determine the vision candidate and develop it into a cohesive picture of your desired future.

6. Visualize your vision with your own drawings or photo collage on paper or in file form.

7. Align your vision to your assumptions about the future (blue futures glasses).

8. Align your vision to the potential surprises (red futures glasses).

9. Discuss your vision with your partner, good friends or other "stakeholders".

10. Ensure that you regularly see your vision, either by storing it as a file on your desktop or by hanging it up in your bathroom. The latter has the advantage, or disadvantage, that those living with you will measure your progress.

Checklist of methods and techniques

The method checklist for future management professionals provides information on how you can enrich and improve your work with the yellow futures glasses.

Professional checklist:
Methods for the yellow futures glasses and suggested literature
(see Bibliography)

Developing vision questions
- Critical success factors (Rockart, 1979)
- Comprehensive situation mapping (CSM) (Georgantzas and Acar, 1995)
- Vision questions / Delphi (Mićić, 2006)

Developing or reviewing the mission
- Structured discussion
- Internal Delphi (Helmer, 1983)
- Analytic hierarchy process (Saaty, 1996)

Developing vision candidates
- Creative imagery (May, 1996)
- Personal visioning or group visioning (May, 1996)
- Mind mapping (Buzan, 2006)
- Participant interviews (external and internal)
- Morphology (Glenn and Gordon, 2003; Godet, 1994)
- Field anomaly relaxation (Coyle, 2003; Rhyne, 1981)
- Retrograde success report (Mićić, 2003)

Evaluating vision candidates
- Structured discussion with pro and contra arguments
- Scoring procedures
- Analytic hierarchy process (Saaty, 1996)
- Multiple perspective concept (Linstone, 2003)

Determining the core of the vision
- Analytic hierarchy process (Saaty, 1996)
- Multiple perspective concept (Linstone, 2003)

Developing strategic guidelines
- Morphology (Glenn and Gordon, 2003)
- Internal Delphi (Helmer, 1983)
- Analytic hierarchy process (Saaty, 1996)
- Strategic conversation (van der Heijden, 1996)

Professional checklist (cont'd)

Ensuring completeness, correctness and consistency
- Matrix for linking the vision elements with each other
- Matrix for linking the vision elements with assumptions about the future
- Matrix for linking the vision elements with surprises

Presenting results
- Text, structured or prosaic
- Diagrams, charts and mind maps
- Drawings
- Film and animation
- Play acting

8 Your violet futures glasses: What are you planning to do?

The crew on the windjammer needs a plan in order to be able to achieve the vision they are aiming for through practical action. The plan must include goals, projects, processes and systems, together with guidelines for their daily work. In the analogy of the captain, we associated the violet color of the appropriate glasses with the color of bruises, which are more or less inevitable when working on a ship.

In connection with the future, we generally first think about forecasts, meaning the blue futures glasses in the widest sense, and then secondly about planning. That is what you need the violet futures glasses for. From the things that are perceived as being fundamentally imaginable and essentially doable with the green futures glasses, you select what you really desire with the yellow futures glasses and then plan the necessary actions for realizing the vision with the violet futures glasses.

> The violet futures glasses are the ones that entrepreneurs and managers wear in their daily business. Unfortunately, they generally forget that they can only meaningfully wear them, if they have previously seen the future through the other four glasses.

The reverse is also true, that looking at the future is only of artistic and entertaining value if the main results are not transformed into concrete plans and actions. How many enthusiastically developed visions and strategies have fizzled out, been forgotten or failed in daily business life? You need the violet futures glasses to make your futures strategy complete. Future management can only lead to success with the commitment of goals, processes, projects and systems in your daily business.

A lot has already been thought and said about the violet futures glasses in connection with other things. Just think of the following areas:

- project management
- strategic planning
- operative planning (balanced scorecards and so on)

- critical path analysis
- time management.

Because the violet futures glasses provide a view of the future that is well known to and used by entrepreneurs, leaders and managers, we will concentrate on the essential characteristics within the framework of our model here. The violet futures glasses fulfill two main functions:

1. They ensure that the strategic vision is achieved within the frame of the mission and the strategic guidelines.
2. They help to develop and implement eventual strategies as a response to potential surprises.

Your violet futures glasses: Overview

Table 8.1 summarizes the characteristics of the violet futures glasses.

Table 8.1 The violet futures glasses: Overview

Objective: To determine the futures strategy, which as part of the mission, leads to the realization of the strategic vision, taking the strategic guidelines into consideration.

Work step and key question:
- Strategy development
- How should we design our futures strategy as the path to our vision?

Purpose:
- You increase the probability and degree of success.
- You form orientation and responsibility in your daily business.
- You improve your efficiency by concentrating your efforts.
- You form values.
- You enable regular monitoring of your success.

Principles:
- Strategic goals are the mid-term stages on the path to the vision.
- Base strategic goals on the analysis of the future of the environment.
- Create flexibility towards strategy elements that arise.
- Guarantee robustness against surprises.
- Support by a critical number of actors within the organization.
- Support the strategy through systems and resources.
- Create space for actions.
- Use meaningful measurements for goals.
- Goals need to be important to the subconscious, not the conscious.
- The results of the violet futures glasses should be documented.

Table 8.1 (cont'd)

Attitude:
- Focus on achieving a promising and advantageous position.
- Concentrate on challenging and achievable goals.
- Concentrate on the essentials.
- Be enthusiastic about your goals.

Core concepts involved:
- Strategy
- Goals
- Projects
- Processes
- Systems
- Eventual strategies
- Developing opportunities

Typical methods:
- Planning
- Roadmapping
- Project management
- Time management

Procedure:
1. Determine the strategy questions.
2. Derive your strategic goals from the first part of your futures strategy.
3. Determine the developing opportunities.
4. Derive projects, processes and systems.
5. Integrate eventual strategies.
6. Review your futures strategy using your assumptions about the future.
7. Summarize the futures strategy in a sentence or term.
8. Check that your strategic vision can actually be achieved.

Results:
A consistent futures strategy which leads in an efficient way to the realization of the strategic vision and which has measurable goals, projects, processes, systems, developing opportunities and eventual strategies.

Case studies on the violet futures glasses

As these are the standard futures glasses for entrepreneurs and managers there are numerous examples of their use; typical examples are described below.

From the vision via the goal to the project, process and system

We will use a major Swiss consumer goods producer as an example here. Its procedure corresponds to the well-established method of breaking a vision down into goals that in turn are broken down into projects, processes and supporting systems.

Around the millennium, the company's management team used the yellow futures glasses to develop the strategic vision of transforming the company from a producer for the domestic market only, into a Europe-wide developer of private labels. The cornerstones of the strategic vision were internationalization and a focus on providing solutions rather than production. Goals were determined for interim stages. Among other things, the unit cost was to be reduced by thirty percent within three years and an export team built up.

The company thus planned the individual steps to be taken, some immediately, some in the coming years on the long road to the strategic vision. This had a series of positive effects. For one thing, the vision became more tangible, as it was easy to recognize if and how it would be achieved. For another, deviations could be seen more quickly and appropriate actions therefore taken earlier.

This breaking-down process can also be referred to as roadmapping, although roadmapping largely belongs to the blue futures glasses. Others refer to the central activity of the violet futures glasses as a "Strategy Map"[1] or "Transformation Map".

Business plans are developed with the violet futures glasses

Successful business startups are usually based on early perception of an attractive future opportunity and the dominance of the founder's vision. These two things are basic preconditions for success in a startup. Yet an implementation plan is essential to successfully build a business. A business plan with the violet futures glasses shows how the vision can be turned into marketable performance with successful sales and marketing and an efficient organization and how sufficient profit can be generated.

Planning the future in a business plan serves as the acid test for the business model. It is furthermore an important means of communication in negotiating with financiers, business partners and suppliers. Monitoring and managing ongoing performance can only be achieved through such planning.

Tuvalu develops a plan for evacuation due to climate change

The North Pole could be completely free of ice within a few decades. If sea level rises as a result of climate change, the existence of some Pacific archipelagic states is threatened. The future assumption of the government of Tuvalu, a small state with 11,000 inhabitants, whose highest point is only five meters above sea level, should therefore be that their country will sink. Tuvalu has entered into an agreement with New Zealand: seventy-five inhabitants are admitted each year, but only those who can prove that they have a certain income. Australia rejected such an agreement and therefore refused to admit the Tuvalu people. There is also a plan to relocate all inhabitants to the Fiji island of Kioa. The Tuvalu government wants the industrialized nations to bear the costs of these measures, as they are the ones who caused climate change.[2]

McDonald's becomes more flexible through a supply chain solution

When the BSE scandal (mad cow disease) was at its peak, McDonald's was already long prepared for such a surprise. Supply chains are highly sensitive as a result of the so-called bullwhip effect. With the bullwhip effect, the effects of the smallest variations in sales are amplified up the supply chain to the suppliers. Thanks to the early development and implementation of a special supply chain management system, McDonald's only needed four days to adjust the supply chain after demand for beef collapsed as a result of the BSE scandal.

Trier prepares for possible surprises

The city of Trier not only developed a strategic vision, but also safeguarded itself against potential surprises. The core elements of the vision are maintaining the population at 100,000 inhabitants and pursuing close integration and cooperation with neighboring Luxemburg, which is expected to prosper in the foreseeable future. Table 8.2 shows some of the potential surprises developed and analyzed together with their appropriate eventual strategies. Both the surprises and the eventual strategies are only a selection and have been reproduced in a shortened form. Since this is public it can be used here as an example.

Many of the eventual strategies have led to the strategic vision being reworked and improved and made more robust against potential surprises in the future.

Table 8.2 Eventual strategies for the city of Trier

Surprise	Eventual strategies (excerpts)
Luxemburg suddenly rejects close cooperation.	■ Show the win–win advantages of a cooperation from the very beginning with regard to the employment market, the living situation and further fields of action and support them with implied action ■ Enter into stronger cooperations with other municipalities in the region and neighboring countries
The population threatens to decline from 100,000 to 75,000.	■ Prepare a plan to scale Trier back in favor of parks and open spaces ■ Prepare a program to considerably strengthen activities to attract new citizens
Most citizens are not willing to take on civil responsibility.	■ If the financial situation is difficult: organize the community on a greater need-based approach, i.e. do less as an administration ■ If the financial situation is good: add tasks to the community, i.e. do more as an administration ■ Start to form qualitative incentives to reward civil responsibility
Trier is threatened with above-average aging. More than half the population are over 60.	■ Think in advance of a concept for a program with active "rejuvenation measures" ■ React if and when the situation occurs
Radical downsizing of the social network.	■ Start to promote voluntary civil responsibility through qualitative incentives (see above) ■ Develop a concept to attract financially well-situated seniors to balance out the financial situation and needs of the older people in Trier (as done in Constance for example)
The number of people in employment in Trier falls dramatically and income from taxes is reduced to 30 percent.	■ Start to concentrate on the really indispensable tasks ■ Start to qualify Trier as a place of residence for Luxemburg
Political change in Trier.	■ Include the city council closely in the futures strategies as already happens

Purpose of the violet futures glasses

The violet futures glasses, the planning and strategy glasses, are based on the results of the other four futures glasses. The results of the blue and red futures glasses provide the future analysis of the environment and the green futures glasses the material from which the yellow futures glasses then form the strategic vision. Finally, the violet futures glasses ensure that this knowledge is transformed into planned action. With the violet futures glasses you are on your way to the desirable future that you determined using the yellow futures glasses. At the same time, you safeguard yourself against surprises that you perceived with the red futures glasses.

You form an interface to strategic planning

The violet futures glasses build the left side of the bridge from strategic management to futures research and back again as described in the "Future management" section of Chapter 2. The violet futures glasses are related to strategic management in their characteristics.

By planning your activities and resources, you bring the vision into your daily business

With the violet futures glasses of strategy development, you break the yellow futures glasses' desirable future down into manageable action. How many visions, developed with great enthusiasm, have failed thanks to business routine? Even if it is a really good common vision, daily business often soaks up all your attention and causes the vision and the strategy to disappear from your consciousness.

> The violet futures glasses combine the knowledge gained with the other four futures glasses into an organized system of planned action in your daily business.

You embed responsibility in your daily routine

With the violet futures glasses, you develop your company's strategy by determining binding strategic goals, projects, processes and systems to achieve your vision step by step. Employees and managers taking personal responsibility for the achievement of their individual goals creates commitment to the implementation of the strategy.

You increase the probability and degree of your success

The fundamental aim behind the development, implementation and pursuit of a strategy is to increase the success of a person, a company or an organization. Without a strategy developed and implemented using the violet futures glasses, the probability and degree of success are ultimately left to chance.

> It is only through planned action that a vision can be acheived with an acceptably high probability.

You increase your efficiency by concentrating your efforts

A strategy focuses money, time and minds, in other words your most important resources, onto the activities and factors decisive for success, which all aim in the direction of the strategic vision and therefore ensure effectiveness and efficiency. Using the violet futures glasses, all goals, projects, processes and systems are directed towards achieving the vision, taking the guidelines into consideration. The strategy provides an organization with the direction it needs to become more efficient. With regard to efficiency therefore, a vision and a strategy have a value even if they turn out to be less than optimal or even wrong.

You enable success monitoring and navigation towards your goals

By establishing intermediate goals on the way to your strategic vision, you can regularly check whether and to what extent you are going in the right direction. As a result, you make it easier to navigate towards your goals by supportive and corrective measures.

You safeguard your futures strategy and your existence

The red futures glasses show that and how the future can surprise you. The violet futures glasses are there to protect your futures strategy and ultimately your economic existence against the most important surprises. You develop eventual strategies for this purpose, which you either implement immediately as preventive strategies or as acute strategies that you prepare for implementation if the surprise actually occurs.

Core concepts of the violet futures glasses

The violet futures glasses are concerned with strategy and planning. The word strategy comes from the Greek terms *stratus* (army, something comprehensive or superior) and *agein* or *igo* (lead, act).

Together, they refer to either the art of war or the art of leadership and comprehensive action.[3] In recent years, "strategic" has been used for everything long-term or simply for everything that is important. The term plan comes from the French and only appeared in the 18th century. Even though the violet futures glasses are characterized by the planned future, we will leave plans out of the core concepts, as the term is too general.

What exactly strategy and planning are has been a popular topic with management practitioners and theorists since the 1950s. There are several dozen definitions of the concept of strategy alone. Some people are even in favor of stopping trying to provide a definition of the complex term strategy.[4] However, at this stage we want to provide a basic understanding for use in practice (see Figure 8.1).

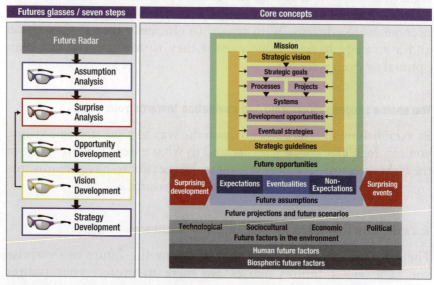

Figure 8.1 The violet futures glasses and their core concepts

Strategy and futures strategy

Figure 8.2 shows four possible ways of understanding the term strategy, which make clear at a fundamental level, how strategy and thus planning can be understood in various ways:

- *First understanding:* Strategy refers to activities in the pursuit of long-term goals.

- *Second understanding:* Strategy also refers to the setting of long-term goals.
- *Third understanding:* Strategy additionally refers to the setting of a mission, vision and guidelines.
- *Fourth understanding:* Strategy additionally refers to anticipating futures.

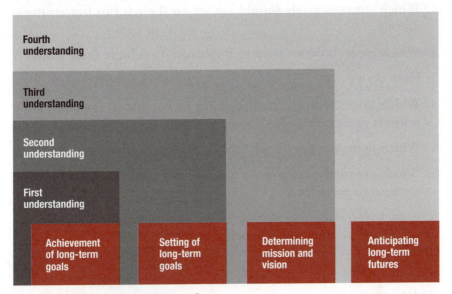

Figure 8.2 Understandings of "strategy"

We suggest two definitions within the framework of the five futures glasses and the *Eltville Model*. The strategy is the result of the violet futures glasses.

> Strategy is the totality of decisions, guidelines and activities for setting and pursuing long-term goals.

The futures strategy is the combined result of all five futures glasses.

> Futures strategy is the totality of the core concepts that are necessary for anticipating the future, the setting of mission, vision and guidelines and for setting and pursuing long-term goals.

Strategy questions

> You use strategy questions to determine the fundamental things you need to know and to decide about the best way to achieve the mission and vision within the framework of the guidelines.

The strategy questions are just as numerous and varied as the violet futures glasses' core concepts:

1. Which strategic goals should we set on the road to our strategic vision?
2. Which projects do we need to implement to achieve these goals?
3. How do we need to design processes to achieve these goals?
4. Which systems do we need to have to be able to implement the projects and processes?
5. Which opportunities do we need to develop further?
6. Which eventual strategies do we need to implement and which do we need to prepare?

In principle, you could also use the violet futures glasses to ask questions about necessary and supporting strategic guidelines. The characteristics of the yellow and the violet futures glasses touch at this point.

Strategic goals

We will have built up a new business in optoelectronics by the end of next year. This could be the strategic goal of a management team. Strategic goals are of particular importance in the perspective of the violet futures glasses because they form the link between the vision and daily business. We define strategic goals as follows:

> A strategic goal is the desired state of a field of action that is defined clearly according to its characteristics and to the point in time.

What is more or less common knowledge is summarized here for the *Eltville Model*:

1. *Name of the goal:* A goal needs to describe in one sentence (as above) the desired state at the point in time in the future concerned.

2. *Measurement criteria:* It must be totally clear how you would recognize that you have achieved the goal.

3. *Image of the goal:* Ideally, the goal can be visualized as an image.

4. *Path to the goal:* Determining the basic path that will be taken to achieve the goal is part of the description of the goal.

5. *Resources:* Goals can only be achieved using resources.

6. *Goal manager:* Every goal needs a person who keeps it to the forefront of management's attention with passion, know-how and resoluteness and thus drives it forward.

Additional core concepts

The additional core concepts of the violet glasses are relatively well-known terms that, at least for practical application, do not require detailed explanation:

1. *Process:* Regular sequence of tasks and activities to achieve a goal or result in the value chain. Example: the operation of quality management.

2. *Project:* Once-only sequence of tasks and activities to achieve a goal. Example: the introduction of quality management.

3. *System:* A device or facility for supporting processes and projects. Example: a quality management system. The term system comprises all material and immaterial resources and tools.

4. *Developing opportunity:* Highly rated future opportunities that cannot yet be part of the futures strategy, because their value and their achievability are not yet clear. Example: *We could introduce an automatic competitor intelligence system, but don't know if such systems really provide meaningful information.*

5. *Eventual strategy:* Possible measures that can be carried out in the case that surprises (unexpected events and developments) and significant changes to the assumptions about the future occur. Example: *Should a substitute technology appear on the market, we will change to technology X.*

Attitude and principles of the violet futures glasses

The violet futures glasses require a realistic, pragmatic and analytical attitude. Your experience is valuable because you can decide and act more intuitively und thus more quickly using it. To a certain extent, the violet futures glasses also describe progressive thinking

> The violet futures glasses transform your current reality into a reality you desire in the future.

Using the violet futures glasses, you look at your world from a micro perspective and turn your attention inwards. You are an involved, active and intervening driver of what is happening.

Notice the relationship to the yellow futures glasses

A whole series of attitudes and principles of the yellow futures glasses (see Chapter 7) are also valid in a certain way for the violet futures glasses, although these do however place more emphasis on planning and executing the action towards the desired future. The following sections make the relationship between the attitudes and principles clear.

The quality of your strategy determines the quality of your future[5]

The quality of your strategy and plans is not the only factor influencing the quality of your future and your present, but, after the vision, it is one of the most important factors. With the violet futures glasses, you determine where you want to focus your scarcest resource, your attention. The rule could be: *Show me your goals and I will tell you your future*. Visionary and ambitious goals form fantastic futures. Purely extrapolatory goals form modest futures.

> *What I experience is what I have decided to focus my attention on.*
> (William James)

Backcast based on your vision

The goals, projects, processes and systems that you develop with the violet futures glasses must always lead towards the vision. The violet futures glasses are related to the yellow lead ones. Both strive towards a desired future. Whereas the yellow futures glasses are primarily used for the visionary and normative decisions on direction, the violet futures glasses follow the goal of finding pragmatic and practicable ways of realizing the vision.

Do *not* put the financials right at the top

Norton and Kaplan put well-known concepts into two catchy and marketable names: Balanced Scorecard[6] and Strategy Map.[7] The financial perspective tends to be at the top of the chain of goals. Shareholder-value or profit appears as a *causa finalis*, as the most important thing. However, we view profit as the result, not the goal.

> You will find it difficult to motivate people with turnover and profit growth, and almost impossible with balance sheet figures.

Concentrate on gaps and -surpluses

Together with the mission, vision and guidelines, the yellow futures glasses provide the model for the future. As already recommended with the yellow futures glasses, you can mentally place this image over your current reality and thus recognize where the strategic gaps are that you need to fill and where you need to reduce strategic surpluses. The "gap analysis" creates clarity about the results to be achieved, if not about the activities that need to be planned and implemented. The goals will become clear, yet they can be achieved in many different ways.

Be clear about the goals

Your goals need to be described so concretely and unambiguously, that there is no doubt, at least at the beginning, that they can be achieved. We don't mean the wishy-washy goals usually formulated in millions of companies. To improve a product is not a goal, but a process. To be rid of a competitor is not a goal, because it is directed against someone else, and its achievement is largely beyond our power. To become established in a market is not a goal, because it isn't clear what "become established in a market" exactly means. However, if we determine that by the end of the next financial year we will have gained 25,000 new customers, each with a minimum turnover of 1,200 Euros, then that is a clear goal.

> As soon as the mind is directed towards a goal, much comes towards it. (Johann Wolfgang von Goethe)

Setting a goal means not setting ten other goals

Determining the mission, the vision and the strategic guidelines makes the selection of the goals much easier. After all, only those goals that serve the realization of the strategic vision can be set in this framework. Nevertheless, many roads lead to the vision and the roads can be taken in different ways. Concentrate on the essential. Someone who has great goals doesn't let himself be diverted by insignificant things and doesn't get worked up about trivia.

■ The art of strategy is often to say what you do not want to do anymore.

Differentiate between strategic goals and routine business goals

Surely customer satisfaction can't not be a goal this year, many an employee will exclaim in outrage when his goals are being discussed. The misunderstanding can be quickly clarified if you agree that there are routine business goals, which are always valid, and strategic goals that are to be particularly focused on by the management and all employees in the time period concerned.

Get the support of key actors

The written strategy alone does not achieve much. You can multiply the number of actors in your organization who really know the strategy by their position in the hierarchy and their influence on other members of the organization. The higher an actor's hierarchical level, the stronger the influence of his support will be for the strategy's chance of success. This does, of course, work in both directions. An unruly temporary employee obviously creates less damage than a member of the board who opposes the strategy.

First think of the strategy and then the structure

"Structure follows strategy", is Chandler's old rule.[8] Every material thing in your company, that is, buildings, plant, machines, equipment, and furniture, and all the systems you operate, from the organizational chart or the process model to the job descriptions, need to be in accordance with the strategy, which in turn is oriented towards the mission and vision. This sequence is valid for thinking, but not for action as the following principle shows.

> Structure follows strategy where thinking is concerned, but strategy follows structure where action is concerned.

First form the structures and the resources before you implement the strategy

Whereas the strategy has priority in thinking, the structure needs to take first place where action is concerned. A strategy cannot be effective without the structures, processes and resources necessary for its implementation. Against this background, it can be right to first start changing the structures, as long as these changes are based on a clear strategy.

Summarize all activities in *one* strategy

What seems so obvious in theory is generally not obeyed in practice. There are sometimes several strategies and catalogs of measures that are all valid and that are being followed in parallel. You need a comprehensive schedule of goals, projects, processes and systems, regardless of whether this is called a master plan, strategy map or roadmap. If a management team cannot achieve this then, seen objectively, its right to exist is in question.

Choose the optimum degree of challenge

It is well known that people perform suboptimally if they are either not challenged enough or challenged too much. Happiness researchers report that this is also true of their satisfaction. Find out step-by-step the amount of challenge which you personally and, above all, your colleagues and employees need to drive them to best performance and satisfaction. The degree of challenge is determined by two things: first, by the difference between the current and future desired competence and second, by the difference between the current reality and desired reality.

Balance efficiency and flexibility

We have already mentioned the rule "flexibility replaces foresight" a few times. Your company is most vulnerable where you sacrifice most flexibility in favor of efficiency. If you have the choice, choose the option with the lowest flexibility sacrifice, even if it costs more.

■ Get used to paying for flexibility.

Be open to strategy elements that arise

How often have you experienced a developed and agreed strategy being implemented in detail? Henry Mintzberg[9] pointed out that every strategy, however carefully, comprehensively and intelligently it has been developed, can be divided into realized and not-realized strategy and that the strategy that is finally actually realized only consists in part of the planned strategy and to a not insignificant part of unplanned and "emerging" strategy (see Figure 8.3). It is realistic and advisable to assume that this will always also apply to every strategy you develop.

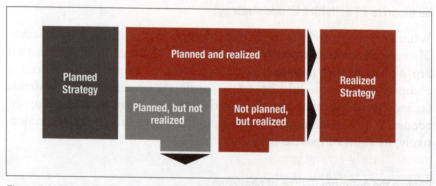

Figure 8.3 Planned and realized strategy (Mintzberg, 1994)

Learn from mistakes

Although the planned strategy hardly ever corresponds to the realized strategy, the planning and setting of goals as a means to compare planned results with achieved results is a well-known fruitful feedback system.

■ Planning replaces coincidence with mistakes, yet you can learn more from mistakes than from coincidences.

Maximize the congruence of individual and common goals

With the violet futures glasses, you face the great challenge of setting goals that are really important to each individual member of the management team and others who carry responsibility. The company's goals should be as congruent as possible with the goals that the actors consider personally important, in order for them to also be coherent. Such goals are achieved with a much higher probability than the usual goals that are derived purely from business necessities.

Goals and strategies need to be important to your subconscious mind, less so to your conscious mind

A person's subconscious mind can perceive much more information than his conscious mind. In a quantitative comparison, the difference in information quantity between the subconscious and the conscious is equivalent to eleven kilometers to five millimeters. The subconscious, that mysterious object which, at least as far as information is concerned, makes up such a large part of human beings, decides much earlier and much more decisively than our conscious mind what is really important to us and what we really want.

> We achieve what is important to our subconscious. And what we have achieved is what was really important to our subconscious.

So how important are conscious, deliberate decisions made by people or even a management team for the realization of a futures strategy? Contemporary psychology assumes that our behavior is based to only a very small extent on our conscious decisions and to a much greater extent on the subconscious ones. And that doesn't just apply to anyone who has managed to lose five kilos for the fourteenth time. It applies to the same extent to the ability of a management team to realize a commonly developed strategy. You could think that our conscious mind is the tail that believes it is wagging the subconscious dog. People do nothing that their subconscious – or the limbic system – believes would disturb its emotional balance. It often decides what we later believe we consciously want.

> With our subconscious, we are sometimes like a government spokesperson who announces and explains decisions without knowing anything about the background.[10]

The question of the subconscious and conscious mind is particularly decisive in politics. At least those politicians with some business knowledge know that if the state continues to go into debt, then at some point this will lead to a dramatic collapse. However, the politician, or at least his subconscious, is most interested in being reelected; he therefore has no other choice than to spend money for the short-term benefit of the voters.

The situation becomes even more dramatic if we believe psychologists that the personality of the subconscious develops in the first few years of our life and thereafter can only be changed with a great and constantly increasing effort. All the books and seminars that train soft skills would therefore be meaningless.

> *Knowledge and comprehension cannot be imparted, they have to be created anew in every brain.* (Gerhard Roth)[11]

If we agree with Gerhard Roth, then that has serious consequences. It would mean that in reality it is not possible to make people into futures managers if they don't already see themselves as such and if basically they aren't one already. Anyone reading this book is therefore either a vehement critic of the thought that the future can be managed, or – which is more probable – he is already a good future manager.

In view of the power of the lazy subconscious, does it then make any sense to develop a vision, derive goals and plan projects? We would say yes for two reasons: first, the point is not to develop a vision and set goals that contradict the subconscious. On the contrary, the point is to discover a vision that corresponds to the subconscious, which obviously cannot primarily be achieved through rational and analytical methods. Second, a company won't be successful if everyone only follows his own vision. A common vision is needed, which is an acceptable compromise between all the real individual professional visions of those developing it.

Make your futures strategy robust

The development of goals and projects as the path to the vision, as described above, is only one side of the violet futures glasses. The other side is concerned with preparing for possible serious surprises. The red futures glasses made you aware that surprises are the only sure thing about the future. A good futures strategy needs to be robust to the most important surprises. This is true for all elements of the futures strategy, from the mission, the vision, the guidelines, goals, projects and processes to the systems and developing opportunities.

Your futures strategy is robust if the effects of important potential surprises would not threaten your existence because you have already immunized yourself against them or because you know how you can protect yourself should they occur. However, a greater degree of robustness is often accompanied by a less original and ambitious strategy. The more robust a strategy, the more it tends to be a rather conservative standard strategy, being followed in the same way by other actors in the market. Opportunities and threats or risks need to be carefully weighed up. Figure 5.5 on page 123 shows the thought structure for checking strategy elements against surprises.

Choose one of seven types of eventual strategy

What can you do to be prepared for surprises? Basically, the following types of eventual strategy are available (see Table 8.3). An example for developing eventual strategies can be found in Table 8.2. The preventive strategies among the eventual strategies become normal goals, projects, processes and systems, whereas the acute strategies as such are a part of the futures strategy.

Table 8.3 The seven eventual strategies

Name	Description	Type
Neglect	After careful examination, evaluate as not worth working on	Preventive strategy
Prevention	Prevent the surprise, for example by eliminating preconditions	Preventive strategy
Preparation	Include defensive and securing elements in the strategy which are already available	Preventive strategy
Precautions	Keep a protective plan in the drawer for the acute case should it actually occur	Acute strategy
Transformation	Keep an offensive plan in the drawer for the acute case should it actually occur, which enables the surprise to form relative advantages	Acute strategy
Reduction	Reduce the potential damage (e.g. insure)	Preventive strategy
Anticipation	Actively bring about the surprise yourself, to generate benefits	Preventive strategy and acute strategy

Neglect

The simplest thing to do is to close your eyes to the future's possible surprises. The dangerous thing about doing so is that the fact that the red futures glasses are missing doesn't hurt and you don't notice it until the surprise happens. You can't recognize that the celebrated Entrepreneur of the Year is operating at full risk and therefore risking the existence of his company and his employees' jobs. It takes time and money to take possible serious discontinuities in the company's strategy into account. By ignoring them, you save resources and thus create an advantage at the price of a much higher risk. Many fantastic company successes could have ended quite differently if history had taken an only slightly different course.

> Many a celebrated "Entrepreneur of the Year" sits in front of the bankruptcy court or even in prison a few years later.

And yet you have to neglect the majority of imaginable surprises. Someone who tries to eliminate all risks takes the greatest risk because he invests too much money, time and intellect in protection and thus loses valuable flexibility and time in competition. You should neglect all imaginable surprises that you could cope with without existential damage.

Prevention through preventive strategies

You cannot prevent most of the imaginable surprises in your market environment. Even the most expensive reeducation campaign will not prevent your customers from rearranging their values. You are equally powerless to prevent a terrorist attack on the football stadium you sponsor. The eventual strategy "prevention" is therefore only applicable in cases where you have a direct influence, in the choice of different business partners for example.

Preparation through preventive strategies

With this eventual strategy, you enrich your futures strategy with preventive elements that protect you from the surprise in question. If you invest a lot of money in developing a business area and thus bind yourself for a long time, a preventive strategy would consist of a parallel low-level investment in an alternative business area. At the beginning of 2003, Gillette announced that, together with the research company Palomar Medical Technologies, it would develop a patented laser for long-term hair removal for home use. An important aspect of this project is no doubt its preventive character. After all, Gillette's core business of daily shaving would be severely threatened by the development of a laser-based alternative. Further examples have already been described from page 97 onwards.

Taking precautions through acute strategies

Acute strategies are emergency strategies or those you keep in the drawer. Contrary to preventive strategies, acute strategies need no action a priori, just the appropriate planning. If the damage actually occurs, then the only thing that sometimes helps is to limit it. If for example, a food manufacturer is faced with mass poisoning of its customers, then everything needs to be done in advance to limit the damage to the image of the company through well-prepared crisis communication and crisis management.

■ **"What will we do if ..." is the typical search question for acute strategies.**

If the competition suddenly drastically reduces its prices, then you can either follow suit as a result of a pre-prepared cost-reduction program or carry out a campaign you have planned in advance with which you make the dubiousness of the competition's strategy clear to your customers. Identify alternative locations, negotiate contracts or prepare a massive, quickly implementable "home office program" for the case that your headquarters burns down at some stage.

Transform through acute strategies or preventive strategies

The above example of the radical cost-reduction program and, above all, the home office program show that the red futures glasses often lead to ideas that can also be useful in the normal situation. Targeted transformation through preventive strategies is the same as taking precautions through acute strategies except that attention is consciously turned to searching for potential relative advantages. The Gillette example above could also have been triggered through "transformation".

Reduce the potential damage though preventive strategies

The insurance business offers a great variety of solutions to insure against the financial damage arising from surprising events and developments. You can insure against financial losses from robbery, transport damage and even the failure of a product introduction. The insurers have come up with creative solutions such as completion insurance. However, the instrument of insurance generally fails when you want to protect yourself against the sudden acceptance of a competing technology in the market. And no insurer will insure you against bankruptcy. To reduce the potential damage, you therefore have to consider doing the insuring yourself, in the form of built reserves.

Anticipation through preventive strategies and acute strategies

The most offensive eventual strategy consists of causing the potential surprise yourself. If a company – in the above case Gillette, or many music publishers for example – recognizes that its current products could be substituted by a new technology, then it basically has the option of bringing about this substitution itself, in order to be the first to start off well prepared into this new future. In practice however, this rarely happens because the forces for consistency tend to favor the old concepts.

> *It wasn't the postmasters who founded the railway.*
> (Joseph Alois Schumpeter)

Methodology checklists

You will be very familiar with the methodology of the violet futures glasses if you have already been involved with goals, time management or project management. Experience shows that this is the case with most readers who are interested in a book on methodologically substantiated future management. Norton and Kaplan summarized the essentials for practical use in their works *Balanced Scorecard* and *Strategy Maps*, although they certainly didn't develop anything new with it.

The first checklist is for your work in your company, and the second for you as a life entrepreneur. The method checklists are aimed at future management experts.

Procedure for companies

1. **Assemble your futures team.**

2. **Determine your strategy questions** using the description and examples on page 222.

3. **Determine the time horizon.** Your strategic vision should follow the time horizon already recommended in the checklists for the blue and yellow futures glasses. If your vision has a very long time horizon of ten or more years, you should formulate strategic goals

for the next three years and additionally to the end of next year. You thus have two goal levels underneath the vision. If your vision reaches no further than five to eight years into the future, you can concentrate on one level with annual strategic goals.

4. **Identify the differences between the vision and the present.** Make the gaps and the surpluses into part of your strategy.

5. **Develop the necessary eventual strategies.** You will find guidelines on doing so on page 231 ff. The green futures glasses provide you with a large pool of approaches. The eventual strategies can flow into the futures strategy in any form, whether as vision elements or mission elements or as any other strategy element described in the following steps.

6. **Develop goal candidates.** You can achieve your vision and your guidelines in numerous ways. Develop alternative strategic goals, also with the help of the opportunity panorama from the green futures glasses. These goal candidates can then be evaluated according to criteria such as effectiveness and efficiency and prioritized in order to ultimately determine the most suitable strategic goals.

7. **Derive your strategic goals from your strategic vision and your mission.** The strategic goals denote milestones on the road to the strategic vision. Therefore break the elements of the strategic vision and if necessary the mission, into smaller units. You thus turn the longed for technical breakthrough into a partial development realizable in three years or even in one year. This process is referred to as backcasting. You draw the path back from your strategic vision to your present. Determine the goals according to the requirements shown on page 222.

8. **Determine the developing opportunities.** Which opportunities (green futures glasses) did you give a high value to, but which need to be examined and therefore further developed with regard to their value and implementability?

9. **Determine the projects and processes for achieving your strategic goals.** Projects and processes are the two types of activity with which you spend more or less the whole of your working life. Projects need to be implemented and processes need to be operated to achieve goals. The developing opportunities also need to be followed with a certain amount of resources.

10. **Define the projects and processes needed to realize the most ambitious strategic guidelines.** The strategic guidelines are the rules for your external and internal strategic behavior. They need to be observed in the present. Many guidelines however are so ambitious that you need to develop special activities in order to keep to them within a foreseeable period. Cultural guidelines in particular can be observed very quickly.

11. **Determine the systems needed to support the projects and processes.** What do you need to implement your projects, operate your processes and thus achieve your goals? The term system is used to encompass all material and immaterial resources.

12. **Align your strategy to your assumptions.** You have already checked the compatibility of the normative elements of your futures strategy, that is, the mission, vision and guidelines, with your assumptions about the future. Now ensure in the same way that your goals and the other elements of your strategy fit your assumptions about the future and, ideally, are supported by them. Link the strategy elements and the assumptions about the future in a matrix that will help your systematic alignment. Where conflicts appear, you will need to change the element of your futures strategy concerned.

13. **Consolidate everything into a "strategy map".** Bring all goals, projects, processes and systems together in an overview of your strategic action. We use the terms strategy map,[12] transformation map and roadmap synonymously here. As already recommended in the section on the principles of the violet glasses, you should put the strategic vision as a fascinating future image at the top of your strategy map and not shareholder value and profit.

14. **Determine goal managers.** Ensure that every goal, every project, every process and every system has a manager. In our experience, the goal managers are particularly valuable instruments, because they unite responsibility and the orientation towards goals. Your goals are then also sitting at the table in every management meeting so to speak.

15. **Install a future radar.** Ensure that the members of your futures team attentively monitor the completeness and correctness of your assessments in the assumption panorama, surprise panorama and opportunity panorama. We would like to refer at this point to the book *FutureRadar*,[13] which covers this subject in detail.

16. **Agree a communications plan.** Ensure that you can think and talk about your futures strategy regularly and with enough time and peace and quiet.

Procedure for life entrepreneurs

For your personal life enterprise, you can focus the violet futures glasses on a few essential steps, the results of which you should make a note of in writing:

1. Determine the annual goals on the road to your vision using the criteria listed on page 222.
2. Review the guidelines developed with the yellow futures glasses, which you want to work and live by in future.
3. Determine a project for every goal and every particularly ambitious guideline.
4. Divide every project into tasks and distribute the tasks in your diary such that you can carry them out.
5. Make sure that you are not trying to achieve too much with the vision, the guidelines or the projects. Very ambitious people tend to plan to achieve around twice as much as they can actually achieve.
6. Schedule regular times to think, for example one afternoon per month or one day per quarter.
7. Enjoy the realization of your futures strategy.

Checklist of methods and techniques

The methods checklist for future management professionals lists the most important methods and techniques for the violet futures glasses.

> **Professional checklist:**
> **Methods for the violet futures glasses and suggested literature**
> (see Bibliography)
>
> **Developing strategy questions**
> - Critical success factors (Rockart, 1979)
> - Comprehensive situation mapping (CSM) (Georgantzas and Acar, 1995)
> - Value chain (Porter, 1985)
> - Strategy questions / Delphi (Mićić, 2006)

Professional checklist (cont'd)

Deriving possible goals, projects, processes, systems and developing opportunities
- Retropolation / backcasting (Cornish, 2004)
- Roadmapping (Möhrle and Isenmann, 2002)
- Balanced scorecard (Kaplan and Norton, 1996)
- Strategy map (Kaplan and Norton, 2004)
- Value chain (Porter, 1985)
- Critical path analysis
- Opportunity panorama (Mićić, 2005)

Evaluating, prioritizing and deciding
- Analytic hierarchy process (Saaty, 1996)
- Cost–benefit analysis (May, 1996)
- Risk analysis (May, 1996)
- S-curve analysis (Pengg, 2003)
- Opportunity panorama (Mićić, 2005)

Developing and integrating eventual strategies
- The seven strategies as described above

Aligning the futures strategy with the assumptions about the future
- Matrix of futures strategy elements and assumptions about the future

Presenting results
- Balanced scorecard (Kaplan and Norton, 1996)
- Strategy map (Kaplan and Norton, 2004)
- Roadmapping (Möhrle and Isenmann, 2002)

9 See more of the future

The five futures glasses and the *Eltville Model*

The *Eltville Model* of future management is based on the five futures glasses. The *Eltville Model* helps you to think about futures in a systematic and structured way, whilst always keeping an overall view of everything.

Process model and object model

The *Eltville Model* comprises two parts: the process model and the object model (see Table 9.1). The process model consists of seven steps: the five futures glasses, together with an introductory step, the "future radar" for collecting futures information and a closing step, "institutionalization", which turns future management into a regular and ongoing process. These seven steps form a thought process. They answer the key questions in future management, which every person, every company and every organization needs to ask itself and to answer. If you carry out these work steps, you will get the results that can be shown in the object model. The object model contains the core concepts that result from the application of the five futures glasses. In it, the core concepts are defined as such and in their relationship to each other.

Table 9.1 The two partial models of the *Eltville Model*

The process model	The object model
■ Description of a general process in seven steps.	■ Description of interconnected core concepts.
■ Five of the seven steps are characterized and described by the five futures glasses.	■ The core concepts form a "mental map" for all important future management terms.
■ The introductory step, "future radar" and the closing step "institutionalization" round off the process model.	■ With their clear relations, the core concepts form a semantic network.

The core concepts of the *Eltville Model*

In the preceding chapters, the core concepts for each of the futures glasses have been described in detail. The system of the five futures glasses and their core concepts was determined and conceived based on 250 interviews and more than 1,000 workshops and seminars with management teams in various industries and on the basis of the specialist literature. Using phenomenological analysis, we developed the essence of the meaning of the terms and their interactions and derived a mental model[1] and a cognitive map[2] from them.

The core concepts are connected into a semantic network. That means that every object is not only unambiguously described as a term, but also in its connections and relations to the other core concepts. Figure 9.1 shows a simplified version of this semantic network. In fact there are 113 connections between the core concepts – without considering the futures questions.

In Figure 9.1, the core concepts are clearly assigned to one of the futures glasses using color. The signals and future factors were introduced earlier as part of the core concepts of the blue futures glasses, but they really belong to the process step Future Radar, described in the book *The FutureRadar*.[3]

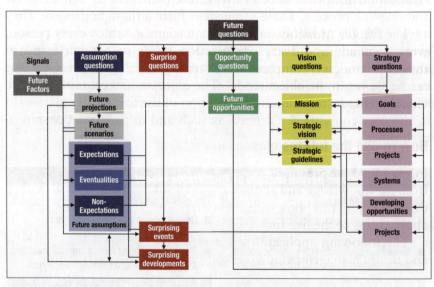

Figure 9.1 The core concepts as a semantic network

A detailed tabular overview of the core concepts with definitions and examples can be found in the Appendix.

Processes and core concepts of future management

Figure 9.2 shows the process model and the object model together in a cognitive map.

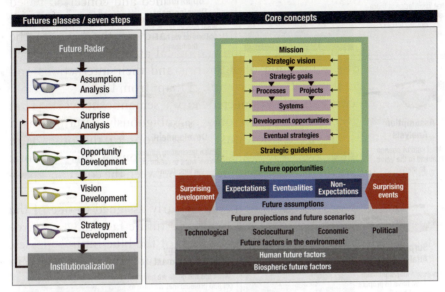

Figure 9.2 The *Eltville Model* with steps and core concepts

The *Eltville Model* is simple enough to provide a complete framework for thinking and acting in practice as a kind of mental map. On the other hand, it is complex enough to fully portray the processes and results of future management while remaining neutral towards individual methods, techniques and tools (see Figure 9.3).

How to use the futures glasses in practice

In Chapter 1 we promised you a number of benefits that can be gained from the knowledge and application of the five futures glasses. We will therefore close this book with a summary and overview of the possible applications of the five futures glasses and the *Eltville Model*.

The following applications relate to your personal life enterprise and future management in your company or your organization.

Organize your thoughts

In Chapter 2, from page 15 onwards, you learned about the most

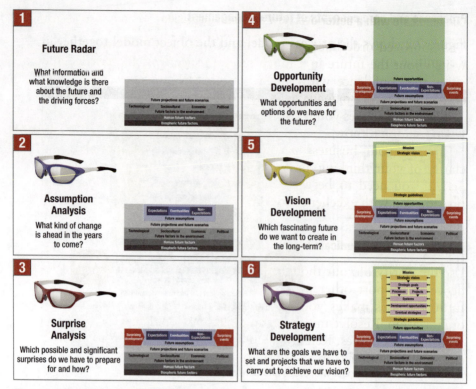

Figure 9.3 The *Eltville Model* step by step

important futures confusions, which you can now avoid using your knowledge of the five futures glasses.

Who isn't confused when they think about the future? Your thoughts keep going around in a circle in an unpleasant way: What do I consider to be probable? Which future would I like to form? What is possible at all? What if something completely different happens? How can I form my future? These are the questions we frequently ask ourselves about the future. The solution appears obvious: Just read an advice book on the future or employ one of those futures researchers. However, after the latter has finished his work either in a book, a lecture or even a consultancy project, most people are more confused than they were before.

The five futures glasses support you through clear, interrelated definitions of the thought processes and the core concepts of future management unambiguously connected to them. You are now in a position to clearly differentiate the various futures and handle them in an experienced way.

Communicate with a better overview and more precision

The improved orderliness in your mind will enable you to talk and write about the future in a much more precise way. Experience and enjoy the confidence with which you use the processes, terms and concepts of future management. The holistic approach of the *Eltville Model* also provides you with a good overview of what you know and what you don't know.

Impress your business partners with the holistic approach and clarity of your thinking and your language. The five futures glasses and, if you need to be even more precise, the *Eltville Model* will provide you with excellent support.

Help others to communicate better

Use the clarity of your thoughts and communication and your confidence to support other people's discussions. Knowledge of the five futures glasses makes you into a highly suitable facilitator in your organization. Resolve misunderstandings and conflicts with just a few words and examples. Refer to a few appropriate principles to possibly end year-old conflicts in a very short time.

> In your company, the *Eltville Model* provides you with a precise and uniform language for thinking about and working on the future.

You can more or less eliminate the usual misunderstandings that lead to huge costs and often existence-threatening wrong developments.

Gain more insight from newspapers, books, lectures and films

At the start of Chapter 1, you learned how statements about the future can be, metaphorically, "colored". Now that you know the five futures glasses, their characteristics and principles, you can much better understand, evaluate and use texts, statistics, novels and films about the future. Your new knowledge on methodology will, in particular, help you to better use the "idea cathedrals" described by futures researchers and separate the wheat from the chaff.

> You can better and more quickly recognize the essential and immediately identify the less relevant and ignore it with a good conscience.

Use the futures glasses as a template for designing futures projects

The *Eltville Model* is an ideal template for designing futures projects. Save time and money in developing a model for thinking and communicating about the future. Benefit from the soundness of the model described, achieved through hundreds of applications.

Whether you want to compile a study, give a talk, hold a seminar, carry out a workshop or organize and plan a complete strategy project for your company – the seven process steps and the core concepts in the *Eltville Model* provide you with a tried and tested template for designing futures projects. The Future Radar is the preliminary phase for the research: for each of the futures glasses you need to plan a workshop day with preparation and follow-up. Depending on the emphasis of the objectives, you can plan more or less time for the individual futures glasses.

The core concepts give you a structured template for the types of results from your futures project. You can therefore explain right at the beginning to those involved in the project what the objectives are and what they can expect at the end as a result.

The checklists provided for each of the futures glasses show you each individual work step on the road to valuable and cohesive results.

Structure your futures strategy

The future management object model more or less provides you with the structure for your futures strategy and additionally interconnects the terms in a knowledge network. You save the need for extensive explanation due to the precise definitions and their interconnections.

> A sound model provides you with the basis to put forward arguments to your employees, colleagues, supervisory boards, partners and other stakeholders.

Organize your toolbox

The *Eltville Model* is deliberately not method-specific. You can use several different methods to work on the process steps and the core concepts. The checklists of methods and techniques, which we have primarily added for future management professionals, are structured firstly according to the futures glasses and secondly according to the partial steps to each pair of glasses. In this way, the futures glasses are an ideal structure for your toolbox. Every step, every partial step and every core concept becomes a "compartment" in your toolbox. In future, you can evaluate the unstructured method lists in specialist literature in a way that suits you and use them to your advantage.

See more of the future than the competition

We have experienced hundreds of times that even the most professional management teams can be totally helpless with regard to a clear structure and methodology for looking at the future. Since the turn of the millennium, a competition for foresight has developed between companies, organizations and even countries. Anyone who is better at handling the future than others will recognize the threats and, above all, opportunities that lie in it earlier and is therefore better able to use them to his advantage.

> Use your ability to look clearly at the future and communicate about it as a strategic advantage in the competition for foresight.

Make more of your future

If we summarize all the applications mentioned, the five futures glasses and the *Eltville Model* put you in a position to make more of your life, your company, your city, your country and thus of your future. Seize this great opportunity!

Have a bright future!

Appendix

Core concepts of the *Eltville Model*

Table 1 Core concepts of the *Eltville Model*

Core concept	Definition	Example
Assumption questions	You use assumption questions to determine the essential knowledge requirement about the probable development of your environment.	■ To what extent will the increase of videophones and videoconferences limit business travel?
Future factor	Future factors are trends, technologies and issues that act as driving forces of future changes.	■ Individualization (trend) ■ Nanotechnology (technology) ■ Climate change (issue)
	A trend is a clearly directed change to one or more variables in the environment.	■ The number of kilometers traveled per person and per year will increase.
	A technology is a tool to expand human capabilities.	■ Nanotechnology ■ Photonics ■ Human–machine interfaces
	An issue describes a phenomenon that creates future changes in one or more directions.	■ Religious conflicts ■ Military conflicts
Signal	A signal is a piece of information about possible developments and events in the future.	■ Twenty percent of young foreign nationals and ten percent of young home nationals leave school with no qualifications.
Future projection	A future projection is a statement about the possible state of an observation object in the environment at a given point in time in the future.	■ Sixty percent of the people in city X will live in single households in the year 2015.
Future scenario	A future scenario is a system of projections that describes a complex picture of a possible future and possibly the path to it.	■ See the Battle of Dorking on page 91 as an example – a complex story about a fictitious future war.

Table 1 (cont'd)

Core concept	Definition	Example
Assumptions about the future	An assumption about the future is a conviction about the probable future, expressed in a projection or a scenario of measured expectational probability.	■ We assume with eighty percent certainty that in the year 2020, sixty percent of the people in city X will live in single households.
	An expectation is an assumption about the future that expresses a high expectational probability.	■ See above: We assume with *eighty* percent. …
	An eventuality is an assumption about the future that expresses a medium expectational probability.	■ See above: We assume with *fifty* percent. …
	A non-expectation is an assumption about the future that expresses a low expectational probability.	■ See above: We assume with *ten* percent. …
Surprise questions	You use surprise questions to determine the essential knowledge requirement about possible surprises in your environment that would have serious effects.	■ How could our customers' demand for our services suddenly dramatically fall?
Surprise	A surprise is a projection or a scenario of an event or a development in the environment with low probability but potentially serious effects.	■ Process-based surprise: A music market that needs no physical storage medium. ■ Event-based surprise: Tsunami on 26.12.2004.
Opportunity question	You use opportunity questions to determine the essential knowledge requirement about possible advantageous action to form something in your company's important fields of action.	■ Which new products and solutions can we develop and offer?
Future opportunity	An opportunity is a possible advantageous action.	■ We will enter the Chinese market. ■ We will found a logistics company.
Vision questions	You use vision questions to determine the essential decision requirement about your desired future.	■ Vision: What will our company look like in the year 20XX? ■ Mission: What will the purpose of our company be in the future? ■ Guidelines: How do we want to decide and act in future?

Table 1 (cont'd)

Core concept	Definition	Example
Strategic vision	A strategic vision is the concrete image of a fascinating, jointly desired and achievable future.	■ In 2018, we will be the quickest developer of individual cosmetic products in Europe.
	Vision elements (parts of the vision), which are complex and visionary long-term objectives, are pulled together into a vision. The vision is the totality of the vision elements.	
Mission	A mission is the general long-term purpose that an organization fulfills (for its customers). The mission is the totality of the mission elements.	■ We reduce the financial consequences of accidents (insurance company).
Strategic guidelines	Strategic guidelines are rules and principles on strategic values and behaviors.	■ We invest five percent of our turnover in research and development.
	Guidelines can be determined 1. at a normative-strategic level (together with the vision and mission), 2. at a cultural-strategic level and 3. at an operational-strategic level (together with objectives, projects, processes and systems).	
Strategy questions	You use strategy questions to determine the essential knowledge and decision requirement about the best way to achieve the mission and vision as part of the guidelines.	■ Which strategic objectives will we set ourselves on the road to our strategic vision? ■ Which projects do we need to realize to achieve the objectives?
Strategy	Strategy is the totality of decisions, guidelines and activities for setting and pursuing long-term objectives. Futures strategy is the totality of core concepts that are necessary for the anticipation of the future, the setting of the mission, the vision and the guidelines and the setting and pursuing of objectives.	■ See definition of partial objects (Chapter 8).
Strategic goal	A strategic goal is the desired state of a field of action, which is clearly defined by characteristics and point in time in the future.	■ By the end of next year we will have established a new business area in optoelectronics.

Table 1 (cont'd)

Core concept	Definition	Example
Process	Regular sequence of tasks and activities to achieve a goal or results in the value chain	■ Operation of a quality management system
Project	One-off sequence of tasks and activities to achieve a goal	■ Introduction of a quality management system
Task	Activities for achieving a goal within a process or project	■ Development of a concept for a quality management system
System	Device for supporting processes or projects The term system is used to encompass all material and immaterial resources and tools.	■ A quality management system ■ A manufacturing plant
Developing opportunity	Highly rated future opportunity that cannot yet be part of the futures strategy as its value and implementability are not yet clear	■ We could introduce an automatic competitor intelligence system but don't yet know if such systems provide really meaningful information.
Eventual strategy	Possible measures that can be carried out if surprises (unexpected events and developments) and significant changes to the future assumptions occur	■ Should a substitute technology appear on the market, we will change to technology X.

Notes

1 About this book
1. De Bono, 1985

2 Why we need futures glasses
1. Berlyne, 1974
2. Kierkegaard, 1844
3. Heidegger, 1993
4. Maslow, 1971
5. www.worldvaluessurvey.com and others
6. Mićić, 2007
7. Laswell, quoted in Bell, 1997
8. The image of climbing a mountain is by Steven Covey
9. Prahalad and Hamel, 1995
10. Schwartz and Randall, 2003
11. This refers to the work of Jay Forrester on systems dynamics
12. Mićić, 2006

3 Many futures and five futures glasses
1. Bell, 1997; Godet, 1997; Dator, 2000; Bezold, 2000
2. Polak, 1973; Bell, 1997; Friedman, 1977
3. Loye, 1998
4. Fahey and Randall, 1998; Voros, 2003
5. Friedman, 1977
6. *Financial Times Deutschland*, short edition, 31 May 2006
7. Bishop, 2002; Loye, 1998; Bell, 1997; Garrett, 2000; Lindgren and Bandhold, 2003; Voros, 2003
8. Bell, 1997; De Jouvenel, 1967; Bishop, 2002; Slaughter, 2000; Lindgren and Bandhold, 2003; Voros, 2003; Godet, 1994; Selby, 1993; Nanus, 1990
9. *Frankfurter Allgemeine Zeitung*, 25.10.2006: Die fast perfekte Tarnkappe für die Mikrowelle.
10. Bishop, 2002; Bezold, 2000; Hancock und Bezold, 1994; Voros, 2003
11. We could also talk about realistic futures here (Razak, 2000). However, the word "realistic" can also be used for assessing plans that, if possible, should not be considered in the category of probability in the classical sense, as one's own intervention in the environment has to be taken into account
12. Hancock and Bezold, 1994
13. Petersen, 1999; Steinmüller, 2003
14. Helmer, 1983; Friedman, 1977
15. Godet, 1994
16. Cunha, 2004
17. Bell, 1997; De Jouvenel, 1967; Bishop, 2002; Hicks, 2000; Bezold, 2000; Godet, 1994; Lindgren and Bandhold, 2003
18. Loye, 1998; Bell, 1997; Helmer, 1983; Sandi, 2000; Voros, 2003
19. Bell, 1997; Selby, 1993; Razak, 2000
20. Henderson, 2000

21 Hancock and Bezold, 1994
22 Mintzberg, Ahlstrand and Lampel, 1999
23 Petersen, 1999; Steinmüller, 2003
24 Kierkegaard, 1844
25 In other words, "five factorial"
26 Wave theory used to be linear. Freak waves therefore could not be possible. Nowadays, we know that waves require non-linear consideration, like practically everything in nature

4 Your blue futures glasses: What lies ahead?
1 Murray, 1943
2 AP, 2006: Boeing Shares Drop After Downgrade, http://biz.yahoo.com/ap/070122/boeing_mover.html, Published on: 22.01.2007
3 Stieler, 2006
4 Just, 2004
5 www.DieWeltwoche.ch, issue 50/06,
6 Miersch, 2006
7 *Die Welt*, 24.03.2001
8 Dewar, 2002
9 Dewar, 2002
10 Mason and Mitroff, 1979
11 Interview with Heinz Goldmann on 10/11/2004
12 *FutureRadar*, Mićić, 2006
13 Gausemeier et al., 1996
14 Bishop, 2003
15 Armstrong, 2001
16 Ruthen, 1993
17 Gleick, 1987; Gell-Mann, 1994
18 Lorenz, 1963
19 Heisenberg, 1959
20 Breiing and Knosala, 1997
21 Helmer, 1983
22 Helmer, 1983
23 Mićić, 2006

5 Your red futures glasses: How could the future surprise you?
1 Petersen, 1999
2 The assumption that within 5 weeks you lose 50 percent of turnover
3 Schwartz and Randall, 2003
4 Dennis and Donella Meadows, 1972
5 www.Heise.de (2004): Sharp steigt bei Loewe ein, http://www.heise.de/newsticker/meldung/48508, Managermagazin, 09/2004, S. 30 ff, published: 23.06.2004
6 *Technology Review*, 04/2006
7 www.Portel.de quotes "Wirtschaftswoche" on 03.02.2007: "Telekom-Studie stellt eigenen Netzbetrieb in Frage"
8 USAFA, 2006
9 www.Networld.de; 12.03.2001

10 French original: "L'éducation, c'est passer de la certitude ignorante à l'incertitude réfléchie", or "la prospective nous aide à passer de la certitude ignorante à l'incertitude réfléchie" (used by Ute von Reibnitz)
11 Fahey and Randall, 1998
12 Schwartz, 1996
13 Gausemeier et al., 1996
14 van der Heijden, 1996
15 Barber, 2003
16 Bishop, 2003
17 Ansoff, 1975
18 Prognosticon is an Ancient Greek word for an early sign of future events or developments
19 Fahey and Randall, 1998
20 Caplan, 1964
21 "Realtime decisional innovation" according to Mendonca and Cunha, 2004
22 Ansoff, 1975
23 Petersen, 1999
24 Petersen, 1999
25 Schwartz, 1996
26 *Der Spiegel*, 01.09.2004
27 Thom, 1975
28 Janis, 1972
29 Schwarz, 1996; van der Heijden, 1996
30 Geschka and Hammer, 1992; von Reibnitz, 1992; Georgantzas and Acar, 1995; Gausemeier et al., 1996; Godet, 2006
31 Neuhaus, 2006
32 Fahey and Randall, 1998
33 Wack, 1985
34 von Oetinger, 2003
35 Dunningan, 2000

6 Your green futures glasses: Which future opportunities do you have?
1 *Handelsblatt*, 03.06.2003,
2 Reinhold Würth, live in a Club 55 interview, Crete, June 2003
3 Hamel and Prahalad, 1992
4 Eisenstat, Foote et al., 2001; Wolpert, 2002
5 Eisentat, Foote et al., 2001
6 Kim and Mauborgne, 2004
7 May, 1996
8 Kessler, 2004; Bradford, Duncan and Tarcy, 2000
9 Kessler, 2004
10 Inayatullah, 2003
11 Malaska and Holstius, 1999
12 Saul, 2005
13 van der Heijden, 1996
14 Bradford, Duncan and Tarcy, 2000
15 Wells, 1998; de Bono, 1991
16 Cormican and O`Sullivan, 2004: 820

17 Wells, 1998
18 Wolpert, 2002
19 De Bono, 1991; Kim and Mauborgne, 2004
20 Dawkins, 1976; Aunger, 2002
21 Schnaars, 1994
22 *Süddeutsche Zeitung*, 13.10.2006
23 Drucker, 2002
24 Kelley, 2001

7 Your yellow futures glasses: Which future do you want to form?

1 Collins and Porras, 1996
2 In Austria, this statement is also attributed to the former Chancellor Franz Vranotzky. Herman Josef Abs, former Chairman of the Board and Chairman of the Supervisory Board of the Deutsche Bank is also sometimes cited as the author
3 IBM Anual Report 2005
4 IBM Anual Report 1994
5 Polak, 1973
6 Mewes, 1991
7 Collins and Porras, 1996
8 Collins and Porras, 1996; Bleicher, 1994
9 *Die Zeit*, 28.04.2005
10 Senge, 1993
11 Davis, 1988
12 Campbell and Park, 2004
13 Sprenger, 2004
14 Mary, 2005
15 Mary, 2005
16 Senge, 1993
17 Bishop, 2002
18 Malaska and Holstius, 1999
19 Lindgren and Bandhold, 2003
20 Senge, 1993
21 Tschirky and Müller, 1996
22 Berth, 1996
23 Campbell and Park, 2004
24 Csikszentmihalyi, 1998
25 Tschirky and Müller, 1996
26 Bishop, 2003
27 Weick and Sutcliff, 2003
28 www.harley-davidson.com
29 www.basf.com/group/corporate/en/about-basf/strategy/index
30 Saaty, 1996

8 Your violet futures glasses: What are you planning to do?

1 Kaplan and Norton, 2004
2 Sardemann, 2004
3 Hammer, 1998; Gälweiler, 1987

4 Hammer, 1998
5 Josef Schmidt
6 Kaplan and Norton, 1996
7 Kaplan and Norton, 2004
8 Chandler, 1966
9 Mintzberg, 1994
10 Roth, 2004
11 Quoted in Mary, 2005
12 Kaplan and Norton, 2004
13 Mićić, 2006

9 See more of the future
1 Spicer, 1998
2 Spicer, 1998
3 Mićić, 2006

Bibliography

Ansoff, Igor (1975): Managing Strategic Surprise by Response to Weak Signals, in: *California Management Review*, **18**(2): 21–33.
AP (2006): Boeing Shares Drop After Downgrade, http://biz.yahoo.com/ap/070122/boeing_mover.html (published: 22.01.2007).
Armstrong, J. S. (ed.) (2001): *Principles of Forecasting: A Handbook for Researchers and Practitioners*, New York: Springer.
Aunger, Robert (2002): *The Electric Meme: A New Theory of How We Think*, New York: Free Press.
Barber, Marcus (2003): *Wildcards – Signals from a future near you.*
Bell, Wendell (1997): The Purposes of Futures Studies, in: *The Futurist*, November/December, pp. 42–5.
Berlyne, Daniel E. (1974): *Konflikt, Erregung, Neugier*, Stuttgart.
Berth, Rolf (1996): *Marktmacht: Mind-Profit-Management wagt den visionären Quantensprung*, Düsseldorf.
Bezold, Clement (2000): *Knowledge Base of Futures Studies*, Volumes 1–4, Futures Studies Centre Resource Pages, The Visioning Method, Indooroopilly (Australia).
Bishop, Peter (2002): Course in Social Change at the University of Houston Clear Lake, Summer 2002.
Bishop, Peter (2003): Interviews with Professor Peter Bishop, September 23 to 26, 2003.
Bleicher, Knut (1994): *Das Konzept integriertes Management. Visionen – Missionen – Programme*, 5th edition, Frankfurt/New York.
Bradford, Robert W.; Duncan, J. Peter; Tarcy, Brian (2000): *Simplified Strategic Planning*, Worcester: Chandler House.
Breiing, A.; Knosala, R. (1997): *Bewerten technischer Systeme*, Berlin: Springer-Verlag.
Buzan, Tony (2006): *The Ultimate Book of Mind Maps*, Harper Thorsons.
Campbell, Andrew; Park, Robert (2004): Stop kissing Frogs, in: *Harvard Business Review*, July/August, pp. 27–8.
Caplan, Gerald (1964): *Principles of Preventive Psychiatry*, New York: Basic Books.
Chandler, Alfred Dupont (1966): *Strategy and Structure: Chapters in the history of the industrial enterprise*, 3rd edition, New York.
Collins, James C.; Porras, Jerry I. (1996): Building your company's vision, in: *Harvard Business Review*, September/October, pp. 65–77.
Cormican, Kathryn; O'Sullivan, David (2004): Auditing best practice for effective product innovation management, in: *Technovation*, **24**: 819–29.
Cornish, Edward (2004): *Corporate Radar.*

Coyle, R. Geoffrey (2003): Morphological Forecasting: Field anomaly relaxation (FAR), in: Glenn, J. C. and Gordon, T. J. (eds) *Futures Research Methodology*, V. 2.0.

Cunha, Miguel Pina F. (2004): Time traveling: Organizational foresight as temporal reflexivity, in: Tsoukas, Haridimos; Shepherd, Jill (eds): *Managing the Future, Foresight in the Knowledge Economy*, Blackwell.

Czikszentmihalyi, Mihaly (1998): *Finding Flow: The Psychology of Engagement with Everyday Life*, New York: Basic Books.

Dator, Jim (2000): *Knowledge Base of Futures Studies*, Volumes 1–4, Futures Studies Centre Resource Pages, From Future Workshops to Envisioning Alternative Futures, Indooroopilly (Australia).

Davis, Stanley, M. (1988): *Future Perfect*; deutsch: *Vorgriff auf die Future*; Freiburg.

Dawkins, Richard (1976): *The Selfish Gene*, Oxford: Oxford University Press.

de Bono, Edward (1985): *Six Thinking Hats*, Boston.

de Bono, Edward (1991): *Opportunity: Das Trainingsmodell für erfolgreiche Ideensuche*, Düsseldorf and Wien.

de Geus, Arie (1988): Planning as learning, in: *Harvard Business Review*, March–April.

de Jouvenel, Bertrand (1976): *The Art of Conjecture*, New York: Basic Books.

Dewar, James (2002): The essence of assumption-based planning, in: Dewar, J. *Assumption Based Planning*, New York: CUP.

Drucker, Peter F. (2002): The Discipline of Innovation, in: *Harvard Business Review*, August, pp. 95–103.

Dunnigan, James F. (2000): *Wargames Handbook, How to Play and Design Commercial and Professional Wargames*, 3rd edition, Lincoln: Writers Club Press.

Eisenstat, Russell; Foote, Nathaniel; Galbraith, Jay; Miller, Danny (2001): Beyond the business unit, in: *McKinsey Quarterly*, No. 1, pp. 54–63.

Fahey, L.; Randall, R. (1998): *Learning from the Future: Competitive foresight scenarios*, USA: John Wiley & Sons.

Friedman, Yona (1977): *Machbare Utopien: Absage an geläufige Futuresmodelle*, Frankfurt/M., S. IX–XIV.

Gälweiler, Aloys (1987): *Strategische Unternehmensführung*, Frankfurt/New York.

Garrett, Martha J. (2000): *Knowledge Base of Futures Studies*, Volumes 1–4, Futures Studies Centre Resource Pages, Planning and Implementing Futures Studies, Indooroopilly (Australia).

Gausemeier, Jürgen; Fink, Alexander; Schlacke, Oliver (1996): *Szenario-Management. Planen und Führen mit Szenarien*, 2nd revised edition, München/Wien.

Gell-Mann, Murray (1994): *The Quark and the Jaguar: Adventures in the Simple and Complex*, New York.

Georgantzas, Nicholas C.; Acar, William (1995): *Scenario-Driven Planning*, Westport, CT: Quorum Books.

Geschka, H.; Hammer, R. (1992): Die Szenario-Technik in der strategischen Unternehmensplanung, in: Hahn, D.; Taylor, B. (Hrsg.): *Strategische Unternehmungsplanung – Strategische Unternehmensführung*, 6th edition, Heidelberg.

Geschka, H.; Reibnitz, Ute von (1981): *Die Szenario-Technik als Grundlage von Planung*.

Gleick, James (1987): *Chaos: Making a New Science*, New York: Penguin, pp. 11–31.
Glenn, Jerome C. (2003): Introduction to the futures research methods series, in: Glenn, J. C. and Gordon, T. J. (eds) *Futures Research Methodology*, V. 2.0 CD ROM
Glenn, Jerome C.; Gordon, Theodore J. (eds) (2003): *Futures Research Methodology*, V. 2.0 CD ROM.
Godet, Michel (1994): *From Anticipation to Action, A Handbook of Strategic Prospective*, Paris.
Godet, Michel (1997): *Scenarios and Strategies: A Toolbox for Scenario Planning*, Conservatoire National des Arts et Métiers (CNAM) at www.cnam.fr/lips/toolbox on 11 July 2001.
Godet, Michel (2006): *Creating Futures: Scenario planning as a strategic management tool*, London/Paris/Genf.
Gordon, Theodore J. (2003a): Agent modeling, in: Glenn, J. C. and Gordon, T. J. (eds) *Futures Research Methodology*, V. 2.0.
Gordon, Theodore J. (2003b): Trend impact analysis, in: Glenn, J. C. and Gordon, T. J. (eds) *Futures Research Methodology*, V. 2.0.
Hamel, Gary; Prahalad, C. K. (1992): So spüren Unternehmen neue Märkte auf, in: *Harvard Business Manager*, 2: 44–55.
Hammer, Richard M. (1998): *Strategische Planung und Frühaufklärung*, München/Wien.
Hancock, Trevor; Bezold, Clement (1994): Possible futures – preferable futures, in: *Healthcare Forum Journal*, March/April, pp. 23–29.
Heidegger, Martin (1993): *Sein und Zeit*, Tübingen.
Heisenberg, Werner (1959): *Physik und Philosophie*, Stuttgart.
Helmer, Olaf (1983): *Looking Forward*, Beverley Hill: Sage.
Henderson, Hazel (2000): *Knowledge Base of Futures Studies*, Volumes 1–4, Futures Studies Centre Resource Pages, Transforming Economics, Indooroopilly (Australia).
Hicks, David (2000): *Knowledge Base of Futures Studies*, Volumes 1–4, Futures Studies Centre Resource Pages, Educating for Sustainable Futures, Indooroopilly (Australia).
Inayatullah, Sohail (2003): Ageing: Alternative futures and policy choices, in: *Foresight*, 5(6): 8–17.
Janis, I. (1972): *Victims of Groupthink: A Psychological Study of Foreign-Policy Decisions and Fiascoes*, Boston: Houghton Mifflin.
Just, Tobias (2004): Studie Nr. 294 von DB-Research: Demografische Entwicklung verschont öffentliche Infrastruktur nicht, Frankfurt.
Kaplan, Robert S.; Norton, David P. (1996): *The Balanced Scorecard. Translating Strategy Into Action*, Harvard Business School Press.
Kaplan, Robert S.; Norton, David P. (2004): *Strategy Maps. Converting Intangible Assets Into Tangible Outcomes*, Harvard Business School Press.
Kelley, Tom (2001): *The Art of Innovation*, New York: Random House.
Kessler, Eric H. (2004): Organizational Innovation: A Multi-Level Decision-Theoretic Perspective, in: *International Journal of Innovation Management*, 8(3): 275–95.
Kierkegaard, Sören (1844): *Der Begriff Angst*.
Kim, Chan W.; Mauborgne, Renee (2004): Blue Ocean Strategy, in: *Harvard Business Review*, October, pp. 76–84.
Kreikebaum, H. (1997): *Strategische Unternehmensplanung*, Stuttgart.

Krystek, Ulrich; Müller-Stewens, Günter (1993): *Frühaufklärung für Unternehmen: Identifikation und Handhabung zukünftiger Chancen und Bedrohungen.*

Lindgren, Mats; Bandhold, Hans (2003): *Scenario Planning: Thin link between future and strategy,* New York: Palgrave Macmillan.

Linstone, Harold A. (2003): The multiple perspective concept, in: Glenn, J. C. and Gordon, T. J. (eds) *Futures Research Methodology,* V. 2.0.

Lorenz, Edward Norton (1963): Deterministic nonperiodic flow, in: *Journal of Atmospheric Sciences,* **20**: 130–41.

Loye, David (1998): *The Knowable Future: A psychology of forecasting and prophecy,* New York: John Wiley.

Makridakis, S.; Wheelwright, S. C.; Hyndman, R. J. (1998): *Forecasting Methods and Applications,* 3rd edition, New York: John Wiley.

Malaska, Pentti; Holstius, Karin (1999): Visionary Management, in: *Foresight,* **1**(4): 353–61.

Martino, Joseph P. (1993): *Technological Forecasting for Decision Making,* 3rd edition, New York: McGraw-Hill.

Mary, Michael (2005): *Die Glückslüge. Vom Glauben an die Machbarkeit des Lebens,* Bergisch-Gladbach.

Maslow, Abraham (1971): *Farther Reaches of Human Nature,* New York: Viking Press.

Mason, Richard; Mitroff, Ian (1979): Assumptions of Majestic Metals: Strategy through dialectics, in: *California Management Review,* **22**(2): 80–8.

May, Graham (1996): *The Future Is Ours: Foreseeing, Managing and Creating the Future,* Westport, CT: Praeger.

Mendonca, Sandro; Cunha, Miguel et al. (2004): Wild Cards: Weak signals and organisational imrovisation, in: *Futures,* 36(2): 201–18.

Mewes, Wolfgang (1991): *Die kybernetische Managementlehre: EKS,* Frankfurt.

Mićić, Pero (2003): *Der ZukunftsManager, wie Sie Marktchancen vor Ihren Mitbewerbern erkennen und nutzen.*

Mićić, Pero (2004): *Die Bank von morgen denken und gestalten.*

Mićić, Pero (2005): *30 Minuten für Zukunftsforschung und Zukunftsmanagement.*

Mićić, Pero (2006): *Das FuturesRadar; Die wichtigsten Trends, Technologien und Themen der Future,* Offenbach.

Mićić, Pero (2007): *Morphology of Future Management in Top Management Teams,* Leeds.

Miersch, Michael (2006): Das Debakel von Delphi, in: *Die Weltwoche,* Ausgabe 50/06 (http://www.weltwoche.ch/artikel/?AssetID=15549&CategoryID=91).

Mintzberg, Henry (1994): *The Rise and Fall of Strategic Planning: Reconceiving Roles for Planning, Plans, Planners,* New York/Toronto: Free Press.

Mintzberg, Henry; Ahlstrand, Bruce; Lampel, Joseph (1999): *Strategy Safari: Eine Reise durch die Wildnis des strategischen Managements,* Wien.

Möhrle, Martin G; Isenmann, Ralf (ed.) (2007): *Technologie-Roadmapping: Zukunftsstrategien für Technologieunternehmen,* Berlin.

Murray, Henry A (1943): Analysis of The Personality of Adolph Hitler, with Predictions of His Future Behavior and Suggestions for Dealing With Him Now and After Germany's Surrender, http://library.lawschool.cornell.edu/donovan/hitler/ (retrieved: 12.01.2007).

Nanus, Burt (1990): Futures-Creative Leadership, in: *The Futurist,* May–Jun 1990, S. 13–17.

Neuhaus, Christian (2006): *Future im Management, Orientierungen für das Management von Ungewissheit in strategischen Prozessen*, Heidelberg.
Oetinger, Bolko von (2003): *Das Boston Consulting Group Strategie-Buch*, München.
Pengg, Hermann (2003): *Marktchancen erkennen: Erfolgreiche Marktprognosen mit Hilfe der S-Kurven-Methode*.
Petersen, John L. (1999): *Out of the Blue: How to anticipate Big Future Surprises*, Lanham: Madison Books.
Polak, Fred (1973): *The Image of the Future*. Translated and abridged by Elise Boulding. Amsterdam: Elsevier.
Porter, Michael E. (1985): *Competitive Advantage*, New York: Free Press.
Prahalad, Gary; Hamel, C.K. (1995): *Wettlauf um die Future*, Wien.
Rausch, Erwin with additions from Frank Catanzaro (2003): Simulation and games in futuring and other uses, in: Glenn, J. C. and Gordon, T. J. (eds) *Futures Research Methodology*, V. 2.0.
Razak, Victoria M. (2000): *Knowledge Base of Futures Studies*, Volumes 1–4, Futures Studies Centre Resource Pages, Crafting in a Reflective Circle, Indooroopilly (Australia).
Reibnitz, Ute von (1991): *Szenario-Technik: Instrumente für die unternehmerische und persönliche Erfolgsplanung*.
Reibnitz, Ute von (1992): *Szenario-Technik: Instrumente für die unternehmerische und persönliche Erfolgsplanung*, 2nd edition, Wiesbaden.
Rhyne, Russell (1981): Whole-pattern futures projection using field anomaly relaxation, in: *Technological Forecasting and Social Change*, 19: 331–60.
Rockart, J. F. (1979): Chief executives define their own data needs, in: *Harvard Business Review*, 57(2): 238–41.
Roth, Gerhard (2004): *Fühlen, Denken, Handeln. Wie das Gehirn unser Verhalten steuert*, Frankfurt.
Ruthen, Russel (1993): Trends in nonlinear dynamics: Adapting to Complexity, in: *Scientific American*, Issue 268: 130–35.
Saaty, Thomas L. (1996): *Seven pillars of the Analytic Hierarchy Process*, ISAHP Proceedings, New York.
Sandi, Ana Maria (2000): *Knowledge Base of Futures Studies*, Volumes 1–4, Futures Studies Centre Resource Pages, Visioning a Tender Revolution, Indooroopilly (Australia).
Sardemann, Gerhard (2004): Klimawandel – eine Frage der nationalen Sicherheit?, in: *Technikfolgenabschätzung – Theorie und Praxis*, No. 2, 13th year, p. 120.
Saul, Peter (2005): Strategic Opportunism: Planning for Tough and Turbulent Times, at http://www.petersaul.com.au/strategic-opportunism.pdf (31.01.05).
Schnaars, Steve P. (1994): *Managing Imitation*, New York: Free Press.
Schwartz, Peter (1996): *The Art of the Long View: Paths to Strategic Insight for Yourself and Your Company*, New York: Doubleday.
Schwartz, Peter; Randall, Doug (2003): *An Abrupt Climate Change Scenario and Its Implications for United States National Security*, Pasadena, CA: CIFA.
Selby, David (1993): Futurescapes: Teaching and Learning about the Future, in: *Connections* (the newsletter of the Global, Environmental, and Outdoor Education Council (GEOEC)), May 1993.
Senge, Peter (1993): *The Fifth Discipline*, London: Random House.

Slaughter, Richard (2000): *Knowledge Base of Futures Studies*, Indooroopilly (Australia).
Spicer, David P. (1998): Linking mental models and cognitive maps as an aid to organizational learning, in: *Career Development International*, 3(3): 125.
Sprenger, Reinhard (2004): *Prinzip Selbstverantwortung. Wege zur Motivation*, Frankfurt/New York.
Steinmüller, Karlheinz (2003): *The Future as Wild Card. A short introduction to a new concept*, München.
Stieler, Wolfgang (2006): MP3 für die Buchbranche, in: *Technology Review*, 04/2006, pp. 19–20.
Technology Review (2006) Ist die Telekom noch zu retten? Titelthema 04/2006.
Thom, René (1975): Structural Stability and Morphogenesis, Reading, MA: Benjamin-Cummings.
Tschirky, Hugo; Müller, Roland (Hrsg.) (1996): *Visionen realisieren. Erfolgsstrategien, Unternehmenskultur und weniger Bürokratie*, Zürich
United States Air Force Academy (USAFA) (2006): Air Force America wins NSA cyber defense exercise, http://www.usafa.af.mil/scripts/aweb/newsPopUp.cfm?newsid=786 (published: 21.04.2006, retrieved: 18.03.2007).
Van der Heijden, K.; Schutte, P. (2000): Look before you leap: Key questions for designing scenario applications, in: *Scenario & Strategy Planning*, 1(6).
Voros, Joseph (2003): A generic foresight process framework, in: *Foresight*, 5(3): 10–21.
Wack, P. (1985): Scenarios: Uncharted waters ahead, in: *Harvard Business Review*, September/October, pp. 73–89.
Weick, Karl E.; Sutcliff, Kathleen M. (2003): *Managing the Unexpected. Assuring High Performance in an Age of Complexity*, New Jersey: John Wiley.
Wells, Stuart (1998): *Choosing the Future: The Power of Strategic Thinking*, Boston: Butterworth-Heinemann.
Wolpert, John D. (2002): Breaking out of the innovation box, in: *Harvard Business Review, The innovative enterprise*, August, pp. 77–83.

Index

A

Ability to survive 146
Additive fabrication 72, 132
Aging 257
AIDS 50, 166
Airbus 53 ff, 104
Analogies 85, 104, 126, 129, 154–8
Analytic hierarchy process 159, 163, 206, 210, 238
Anticipation 11, 25, 105, 135, 231, 234, 248, 257
Antiquity 29 ff
Anxiety 8 ff
Arguments (pro, contra, balance) 55 ff
Aristotle 49, 87
Artificial intelligence 66, 121, 140
Assumption
 analysis 14, 42, 50–3, 62, 75 ff, 102, 138, 177, 220, 241
 panorama 51, 83, 86, 122–7, 236
 question 47, 51, 61–8, 81–5, 105, 122, 246
 reversal 89, 126
Atlantropa 165, 194, 207
Attitude 46, 48, 50, 51, 71, 89, 107, 128, 141, 162, 163, 180, 214, 224
Attractors 50, 61, 97
Automatization 65, 67
Automobile 41, 46, 54, 129, 148, 167–9, 197–9

B

Backcasting 235, 238
Balanced scorecard 234, 238, 257
Banking 56, 105 ff, 116, 133, 205
BASF 55
Biodiversity 65
Biometrics 65, 67

Bionics 156
Bionization 65
Biotechnology 65, 131
Blind spots 94
Boeing 53 ff, 132
Brainstorming 25, 85, 122, 143, 158
Braun, Wernher von 143
Bronze and Stone Age 30
BSE 216
Business areas 26, 139, 140, 178, 190, 193, 202
Business plan 215

C

Catastrophe theory 113
Catharsis 30
Causal layered analysis 86, 158
Caesar, Julius 52
Chance 55, 187, 219, 226
Change 8, 50, 62, 64–76, 90, 97, 100, 103, 141, 205, 223, 246
 increased speed of change 87
Chaos research 71 ff
Chernobyl 104
China 164–5
Clarity of goals/objectives 243
Climate change 8, 17, 18, 37, 65, 68, 90, 130, 172, 216, 246
Club of Rome 19
Coca-Cola 192
Cognitive map 4, 241
Coherence 72, 163, 170, 184, 191, 192
Competitiveness 116, 128, 141, 144, 149–51, 157
Complex systems 71, 73
Complexity 25, 29, 41, 50, 60, 66, 82, 96, 112, 113, 170, 171, 184, 200, 205, 259, 260

Comprehensive situation mapping 25, 85, 126, 158, 210, 237
Computer processing power 65
Conception methods 163
Congruence 170, 192, 201, 228
Consistency 83, 111, 119, 169, 197, 211, 234
Convenience trend 66
Copenhagen Consensus 166
Core concepts 46, 51, 62, 89, 101, 128, 137, 163, 177, 214, 219, 223, 246
Corporate culture 12, 58, 114, 153, 200
Cost–benefit analysis 159, 238
Country 45, 52, 74, 91, 155, 161, 172 ff, 207, 216
Creativity methods 129
Crime and terrorism 66
Critical success factors 126, 152, 210, 237
Cross impact analysis 85, 126
Csikszentmihalyi, Mihaly 196
Cyber war 95
Cyberspace 94

D

Daimler 54, 167 ff, 197, 207
de Bono, Edward 7, 250
Decision modeling 85
Decision techniques 48
Delphi method 79, 80, 83
Dematerialization 64, 65, 67, 68
Demography 2
Descriptor 119
Differentiation 8, 25, 26, 28, 32, 104, 163, 169, 176, 187, 189, 190, 200
Digital money 66
Discontinuity 99, 114, 117
Display innovations 65
Disruptive event analysis 126
Dorking, Battle of 69, 91, 105, 246

E

Early recognition 136, 140
Earthquakes 35
E-Book 54, 55
E-Business 65

Efficiency 15, 28, 54, 115, 146, 162, 169, 173, 205, 213, 219, 227, 235
E-Learning 66
Eltville Model 4,5,6,7,27, 111, 169, 221, 222, 239, 241, 243, 244, 245, 246
E-mail 94, 109, 130,
Emancipation 66, 67
Empathy 129, 156, 158
Employees 2, 13, 40, 59, 80, 131, 154, 178, 187, 218, 244
Energy demand 66
Energy innovations 65, 68
Enlightenment 30
Entrepreneurization 66
Environment 14 ff, 23, 36–43, 47, 63, 76, 103–7, 122, 134–9, 169, 178 ff, 196, 213, 217, 246
Ethicalization 66
European integration 66
Eventual strategies 14, 47, 88, 89, 93, 96, 98, 99, 114, 115, 116, 125, 126, 156, 213, 214, 216, 217, 220, 222, 231, 238, 241, 242
Evolution 145, 202
Expectation 5, 16, 22, 26, 35, 43, 49, 57, 70, 71, 82, 86, 102, 138, 177, 182, 220, 240, 241, 242, 247
Expectational probability 69, 71, 77, 79, 82, 247

F

Fast follower 128, 148
Fear 8, 40, 41, 101, 171
Feminization 66
Field anomaly relaxation 85, 158, 210, 256, 259
Fields of action 123, 124, 129, 138, 154, 155, 217, 247
Film 126, 155, 165, 211
Financial services 55, 56, 64, 91, 106, 107, 116
Flexibilization 9, 66, 67, 93
Flow 196
Forecast 16–18, 26, 51, 99, 108, 135, 196–8, 212
Forest dieback 8
Fragmentation 66

Frankl, Viktor Emil 175
Fuel cell 20, 68
Functional food 20, 66
Future
   assumption 53, 84
   confusion 17, 25
   creatable 31–8, 42, 142
   desired 15, 31, 38–47, 162, 174, 191–5, 209, 224
   factor 65, 121, 140, 153, 155, 246
   imagined 31–5, 38, 42, 135, 144
   knowledge 21
   management 10–15, 25, 43, 88, 152, 202, 218, 244
   opportunities 28, 88, 127–57, 160–2, 166, 182, 252
   planned 31 ff, 38, 40, 42, 46, 220
   plausible 31 ff, 34–9, 42
   possible 18, 31–42, 59, 61, 69, 76, 88, 133, 246
   probable 24, 28–32, 39 ff, 44, 50, 69, 71 ff, 78 ff, 96, 134, 203, 247
   question 56, 63 ff
   radar 62, 81, 236, 239–44
   scenario 69, 91, 246
   surprising 16, 31, 35–8, 42–5, 88, 96 ff, 108, 134
Futures wheel 85, 126, 158

G

Gap analysis 158, 225
Gates, Bill 40
Genetic engineering 65
Genius forecasting 85
Global warming 20, 65
Globalization 3, 65
Goal/Objective
   confusion 16 ff, 242
Goethe, Johann Wolfgang von 6, 134, 226
Growth 25, 90, 145, 160, 167 ff, 190, 200

H

Habermas, Jürgen 49, 176
Hamel, Gary 12, 250, 252, 259
Happiness, pursuit of 9, 10

Hayek, Nikolaus 198
Heisenberg, Werner 74, 251, 257
Helmer, Olaf 79, 86, 126, 210, 250, 251, 257
Heraclitus 49
Heuristic 61, 70
Hitler, Adolf 52, 164, 258
Human–machine interfaces 65, 68, 246
Hybrid motor 129
Hydrogen 33

I

IBM 166, 167, 207, 253
IDEO 156
Impact analysis 48, 85, 126, 158, 257
Impact matrix 123, 124
Individualization 66, 68, 206, 246
Industrialization 30
Inflation 91, 230
Informatization 65, 68
Innovation diffusion 20
Innovators 171
Insider 89, 118
Institutionalization 239, 241
Insurance 131, 233, 248
Interculturalization 66
Interdisciplinarization 66
Internationalization 215
Internet 55, 56, 58, 65, 77, 79, 90, 92, 93, 94, 97, 105, 106, 109, 113, 130, 132
Internetization 65
Intuition 158, 181
Investment 13, 53, 57, 58, 92, 140, 145, 150, 169, 170, 232

J

Jesus Christ 52
Judgmental bootstrapping 85

K

Kahn, Herman 25, 108
Kant, Immanuel 49, 194
Kennedy, John F. 164, 179
Key question 6, 15, 50, 88, 118, 128, 162, 179, 213, 239
Knowledge system 8, 66

L

Liberalization 66
Life-balancing 66
Lighthouse function 162
Linking/network 11 ff, 17, 90, 123, 139, 153, 217, 239, 240 ff
Loewe AG 91
Luther, Martin 164

M

Macro perspective 48, 50, 71, 74, 107
Meadows, Dennis 19
Management innovation 66
Mao Zedong 12, 164, 207
Market leadership 179, 194, 200, 201
Market volume 71, 72, 78
Marketing 123, 139, 140, 154, 155, 178
Marx, Karl 164
Material innovations 66
McDonald's 216
Mental map 4, 119, 240, 259
Mercedes 167
Mewes, Wolfgang 174
Microsoft 57, 99, 130, 192
Millennium 19, 168, 215, 245
Mission 123, 177, 220 ff, 240–2
Mitsubishi 168
Monitoring 13, 111, 213, 215, 219
Morphologies 48, 85, 129, 140, 158, 210
Motivation 15, 161,
Motive 8–10, 64, 94, 168
Music market 104, 247

N

Nanotechnology 20, 65, 70, 246
Nike 130
Non-expectations 51, 62, 70, 102, 103, 120, 138, 177, 220, 241, 242
Nuclear energy 65

O

Objective *see* Goal
Observation area/field 59, 154
Oil crisis 93 ff

Opaschowski, Horst W. 174
Opportunity
  advantage opportunity 53, 134
  catching-up opportunity 144
  development 14, 42, 100, 127–9, 142, 177, 220, 241
  horizon 134
  matrix 124, 153–5, 158
  panorama 121, 129, 156–9, 235–8
  question 156, 247
Optoelectronics 222, 248
Overtaxation 196

P

Pandemic 47, 90
Panel 79, 166
Paradigm 10, 97, 143, 200
Participant interviews 210
Past 50, 60, 108, 143, 185
Pepsi-Cola 192
Perception 1, 11, 50, 61, 78, 87, 104, 115, 117, 130, 215
Pericles 38
Permanence 28
Personal responsibility 64, 218
Pesticide 131 ff
Philips 54
Popper, Karl 49
Population 88
Post-it 150
Power 64, 65, 95, 100, 110, 137, 164, 168, 171, 176, 183, 190, 199, 204, 225, 230
Precursor analysis 85, 158
Present 5, 8, 9, 30, 49, 54, 60, 76, 83, 108, 120, 137, 142, 154, 163, 174, 175, 206, 209, 219, 224, 235,
Probability 9, 19, 33, 35 ff, 48, 59, 71, 82–4, 103, 111, 121, 134, 146, 173, 189, 213, 218, 247
Process model 226, 239
Profit 13, 87, 92, 113, 145, 148, 176, 190, 200, 201, 215, 225, 236
Projection matrix 67, 82
Projection/Future projection 47 ff, 51, 55 ff, 67–86, 89, 103–5, 111–22, 138, 140, 177, 220, 240
Prophet 16, 22 ff, 121

Proust, Marcel 6
Puma 130

Q

Quality management 178, 223, 249
Quarterization 66

R

Radar, strategic 76, 94
RAND-Corporation 25
Realism 46, 142
Reconstruction 30
Reformation 30
Religious conflicts 246
Renaissance 29 ff
Replicator 132
Resources 18, 21, 37, 102, 124, 139, 154 ff, 178, 197, 223, 227, 235 ff
Retrograde success report 210
Retropolation 238
Reuter, Edzard 54, 167
RFID (Radio Frequency Identification) 20
Risk
 analysis 159, 238
 management 88, 92, 101, 136
Roadmap 227, 236
Robotics 65
Role
 confusion 16, 22
 playing 85

S

Salutogenesis 66, 98,
Scenario cube 105 ff, 122, 126
Scenarios 16–27, 43, 52 ff, 69, 77, 85, 96 ff, 101–11, 120–6, 129, 155
Schiller, Friedrich 149, 172, 188
Schmidt, Helmut 161, 254
Schrempp, Jürgen 54, 167, 197
Schumpeter, Joseph Alois 201, 234
Science fiction 132, 155
Scoring procedures 206, 210
S-curve 20, 145, 147, 158 ff, 238
Seers 30
Self-advisory software 56
Self-responsibility 163, 187 ff

Seneca, Lucius 1, 181
Senge, Peter 190, 253
Sensor technology 66
Sensors 81
Services 55, 64, 91, 94, 103, 106, 116, 133, 139, 153, 178, 247
Shell 8, 93
Shortage of drinking water 65
Shortage of oil 65, 68, 130
Simulation 19, 51, 85, 89, 120, 126, 158
Software 55 ff, 99, 112, 140, 167
Soil erosion 65
Sörgel, Hermann 165
Specialization 156
Spiritualization 66
Sprenger, Reinhard K. 188
Standstill 30, 95
Statistical modeling 85
Stone Age 30
Strategic conversation 86, 126, 210
Strategic guidelines 47, 156, 163, 180, 210, 248
Strategic vision *see* Vision
Strategically related industries 156
Strategy
 development 14, 42, 213, 218
 question
Strategy Map 215, 225, 227, 236, 238,
Structure analysis 85, 126, 158
Subconscious 36, 58 ff, 128, 142, 213, 229 ff
Substitution technology 93
Suicide 52, 134, 175
Superconductor 9
Supply chain 216
Surprise
 analysis 14, 42, 88, 114 ff
 panorama 89, 124, 236
 question 47, 89, 101 ff, 105, 121, 125, 247
Sustainability 66, 201, 203, 257
Swatch 198

T

Target group 124, 154 ff, 198
Terrorism 65 ff, 68
Tertiarization 66

Thinking hats 7, 256
Thirst for experiences and excitement 66
Threat 8, 41, 92, 100, 124, 136 ff, 140, 194, 196
Time horizon 35, 163, 204, 234
Toyota 129
Traffic innovation 65
Transformation Map 215, 236
Trend
  impact analysis 85, 158, 257
  researcher 11, 15 ff, 22–5

U

Uncertainty 74
Underchallenge 196
Undertaxation 196
Urbanization 66
Utopia 30, 32, 34, 161, 176

V

Value 3, 13, 49, 65, 112, 117–19, 128, 149, 180, 196–9, 248

Videophone 101, 246
Virtualization 64 ff
Vision/strategic vision
  candidate 45, 47, 121, 132, 140, 163, 176, 191–210
  deveploment 14, 42, 162, 177, 204 ff
  question 163, 177 ff, 205–10, 247
Visualization 185
VoIP(Voice over Internet Protocol) 92

W

War game 94, 122
Weak signal 97, 104 ff, 255
Wellness 64
Wild card 48, 88 ff, 104, 119, 121
Wishful thinking 48, 74
World War 25, 30, 141, 165
Würth, Reinhold 130, 173